Semantic Erosion of Middle English Prepositions

STUDIES IN ENGLISH MEDIEVAL LANGUAGE AND LITERATURE

Edited by Jacek Fisiak

Advisory Board:
John Anderson (Methoni, Greece), Ulrich Busse (Halle),
Olga Fischer (Amsterdam), Dieter Kastovsky (Vienna),
Marcin Krygier (Poznań), Roger Lass (Cape Town),
Peter Lucas (Cambridge), Donka Minkova (Los Angeles),
Akio Oizumi (Kyoto), Katherine O'Brien O'Keeffe (Notre Dame, USA),
Matti Rissanen (Helsinki), Hans Sauer (Munich),
Liliana Sikorska (Poznań), Jeremy Smith (Glasgow),
Jerzy Wełna (Warsaw)

Vol. 30

PETER LANG

Frankfurt am Main · Berlin · Bern · Bruxelles · New York · Oxford · Wien

Luis Iglesias-Rábade

Semantic Erosion of Middle English Prepositions

PETER LANG
Internationaler Verlag der Wissenschaften

Bibliographic Information published by the Deutsche Nationalbibliothek
The Deutsche Nationalbibliothek lists this publication in the Deutsche Nationalbibliografie; detailed bibliographic data is available in the internet at http://dnb.d-nb.de.

Cover design:
Olaf Glöckler, Atelier Platen, Friedberg

ISSN 1436-7521
ISBN 978-3-631-61125-8
© Peter Lang GmbH
Internationaler Verlag der Wissenschaften
Frankfurt am Main 2011
All rights reserved.

All parts of this publication are protected by copyright. Any utilisation outside the strict limits of the copyright law, without the permission of the publisher, is forbidden and liable to prosecution. This applies in particular to reproductions, translations, microfilming, and storage and processing in electronic retrieval systems.

www.peterlang.de

To Esperanza, in memoriam

CONTENTS

INTRODUCTION 17

CHAPTER ONE. GRAMMATICALIZATION: SEMANTIC EROSION
AND DECATEGORIALIZATION 19
1. Theoretical framework 19
   1. 1. Definition 19
   1. 2. What motivates grammaticalization? 20
   1. 3. What are the processes which lead to grammaticalization? 22
   1. 4. What are the mechanisms which lead to grammaticalization? 24
   1. 5. Is grammaticalization a unidirectional and continuous process? 26
2. Grammaticalization of English prepositions. Semantic erosion 27

CHAPTER TWO. PREPOSITIONAL PHRASES IN MIDDLE
ENGLISH 31
1. Tools for analysis 31
   1. 1. Syntactic and semantic features 31
   1. 2. Prepositional phrases as counterparts of case forms in Middle
       English 32
2. Methodology 33
   2. 1. A corpus-based study (Helsinki Corpus of Middle English) 33
   2. 2. The database 33
   2. 3. The data 35

CHAPTER THREE. OCCURRENCES AND RATES 39
1. Numbers and rates of p-Phs in Middle English 39
   1. 1. Aboue-Phs 39
   1. 2. After-Phs 40
   1. 3. At-Phs 41
   1. 4. Bi-Phs 43
   1. 5. Bifore-Phs 44
   1. 6. Bihinde-Phs 45

1. 7. Biside-Phs 46
1. 8. In-Phs 48
1. 9. On-Phs 49
1. 10. Ouer-Phs 50
1. 11. Þurgh-Phs 51
1. 12. Under-Phs 53
2. Compilation and appraisal of the data 54

CHAPTER FOUR. DIALECTAL DISTRIBUTION, COMPOSITION TYPE AND TEXT TYPE 59
1. Dialectal distribution 59
2. Type of composition (prose vs. poetry) 66
3. Text type 71

CHAPTER FIVE. SPATIAL AND TEMPORAL SENSES 81
1. Spatial roles 81
2. Temporal roles 101

CHAPTER SIX. FIGURATIVE SENSES: SEMANTIC EROSION 109
1. Aboue-Phs 109
2. After-Phs 110
3. At-Phs 111
4. Bi-Phs 113
5. Bifore-Phs 114
6. Bihinde-Phs 115
7. Biside-Phs 115
8. In-Phs 116
9. On-Phs 118
10. Ouer-Phs 120
11. Þurgh-Phs 121
12. Under-Phs 122

CHAPTER SEVEN. COLLOCATIONAL FRAMEWORK 125
1. Method and criteria for collocational patterns selection 129
2. Corpora 130
3. Data analysis 130
4. French influence on the collocational framework of prepositional phrases 136
  4.1. Aboue-Phs 137
  4.2. After-Phs 138
  4.3. At-Phs 139

4.4. Bi-Phs	146
4.5. In-Phs	160

CHAPTER EIGHT. IDIOMATIZATION 185
1. Theoretical framework 185
　1. 1. Definition 185
　1. 2. Acquisition and processing of idioms 188
　1. 3. Idiom formation 190
2. Idiomatic senses of Middle English prepositional phrases 191
　2.1. Aboue-Phms 192
　2.2. After-Phms 192
　2.3. At-Phms 192
　2.4. Bi-Phms 193
　2.5. In-Phms 193
　2.6. On-Phms 194

CONCLUSIONS 197

APPENDIX 203

PRIMARY SOURCES 209

BIBLIOGRAPHY 219

FIGURES AND TABLES

Figures
Figure 1. *Aboue-Phs* in ME 40
Figure 2. *After-Phs* in ME 41
Figure 3. *At-Phs* in ME 42
Figure 4. *Bi-Phs* in ME 43
Figure 5. *Bifore-Phs* in ME 45
Figure 6. *Bihinde-Phs* in ME 46
Figure 7. *Biside-Phs* in ME 47
Figure 8. *In-Phs* in ME 48
Figure 9. *On-Phs* in ME 49
Figure 10. *Ouer-Phs* in ME 51
Figure 11. *Þurgh-Phs* in ME 52
Figure 12. *Under-Phs* in ME 53
Figure 13. Rates of all *p-Phs* in ME 57

Tables
Table 1. Database structure 34
Table 2. CMALISAU data 35
Table 3. Records for each text and preposition 35
Table 4. Numbers and rates of *aboue-Phs* in ME 39
Table 5. Numbers and rates of *after-Phs* in ME 40
Table 6. Numbers and rates of *at-Phs* in ME 42
Table 7. Numbers and rates of *bi-Phs* in ME 43
Table 8. Numbers and rates of *bifore-Phs* in ME 44
Table 9 Numbers and rates of *bihinde-Phs* in ME 44
Table 10. Numbers and rates of *biside-Phs* in ME 46
Table 11. Numbers and rates of *in-Phs* in ME 48
Table 12. Numbers and rates of *on-Phs* in ME 49
Table 13. Numbers and rates of *ouer-Phs* in ME 50
Table 14. Numbers and rates of *þurgh-Phs* in ME 51
Table 15 Numbers and rates of *under-Phs* in ME 53

Figures and Tables

Table 16. Numbers and rates of all *p-Phs* in ME 55
Table 17. The most common prepositions in ME1 56
Table 18. Dialectal distribution of *aboue-Phs* in ME 59
Table 19. Dialectal distribution of *after-Phs* in ME 60
Table 20. Dialectal distribution of *at-Phs* in ME 61
Table 21. Dialectal distribution of *bi-Phs* in ME 61
Table 22. Dialectal distribution of *bifore-Phs* in ME 62
Table 23. Dialectal distribution of *in-Phs* in ME 63
Table 24. Dialectal distribution of *on-Phs* in ME 64
Table 25. Dialectal distribution of *ouer-Phs* in ME 65
Table 26. Dialectal distribution of *þurgh-Phs* in ME 65
Table 27. Dialectal distribution of *under-Phs* in ME 66
Table 28. *Aboue-Phs* in prose and poetry in ME 67
Table 29. *After-Phs* in prose and poetry in ME 67
Table 30. *At-Phs* in prose and poetry in ME 67
Table 31. *Bi-Phs* in prose and poetry in ME 68
Table 32. *Bifore-Phs* in prose and poetry in ME 68
Table 33. *In-Phs* in prose and poetry in ME 69
Table 34. *On-Phs* in prose and poetry in ME 69
Table 35. *Ouer-Phs* in prose and poetry in ME 70
Table 36. *Þurgh-Phs* in prose and poetry in ME 70
Table 37. *Under-Phs* in prose and poetry in ME 71
Table 38. *After-Phs* and text type in ME 72
Table 39. *At-Phs* and text type in ME 73
Table 40. *Bi-Phs* and text type in ME 74
Table 41. *Bifore-Phs* and text type in ME 75
Table 42. *In-Phs* and text type in ME 76
Table 43. *On-Phs* and text type in ME 77
Table 44. *Ouer-Phs* and text type in ME 78
Table 45. *Þurgh-Phs* and text type in ME 79
Table 46. *Under-Phs* and text type in ME 80
Table 47. Spatial *aboue-Phs* in ME 82
Table 48. Spatial *after-Phs* in ME 83
Table 49. Spatial *at-Phs* in ME 84
Table 50. Spatial *bi-Phs* in ME 85
Table 51. Spatial *bifore-Phs* in ME 87
Table 52. Spatial *in-Phs* in ME 90
Table 53. Spatial *on-Phs* in ME 94
Table 54. Spatial *ouer-Phs* in ME 97
Table 55. Spatial *þurgh-Phs* in ME 99
Table 56. Spatial *under-Phs* in ME 100

Table 57. Temporal *after-Phs* in ME	101
Table 58. Temporal *at-Phs* in ME	102
Table 59. Temporal *bi-Phs* in ME	103
Table 60. Temporal *bifore-Phs* in ME	104
Table 61. Temporal *in-Phs* in ME	105
Table 62. Temporal *on-Phs* in ME	106
Table 63. Temporal *ouer-Phs* in ME	107
Table 64. Temporal uses of *p-Phs* in ME	107
Table 65. Figurative *aboue*-phrases in ME	109
Table 66. Figurative *after*-phrases in ME	110
Table 67. Figurative *at-Phs* in ME	112
Table 68. Figurative *bi-Phs* in ME	113
Table 69. Figurative *bifore*-phrases in ME	114
Table 70. Figurative *bihinde*-phrases in ME	115
Table 71. Figurative *biside*-phrases in ME	116
Table 72. Figurative *in-Phs* in ME	117
Table 73. Figurative *on-Phs* in ME	119
Table 74. Figurative *ouer-Phs* in ME	120
Table 75. Figurative *þurgh-Phs* in ME	121
Table 76. Figurative *under-Phs* in ME	122
Table 77. *Bi*-collocational patterns	159
Table 78. *In*-collocational patterns	182

ABBREVIATIONS

Languages
L   Latin
eME   Early Middle English
lME   Late Middle English
ME   Middle English
ME1   Middle English (1150-1250)
ME2   Middle English (1250-1350)
ME3   Middle English (1350-1420)
ME4   Middle English (1420-1500)
OE   Old English
OF   Old French
ON   Old Norse
PDE   Present Day English

Dialects
EML, EMO   East Midland
WML, WMO   West Midland
NL, NO   Northern
SL, SO   Southern
KL, KO   Kentish

Semantic domains
F   Figurative
S   Spatial
T   Temporal

Miscellaneous
Oc(c)   Occurrences
fr   From
LM   Landmark
Gram   Grammatical item

HCME	Helsinki Corpus of Middle English
MED	Middle English Dictionary
OED	Oxford English Dictionary
Ph(s)	Phrase(s)
Phm(s)	Phraseme(s)
p-Ph(s)	Prepositional phrase(s)
TR	Trajector

INTRODUCTION

The present work deals with Middle English prepositions and is intended to be part of a larger project concerning "Idiomatic Prepositional Constructions in the History of the English Language"[1]. For the sake of putting limits to the study I have restricted my research to the semantic erosion of 12 ME prepositions which express location or/and path.

My analysis is based on textual evidence provided by a large number of samples extracted from the Helsinki Corpus of Middle English (henceforth, HCME) and the Middle English Dictionary (henceforth, MED). The analysis of a single text or a very small number of texts faces many problems. On the one hand, ME texts are not easy to compare, due to the absence of a standard language which led to an enormous variety of texts (different dialects, styles, etc.). On the other hand, ME prepositions present unpredictable meanings and some of them such as *of, on, in, at* and *bi* very frequently interchange their use to cover similar semantic connotations. So it seems reasonable to base the study of prepositions in Middle English on a larger corpus which includes as many texts as possible, texts from different dialects, different types of composition, different styles and different topics.

Thus, I propose a statistical study based on HCME with a detailed account of all records attested in this corpus. In so doing, a great deal of attention has been dedicated to analysing the transition from spatial meanings to other figurative and abstract connotations (semantic erosion) of 12 prepositions which indicate LOCATION and/or PATH (*aboue, after, at, bi, bifore, bihinde, biside, in, on, ouer, purgh* and *under*).

The majority of Middle English prepositions come from adverbs (e.g. *beside, behind*), although some of them come from adjectives (e.g. *near, like*) or participles (e.g. *during, except*). There is, then, a transition from lexical items to grammatical or relational items. For this reason I have dedicated the first chapter to determining the causes and mechanisms which lead both to the process of grammaticalization and

---

[1] *This research has been funded by the Spanish Ministry of Education and Science, grant number HUM2005-00562/FILO. This grant is hereby gratefully acknowledged.*

to the loss of lexical properties (semantic erosion). The second chapter introduces the tools for the analysis of ME prepositional phrases (henceforth, *p-Phs*) and the methodology used in this study, the database structure and the general data. In the third chapter One present a detailed account of occurrences and rates of each type of *p-Phs*. Tabulated and graphic information is provided for the four subperiods of ME so as to view the development and variations of each preposition in the course of Middle English. The fourth chapter is devoted to examining the dialectal distribution of *p-Phs,* their usage in prose vs. verse texts and their usage according the type of text (e.g. religious, technical, etc.). The following chapters are dedicated to analysing the semantic domains of all *p-Phs* headed by the 12 prepositions involved in this study. Thus, the fifth chapter examines the spatial and temporal roles and the sixth the figurative-"erosioned" ones. Finally, the seventh and the eighth chapters are devoted to the collocational and idiomatic framework of *p-Phs*, respectively, with a particular review of French influence on collocational patterns.

CHAPTER ONE

GRAMMATICALIZATION: SEMANTIC EROSION AND
DECATEGORIALIZATION

1. THEORETICAL FRAMEWORK

1. 1. Definition
Some typologists[1] have scrutinized grammaticalization (or grammaticization) processes, particularly in the 1990s. They tried to discover universal principles of language change, and, within the framework of grammaticalization, they have discovered some unidirectional routes of change for certain grammatical items which had developed from an unrestricted expressiveness to increasingly constrained morphosyntactic function, or from a relatively concrete meaning to a progressively more abstract domain. In broad terms, grammaticalization is, then, a process by which a lexical item may change into a grammatical item, or a grammatical item may shift from a less grammatical to a more grammatical status (Kurylowicz 1965: 52; Heine, Claudi and Hünnemeyer 1991: 2; Hopper and Traugott 2003 : 2; Lehmann 1995:11). Grammaticalization, however, is a much more complex phenomenon, as Heine and Reh state: grammaticalization is "an evolution whereby linguistic units lose in semantic complexity, pragmatic significance, syntactic freedom and phonetic substance" (1984: 15). Grammaticalization, then, entails a loss of semantic content in its early stages. Givón (1975) refers to this semantic reduction as "bleaching" and Lehmann (1995) and Heine and Reh (1984) as "erosion". Hopper and Traugott (2003: 87-93) challenge this view by alleging that traces of the original meaning remain in the new grammaticalzed forms, so they prefer the terms "pragmatic enrichment" or "strengthening". Grammaticalization also involves a loss of pragmatic significance and associative content as they become routinized and constrained to a morphosyntactic function. Grammaticalization

---

[1] Kurylowicz (1965), Givón (1975), Heine and Reh (1984), Bybee (1985), Claudi and Heine (1986), Heine, Claudi and Hünnemeyer (1991), Hopper and Traugott (2003 [1993]), Bybee, Perkins and Pagliuca (1994) and Lehmann (1995).

also implies a phonological reduction[2] because grammatical items lose stress and independent tone (Bybee, Perkins and Pagliuca 1994: 6). This reduction is triggered by an articulatory apathy of speakers, producing a gradual weakness and sometimes a loss of the sign itself (Lehmann 1995: 126-127). Consider, for example, OE *na þe læs*, which came to be reduced first to *naðe læs* and then to *naðelas* by the end of the OE period. The phonological reduction continued in ME, *natheles*, and in early Mod.E., *nathless*. By being phonologically and semantically restricted, grams show greater dependency on surrounding units and tend to merge with them, and hence their interpretation is not only dependent on context, but also affected by it (Bybee *et al* 1994: 6). As a consequence of being semantically and phonologically reduced and more dependent on context, the syntactic position of grams becomes more rigid ("rigidification") and increases the range of relations with other elements (Bybee *et al* 1994: 7).

1. 2. What motivates grammaticalization?

The reasons why some lexical items initiate a process of grammaticalization are still under conjecture. Scholars interpret the origin of grammaticalization and its motivating forces differently, depending on their theoretical approach and the purposes of their work. Thus, from a **cognitive background** (Traugott 1989: 49), grammaticalization is viewed as the result of cognitive processes consisting of changes which develop via metaphorical extension, that is, the tendency to shift from a concrete domain to a more abstract one (semantic erosion) and the propensity to express complex concepts, difficult to describe in terms of human cognition, with much more simple concepts close to human reality and experience.

From a **functionalist approach**, Heine *et al* consider that grammaticalization is "the result of a process which has problem-solving as its main goal, its primary function being conceptualization by expressing one thing in terms of another" (1991: 150-151). In line with this perspective, "problem solving" activity is not restricted to grammaticalization as it is also the basic characteristic of metaphor, that is, semantic change must be also interpreted as problem solving (Lehmann 1985). This theoretical approach examines, then, grammaticalization processes according to the principle that every language develops grammatical items motivated by a teleological force, that is, they develop because language needs them. According to this view, in the course of time, languages need new grammatical items to cover the range of functional relations and in due course they recruit lexical items for the implementation of the new grammatical function. In line with this teleological perspective, the grammaticalization of English prepositions, particularly the shift of adverbs to prepositions in the early stages of English, has occurred by way of a

---

2 Lehmann (1995: 126) uses the term "phonological attrition", whereas Heine and Reh (1984: 21ff) use the term "phonological erosion".

"drag-chain mechanism", that is, prepositions stepped into the language system to cover a new range of functional relations produced by the obliteration of part of the inflectional system (Samuels 1972: 80-84). So prepositions emerge to clear up the ambiguity produced by the blurring of case-forms.

In opposition to the functional approach, Bybee (1985: 203-5) and Bybee *et al* (1994: 297-298) state that i) "we cannot claim that a language NEEDS a particular gram-type because no gram-type is universal"; ii) furthermore "two or more markers can arise to fulfill very similar communicative needs" and iii) one may observe that "inflectional markers are often redundant in context, suggesting that speakers do not really NEED them to be there". This theoretical approach favours the view that English prepositions emerged in the early stages of English by way of a "push-chain mechanism" rather than a "drag-chain mechanism". Thus, in a first phase inflectional markers and prepositions matched together to satisfy similar communicative needs, then the use of the prepositional constructions as the alternative and the equivalent of the old case morphology increased by way of pressure of more simple and accommodating rules for effective communication.

Rejecting a teleological motivating force for grammaticalization, Bybee *et al* (1994) propose a **"cross-linguistic and context-oriented"** method of analysis:

> "grammaticization is not goal-directed; grams cannot "see" where they are going, nor are they pulled into abstract functions. The push for grammaticization comes from below—it originates in the need to be more specific, in the tendency to infer as much as possible from the input, and in the necessity of interpreting items in context. This means of course that the grammaticization process has the potential for revealing a great deal about the psychology of language use, but it also means that the method for studying grammaticization must at once be cross-linguistic and context-oriented" (p.300).

In line with this viewpoint, some other scholars highlight social-pragmatic and expressivity needs as the major factor which contributes to initiate a grammaticalization route. Thus, Haiman (1994) and Palander-Collin (1999) view grammaticalization as a cycle of routinized items. As Palander-Collin says, routinization is one of the mechanisms we use in everyday speech to "maximize the effective use of the language system" (1999: 48), we routinize items and they turn old and new ones replace them until they become old again and the cycle continues. The main objection to this perspective is the diffuseness of the embrionic stages of grammaticalization. If a grammatical item is set in motion by discourse pragmatic forces, then the starting point of grammaticalization seems to be rather difficult to determine, unless we can control the constraints and forces which operate on the forms which supply the input to grammaticalization (Hopper and Traugott 2003). Taking into account the cognitive processes and the "pragmatic and associative needs" which seem to be involved in the initial stages of grammaticalization, Hopper and Traugott (2003: 32ff) also emphasise **language internal mechanisms** such as rule change (reanalysis) and rule generalization (analogy) as the basic factors which operate in language change[3]. Acording to them, reanalysis and analogy are useful strategies to trace the paths of grams, although they do not consider them as the ultimate motivating forces of grammaticalization. However, these mechanisms of change should be also analysed in terms of cognitive processes and social-pragmatic needs. By scrutinizing on the origins of grammaticalization processes, Hopper and Traugott state that the cognitive strategies that motivate meaning changes in the early stages of grammaticalization are "initially pragmatic and associative, arising in the context of the flow of speech. At later stages, as grammaticalization continues and forms become routinized, semantic erosion or "bleaching" typically occurs" (1991: 68). Let us consider, for example, the grammaticalization of *withal*. It is originally a compound of two words *wiþ* and *al(le)*, each with its own specific meaning. By c1200, both words are fossilized into an adverbial form with the meaning of "along with the rest; in addition; besides; moreover; likewise; as well" (OED), e.g. *c*1200 *Ormin* 4203 *He beoþ all unnbeshorenn þa swa þwerrt ut wel wiþþ alle*. By 1300 the adverbial form became a preposition used in postposition, especially at the end of a relative clause or its equivalent or of a direct or indirect question, governing a relative (OED), e.g. *a*1300 *Cursor M.* 6374 *Bot tel yew of his suinc i sall, He drou þat fraward folk wit-all*.

1. 3. What are the processes which lead to grammaticalization?

Scholars tend to agree in the description of the stages of the grammaticalization process. Thus the first stage seems to be the shift from concreteness to abstractness ("semantic generalization"/erosion: Hopper and Traugott 2003 :96ff). Every lexical unit initially has a specific meaning for a specific context, but it may gradually tend to lose much of its specificities. So a lexical item which generalises in meaning becomes much more frequent as it occurs in a wider variety of contexts and it is also expected to happen in the contexts in which another grammatical item has been previously used (Bybee and Pagliuca 1985). Increasing generality leads to a wider applicability of use (Bybee *et al* 1994: 6). So the greater generality of meaning a gram achieves, the more increased appropriateness of use it has and the more capacity it also has to relate with other units.

It is also attested that when a unit shifts to a grammatical status it continues to develop after having attained this grammatical status (Bybee *et al* 1994: 5). Grams

---

3   Langacker defines reanalysis as the "change in the structure of an expression or class of expressions that does not involve any immediate or intrinsic modification of its surface manifestation (1977: 58). Analogy "refers to the attraction of extant forms to already existing constructions, [..]. Reanalysis operates along the "syntagmatic axis of linear constituent structure. Analogy, by contrast, operates along the "paradigmatic" axis of options at any constituent node" (Hopper and Traugott 2003: 56; cf. Jakobson and Halle 1956).

correlate, then, on the one hand, generality of meaning and appropriateness to be used in an extensive range of contexts, and on the other hand, when they have achieved a grammatical status they continue to expand their grammatical features and do not move backwards. It is also worth noting that the lexical units that are subject to grammaticalization are basic words, that is, words that are very frequent and so they acquire a polysemic scenery and occur in an extensive distribution.

The second stage involved in grammaticalization is known as "decategorialization" (Claudi Heine 1986: 323ff; Hopper and Traugott 1994: 103ff, Heine and Kuteva 2005). The more grammaticalized a form becomes, the more morphological and syntactical properties it loses. Thus, a given linguistic form belonging, in its origin, to a major grammatical category such as noun is identified by some properties which characterise it, such as case, number and gender, but these properties will be gradually reduced or lost in the process of grammaticalization. Two major and lexically open categories are detected in almost all languages: noun and verb (Hopper and Thompson 1985). Croft (1991) also includes the adjective within the group of major categories. Minor lexically closed categories include preposition, conjunction, pronoun, demonstrative, and auxiliary verb, whereas adjective and adverb appear between the major and the minor categories. The minor categories are very often expressed only as affixes. According to Hopper and Traugott, "it can be hypothesized that diachronically all minor categories have their origins in major categories" (1994: 104). They exemplified, as a type of decategorization, the transition of OE *hwíl* "a period of time, while" to the conjunction *while*. They argue that the original prototypical morphological and syntactical properties of this word (noun) were lost when grammaticalised to a conjunction. They put forward the basic features of *while, when used as conjunction, as follows: it*

a) "cannot take articles or quantifiers.
b) cannot be modified by adjectives or demonstratives.
c) cannot serve as a subject or as any other argument of the verb.
d) can only appear in the initial position in its clause.
e) cannot subsequently be referred to by an anaphoric pronoun". (1994: 104).

The third process of grammaticalization may be depicted as "specialization" and "divergence" of the gram. When an item progresses through the paths of grammaticalization, the range of formal choices decreases because its semantic connotations acquire greater grammatical scope (Hopper and Traugott: 2003: 114; Hoppper 1991: 22). Lexical items may expand indefinitely, whereas grammatical morphemes represent a restricted group whose capacity to arise from items belonging to the lexical class is very limited. These selective paths through which grammaticalization flows produce a certain type of specialization of the grams, although the old and the new forms may coexist. Therefore "specialization does not necesarily entail the elimination of alternatives, but may be manifested simply as textual preferences, conditioned by semantic types, sociolinguistic contexts, discourse genres, and other factors" (Hopper and Traugott 2003: 114). The lexical item from which a clitic or affix arises may continue as an autonomous form and may undertake further changes in the lexical sphere (Hopper 1991: 22). By entering the path of grammaticalization, the clitic or affix covers initially only one of the many contexts that the lexical item has. The grammaticalized context and the other lexical ones may survive as autonomous, "split" (Heine and Reh 1984: 57ff), or "divergent" (Hopper and Traugott 2003: 116ff) elements. It is worth noting, however, that the meaning of the source lexical form very often paves the way to the subsequent grammatical meaning (Bybee et al 1994: 15ff). In like manner "existing meanings may take on new forms: renewal" (Hopper and Traugott 2003: 121).

1. 4. What are the mechanisms which lead to grammaticalization?

Hopper and Traugott (2003: 32 ff) consider reanalysis and analogy as the basic mechanisms by which grammaticalization takes places. By reanalysis[4] is understood the change of the structure of an expression without altering its surface appearance. Thus a typical occurrence of reanalysis is the fusion of two or more forms into one, e.g. compounding (Brinton and Traugott 2005: chapter III). Many English derivational affixes such as *–hood, -dom, -ly* come from lexical items (full nouns with their meaning: "condition/state, realm, body/likeness", respectively). In the course of time they have merged with other nouns forming a single unit. Such a process of merging "involves changes in the assignment of boundaries" and therefore "reassignment of morphemes to different semantic-syntactic categories" (Hopper and Traugott 2003: 41). Thus, when a new grammatical affix appears it initiates a new frequently recurring route by changing its deep structure, but without modifying its surface appearance.

The other mechanism by which grammaticalization occurs is analogy (rule generalization). Analogy is defined as a process in which irregularities in grammar were regularized in the course of time. This process is also viewed as the mechanism of change by means of which a more "constrained" form tends to be replaced by a more general one (Hopper and Traugott 2003: 57). By discussing the importance of token frequency in grammaticalization (Bybee: 2003), Hoffmann (2004: 194-195) maintains that low-frequency complex prepositions in English grammaticalized by analogy, although he conmsiders his proposal as tentative.

There are other mechanisms which lead to grammaticalization, such as methaphorical extension, metonymy, inference and generalization. Metaphorical extension is considered to be one of the mechanisms which monitors the processes of grammaticalization (Claudi and Heine 1986; Sweetser 1990; Lichtenberk 1991; Heine *et al* 1991). Thus by comparing the lexical source of a category and the resulting grammatical form we usually find a transition from a specific and concrete

---

4 Reanalysis has been studied at length by Langacker (1977: 58), Lighfoot (1979: 98-115), Radford (1988: 429-432), Denison (1993).

semantic domain to a more abstract meaning (semantic erosion), although the gram may maintain some semantic features of the lexical source. By exploring the driving forces for the use of metaphors one may posit that the main motivations are: a) the propensity to expand expressiveness; b) the tendency to hide or disguise reality; and c) the trend to express complex experience in much more simple terms, that is, the use of a less complex concept taken from physical phenomena or expereince to convey thoughts far from physical knowledge (Claudi and Heine 1986: 299). As Lakoff and Johnson state, the core of metaphor is "understanding and experiencing one kind of thing in terms of another" (1980: 5). These scholars (1980: 25ff) distinguish three types of metaphors: a) "structural metaphors" (an experience "is metaphorically structured in terms of another", e.g. "I've never *won* an argument with him"); b) "orientational metaphors" (many concepts are understood in spatial orientational terms, e.g. "I *fell* into depression"); and c) ontological metaphors (one may perceive ideas, events etc. as physical realities, e.g. "life *has cheated* me"). Claudi and Heine (1986: 300ff), following Lakoff and Jonhson's metaphorical conceptualization, develop the basic categories of conceptualization, establishing their implicational relationship as follows: quality <-- process <-- space <-- object <-- person. These authors maintain that metaphorical usage restrict semantic complexity to lexical units as these "tend to be reduced essentially to one basic semantic element" (1986: 313) and hence this desemanticization triggers a development towards a grammatical marker.

Bybee et al (1994: 24-25) do not consider metaphor as a major mechanism of semantic change, as they see that metaphor operates "only on the more lexical end of grammaticization paths rather than propelling grams into the more and more abstract domains of grammatical meaning". Heine *et al* (1991b: 113) believe that the processes subject to metaphorical transfer show a "context-induced reinterpretation and metonymy" which incite the appearance of various overlapping meanings. Bybee *et al* (1994: 25) refer to this context-oriented mechanism of change as "inference or the conventionalization of implicature". Heine *et al* (1991: 70ff) explain this process which leads to the "conventionalized meaning" of the gram as follows: a grammatical item in a given context attains a meaning that matches with the original sense and this new sense becomes part of the explicit "conventionalized" meaning of the grammatical item, i.e. the gram *self* was mainly used for reflexive contexts in Old English, although it originally was an emphatic pronoun. This use led speakers to infer that *self* implied reflexive reference, which turned to be its core meaning, whereas the emphatic sense became less important (Faltz 1988). As Bybee *et al* (1994: 285) state, "inference and implicature are the two sides of the same coin: the speaker IMPLIES more than s/he asserts, and the hearer INFERS more than is asserted". So by means of implicature new meanings are being taken for granted to play a role in the context and by means of inference new meanings, different from the original meaning of the gram, are also incorporated to the gram from the context.

Inferencing is also a very important mechanism of change for Hopper and Traugott (2003: 67). Heine *et al* (1991) develop a model of grammaticalization based on metaphorical extension and metonymy conceived as a problem solving activity and motivated by cognitive processes. This activity is unidirectional (from source to target, from concrete to abstract), although it is perceptible as a discontinuous phase because we habitually find metaphorical jumps, whereas metonymy is observable as continuous phase as there are unremitting metonymic connections. Thus Heine *et al* state that metaphor and metonymy are complementary because "a developmemt from a lexical item to a grammatical marker might not be possible unless there is an intermediate stage whereby distinct conceptual domains are bridged by means of metonymical understanding" (1991: 70). Bybee *et al* (1994: 289) include generalization, that is, the shift from concreetness to abstractness, as a mechanism of change, although they also wonder whether generalization is itself a mechanism which contributes to outline the paths of grammaticalization, or whether it is the result of the action of other mechanisms such as metaphorical extension and inference.

1. 5. Is grammaticalization a unidirectional and continuous process?
There is an acceptable agreement with regard to the unidirectionality of grammaticalization: from lexis to grammar (Givón 1975: 96, Heine *et al* 1991: 4-5, Hopper and Traugott 2003:126-129, Haspelmath 2004: 17-46). Unidirectionality seems to be the rule that accompanies the semantic change in grammaticalization processes. Thus, Bybee *et al* (1994: chaps. 6 and 8) show that the changes produced by both inference and generalization seem to be unidirectional. Unidirectionality of semantic change was also attested by Heine *et al* (1991) in their analysis of metaphorical extension. There is also a great deal of evidence that shows that the phonological and grammatical changes that accompany grammaticalization tend towards unidirectionality (Heine and Reh 1984: 74-76; Bybee *et al* 1994: 13). When phonological segments are condensed in the procees of phonological reduction which usually affects the processes of grammaticalization, the resulting grams do not recover the phonological segments which they had before entering the paths of grammaticalization. In like manner, on a grammatical level, when the process of affixation has occurred, affixes do not recover their freedom to be used unbound and freely as independent forms. In fact, they are subject to an increasing "dependency on surrounding lexical material" (Bybee *et al* 1994: 13).

It seems also plausible that there are "common cross-linguistic gram-types", that is, paths (channels, Givón 1979; Heine and Reh 1984) along which delexicalised items move along pushed by similar mechanisms of change in many languages (Heine and Reh 1984; Bybee and Dahl 1989; Heine *et al* 1991; Bybee *et al* (1994). Many scholars have already described the paths of development of many grams, e. g. Bybee *et al* (1994: chap. 3) have analysed the paths leading to simple past and perfective grams. Traugott and König (1991) have also depicted the paths for causal and concessive conjunctions from temporal conjunctions, Rissanen (1997) drew the path for the pronominalization of *one*, etc. Most cases of grammaticalization show changes which operate along a single path; there are, however, some other cases of "polygrammaticalization" (Craig 1991) or multiple development, that is, a single form may develop different grammatical functions. "Thus our claim is not that the source meaning gives a unique grammatical meaning, but rather that the source meaning uniquely determines the grammaticalization path that the gram will travel in its semantic development" (Bybee *et al* 1994: 12). However, it is also arguable whether the multiple grammatical senses that develop from the same source should be considered as multiple paths of development or whether they should be analysed as different stages along the same grammaticalization path (Bybee *et al* 1994: 12). There are still unsolved queries concerning the phases or degrees through which grams evolve. Is grammaticalisation identified in phases or degrees within a continuous process? Lehmann (1995: 121ff) expands the theoretical prerequisites to establish the degree of grammaticalization which a gram has attained, taking as a starting point the autonomy of the sign. The more freedom a sign has in use, the more autonomous it is and the more opposite it is to grammaticality. This author shows three features of autonomy: a) a sign must have a certain weight and prominence in the syntagm; b) when a sign bonds systematic relations (cohesion) with other signs its autonomy decreases; and c) the more autonomous a sign is, the more variability it has. Hopper and Traugott also distinguish three typical phases of grammaticalization that are perceptible in addition to the basic components of generalization and decategorialization: specialization, divergence and renewal. As they say, "specialization, whereby the choice of grammatical forms becomes reduced as certain ones become generalized in meaning and use; divergence,whereby a less grammatical form may split into two, one variant maintaining its former characteristics, the other becoming more grammatical; and thirdly, renewal, whereby old forms are renewed as more expressive ways are found of sayng the same thing" (2003: 113).

Despite the general view that items subject to grammaticalization develop from lexis to grammar and once these items have acquired a grammatical status, they do not degrammaticalize, it is worth noting that some cases of degrammaticalization have been detected. It would be admissible to consider that grammaticalization may move backwards to lexicalization according to the following process: firstly, derivational items grammaticalize to inflectional items which in turn lexicalize to derivational elements (Kurylowicz 1965: 52f; Kahr 1976: 122; Nichols and Timberlake 1991; Wright: 2004; Brinton 2004, Rosenbach 2004).

2. GRAMMATICALIZATION OF ENGLISH PREPOSITIONS. SEMANTIC EROSION

If we look backwards in the history of English we find that, on the semantic level, prepositions and their complements originally represented a conceptual entity with an informative content in OE as they were associated with a spatial or temporal sense. However, in the course of time, particularly in the Middle English period, prepositions lost much of their original "information-content" (Lundskær-Nielsen 1993: 81, 107) as they developed from a spatial or temporal sense to a figurative or abstract meaning. Consequently, they underwent a process of semantic erosion. As has been mentioned, the first stage of grammaticalization is perceived as the shift from concreteness to abstractness ("semantic generalization": Hopper and Traugott 2003 :96ff, "semantic erosion": Heine and Reh 1984). English prepositions entered the paths of grammaticalization by losing much of their originally specific senses. As they generalised in meaning, they became much more frequent and appeared in a wider range of contexts. So increasing generality led to a wider applicability of use (Bybee *et al* 1994: 6). The greater variety of meaning prepositions attain, the greater appropriateness of use they have and the greater facility they also have to interact with other units. The majority of English prepositions were originally adverbs, although some others come from adjectives, participles and other sources. Most of them present the main features previously mentioned as typical of grammaticalization processes. The process of grammaticalaization is much more perceptible in complex prepositions. Consider, for instance, the ME complex preposition *accordant to*. *Accordant* comes from L *ad* + *cord(-is)* "heart", hence, *acorda¤re* "to bring heart to heart". This concrete semantic connotation developed into a more abstract meaning: "to reconcile, reconcile oneself, agree, agree to, agree to give". Thus from Latin and through Anglo-Norman came to be used as *acord(e)*, aphetically *cord(e)* in ME whose pr. pple. *acordant* [*accordant acordaunt, accordaunt*], fr. OFr. *acordant* [pr. pple. of *acorder*], was used as a free lexical word [adjective] with the following meaning: "Agreeing with any one's character, or with circumstances; suitable, fitting, appropriate" (OED). Consider:

1413 Lydgate *Pylgr. Sowle* ii. lviii. 56 (1859) Sothly, this lykenes is **accordaunt**.
1477 Caxton *Dictes* 149 It is **acordaunt** that his [Socrates'] dyctes and sayengis shold be had as well as others.

Acordant is found for the first time in early fourteenth century followed by either *to* or *with* forming a complex preposition. Thus,

c1315 Shoreham 89 **Acordaunt to** thy trauayl, Lord, graunte me thy coroune.
1494 Fabyan cxlvii. 133 (1811) An excedynge nombre, to be **accordaunt with** reason.

By the end of the century this participial form was being used with the native ending *–ing* usually followed by *to* and sometimes by *with*. Consider:

1398 Trevisa *Barth. De P.R.* v. xxviii. (Bodl. MS.), Kinde Seueþ to man vndirstonding instrumentes **according to** his vertues.

Cognitive semantics (Vandeloise 1986, Talmy 2000) and grammaticalization theories (Hoffmann 2004 and 2005 provides a detailed account of grammaticalization of English complex prepositions) have put forward the notion of hierarchy of meanings: the basic spatial meanings of prepositions developed into a network of temporal and figurative meanings by "metaphorical transfer process" (Cadiot 2002).

"Decategorialization" seems to be the second stage in grammaticalization (Claudi and Heine 1986: 323ff; Hopper and Traugott 1994: 103ff). English prepositions have undergone a process of "decategorialization" as they lose the morphological and syntactical properties of adverbs and assume a more grammatical function operating as relational elements (Hopper and Thompson 1985; Croft 1991; Hopper and Traugott 1994). Thus, they cannot be used as argument of the verb (subject, object, etc.), they tend to be restricted to the position in front of its complement; they cannot be referred to by an anaphoric pronoun, etc. (Hopper and Traugott 1994: 104). Thus, the participial adjective *acordant* decategorializes or changes its grammatical category and loses the morphological and syntactical properties of adverbs such as restrictions on adopting a comparative or superlative form, on preceding nouns as qualifiers or on being used as intensive/predicative complements. Its use is restricted to being combined with *to* or *with*, forming a complex preposition. So *accordant* became "specialized". As has been pointed out, "specialization" is recorded as the third process of grammaticalization. The more grammaticalized status an item attains, the more restrictive is its range of formal choices (Hopper and Traugott: 2003: 114; Hoppper 1991: 22). Lexical units tend towards unrestricted expansion, whereas grammatical forms decrease their capacity to spread out. Prepositions tend towards specialization[5], although the meaning of the source lexical form has not been totally removed. Hawkins (1984) has identified the specialization parameters which account for the variation of meaning in prepositions: trajector configuration, landmark configuration and the relational factors that operate between trajector and landmark. According to the trajector configuration, prepositions tend to specialisize in "topological and geometric properties". Thus, the trajector of *around* involves "directionality on a bounded or circuitive path" (Hawkins 1984: 64). By landmark configuration is meant the "relational potential" (*ibid.*) the preposition has, e.g. the

---

5 In the process of grammaticalization prepositions tend to specialize as "linking" units. O'Dowd (1998) states that prepositions (as well as particles) are "pragmatic, discourse-orienting elements". (p. 10) "It is this orientational function that determines their grammatical function as prepositions, particles or other lexical categories, and that drives their semantic extensions into a variety of meanings" (*ibid.*). She also posits that "orientation involves both *situating* (predicating states or changes of state) and *linking* (introducing contextual information" (*ibid.*). According to her "particles situate and prepositions link" (*ibid*).

preposition *in* indicates potential inclusion by the landmark. Finally, the relational factors between trajector and landmark tend towards coincidence or separation. Thus, coincidence is a property of *in*, whereas separation is a property of *out* (O'Dowd 1998:138).

By comparing the ME and PDE topological prepositions *at, on, in* and *bi*, we find that they were very often interchanged either in spatial or temporal references in ME, whereas in (e)ModE they became specialized: *at* specialized as "locative", *by* as "locative-proximity", *on* as "locative surface", including both "on the top of" and "at the surface of"; *in* as "locative interior" (Bennett, 1975: 69). Leech (1969: 249) explains the semantic highlights of topological prepositions in terms of "ascription features of dimensionality". Thus, with *on* we are supposed to perceive a line or surface/area, i.e. as one- or two-dimensional, whereas *in* is perceived as an area or volume, *i.e.* two- or three-dimensional. Dirven (1993: 78) conceptualizes *on* as "contact" positing a radial network which embraces a central notion of "contact with line/surface". From this common core the meaning of *on* extends to "time", which, in its turn, expands to "circumstance". The primary meaning also enlarges to "state", to "area", to "means" and "reason". There is then a notional enlargement in meaningful nets whose centre is more concrete or physical, whereas the peripheral meanings are more abstract or mental.

There is a further distinction worth mentioning: on the one hand, prepositions may occur "fully determined" in a given position and tightly controlled by the terms of the structure in which they appear. Thus *at* in *at large* cannot be replaced by another preposition. On the other hand, prepositions may occur "loosely determined" by the terms to which they relate. Thus we may say *in the garden, up the garden, over the garden, out the garden*, etc. Therefore, the more "determined" a preposition occurs, the more rigidity the prepositional phrase presents.

CHAPTER TWO

PREPOSITIONAL PHRASES IN MIDDLE ENGLISH

1. TOOLS FOR ANALYSIS

1. 1. Syntactic and semantic features

From a syntactic point of view, prepositions express a relation which entails two or more partaking entities: trajector and landmark (Langacker: 1987)[1]. The trajector may be an object, e.g. *the key is in the drawer,* the entity involved in the state, *the key*, functions as trajector, but it may be also a process, e.g. *the children are playing in the garden*, the process *the children are playing* takes the role of trajector. The landmark (NP-complement) is the "reference point entity" (Taylor 1993:153). Although there is a general agreement about the functions of these two terms related by the preposition, there is still a great deal of controversy about the role of the preposition itself, and particularly about its lexical and/or grammatical character. Some scholars consider that it is not possible to separate the meaning of the preposition itself from the meaning conceptualized by its trajector and landmark. Following this line of argument, the meaning of a preposition is not self-governing, as the speaker always has a specific location or orientation, that is, a place or thing in mind. Then the meaning of a preposition depends on the contextual factors. Supporting this view, Rauh (1993:119) states that prepositions "assign roles themselves and do not simply express roles assigned by verbs". Thus in "Bill lives along the road" the verb *live* assigns to its PP-complement the role LOCATION, whereas the preposition *along* assigns to its NP-complement the role PATH. On the other hand, Bennet (1975: 65) insists on the fact that "the differences reside in the context of the preposition" rather than in the preposition itself. In fact, following his line of discussion, we may assume that prepositions have no lexical

---

[1] Langacker (1987: 217ff) has presented the terms *trajector* and *landmark*. The reference (location or orientation) function is the *landmark* (complement of the preposition), whereas the subject of the relation is the *trajector*.

properties, as what matters are the lexical properties allocated to the verb and to the NP-complement. Thus the uses of locative *at, in* and *on* depends basically on the meanings of the words that the preposition relates to each other rather on the meaning of the preposition itself. Thus, these three prepositions may have the same role location, and the differences between them are determined by the context. I would say that "I live in Oxford", but "I have to change trains at Oxford" or "a blind foggy day dropped on Oxford". Then the landmark *Oxford* has no influence on the choice between the prepositions *at, in* or *on*.

From a semantic point of view, it is generally assumed that prepositions express at least one of the following roles: LOCATION (e.g. *at, in, on, by, over, under*, etc), SOURCE (e.g. *from, since, off*, etc.), PATH (e.g. *along, across, through, during*, etc.), GOAL (e.g. *to, towards, for, until*, etc.); and ACCOMPANIMENT (e.g. *with*). However, a preposition, say *over* in PDE, has many different meanings or senses associated with it (Tyler and Evans 2003: 64-106). Scholars have often contended over which meaning or sense should be taken as primary or central. Thus, in the case of *over*, Lakoff (1987) maintains that the primary sense of *over* is "above and across", whereas Kreitzer (1997) suggests that its primary sense is similar to *above*. Tyler and Evans (2003: 35-63) have developed a model of principled polysemy by accounting for a "systematic, motivated network of senses" associated with spatial particles. They suggest both some linguistic criteria for determining the primary sense associated with a semantic network and several principles to show how a network may be extended from that central-primary sense ("proto-scene"). In so doing, they assume that the synchronic network of senses of a spatial particle reflect "many aspects of its diachronic development".

1. 2. Prepositional phrases as counterparts of case forms in Middle English

The increase in the use of prepositional constructions in late OE as counterparts of case morphology forms has been studied from functional and lexical points of view. The functional analysis given by Samuels (1972: 80-84), for example, substantiates the emergence of prepositional constructions as being closely connected (either as cause or as effect) with the disintegration of the case system. However, the functional approach is still divided between two contending theories regarding whether the prepositional constructions ousted case-forms ("push-chain mechanism") or whether prepositions stepped in to fill the gap and avoid the ambiguity produced by the blurring of case-forms ("drag-chain mechanism"). In broad terms, the functional tenets provide an overall theory about language change rather than a detailed explanation based on text analysis, so other scholars such as Traugott (1972), Horgan (1981), Kniezsa (1991) and Lundskær-Nielsen (1993) have put forward evidence of the use of the prepositional constructions as the alternative and the equivalent of the old case morphology, by studying lexical structures in specific texts.

However, the analysis of a text or a very small number of texts faces many methodological problems. Textual comparison is not a reliable procedure in Middle English. The absence of a standard language led to an enormous variety of texts (different dialects, styles, etc.), so it seems reasonable to base the study of prepositions in Middle English on a larger corpus which includes as many texts as possible, texts from different dialects, different types of composition, different styles and different topics.

2. METHODOLOGY

2. 1. A corpus-based study (Helsinki Corpus of Middle English)

My work represents an attempt to measure the use of *p*-phrases in ME, following a statistical method based on the texts available in the Helsinki Corpus of ME[2] (henceforth HCME). Although my study is limited to the semantic analysis of *p*-phrases, I shall try to gather evidence of an increasingly strong tendency towards fixed word order within the prepositional construction creating an incipient process of idiomatisation in ME.

For the sake of putting limits to my work I will concentrate only on 12 ME prepositions: *aboue, after, at, bi, bifore, bihinde, biside, in, on, ouer, þurgh,* and *under*. These prepositions were chosen for two main reasons: a) they all assign their landmark the role LOCATION, whether in spatial or temporal domains, from which they extend to new figurative roles; and b) they all show a certain flexibility to be used indistinctly in many similar contexts. Thus, sometimes there is no semantic difference in ME *p-Phs* such as *aboue þe weorld, at þe weorld; bi þe weorld, in þe weorld; on þe weorld; ouer þe weorld; þurgh þe weorld* to indicate "all over the world" or *in þe niȝt, at þe niȝt, on þe niȝt, bi þe niȝt, ouer þe niȝt* with the meaning "during the night" e.g. *by the vnyuersal worlde* (CMCAXPRO); *and al his progenye in this world* (CMECTPROS); *Is non fairere on werlde her* (CMBESTIA). *he felde on hem in the niȝt* (CMOTEST); *as is in þin house on niȝtes* (CMCLOUD); *To wedden hire bi niȝte* (CMHORN); *ouer-nyȝt* (CMHORSES).

2. 2. The database

The HCME includes sections of 96 texts and a total of 608,570 words. The corpus also incorporates information about the geographical dialect of the texts, their type of composition (prose vs. verse) and text type, i.e. romance, fiction, history, science, document, law, homily, etc.

My database includes two designs. The first incorporates all the *p-Phs* included in this study and found in the whole HCME. The following example, extracted from

---

2 *The Helsinki Corpus of English Texts* is an electronic collection of historical texts, compiled under the supervision of Profs. M. Rissanen and O. Ihalainen (U. of Helsinki). In this study I have analysed the material from the four ME subperiods (M1, M2, M3, M4).

Kyng Alisaunder, shows the structure of this first design which includes 10 fields, namely:

A	B	C	D	E	F	G	H	I	J
N°	*At-Ph*	Context	Text	Date	Dialect	T. type	Comp.	Struct.	Sense
33	At her talent	(hij) dronken wyne and ek pyement, White and red, *at her talent*.	CMALISAU	ME2	EMO	Romance	Verse	At-dnC	Fig.

Table 1. Database structure

Field A (N° **1-n**) lists by reference number the prepositional phrases introduced by any of the prepositions involved in this study (**after, at, bi, bifore, bihinde, biside…**) and found in the HCME.

Field B (**At Ph**) includes the preposition and its complement.

Field C (**Context**) gives the context of the *p-Ph*.

Field D (**Text**) shows the location of the example in the HCME. The text is expressed with the short form used in the HCME, e.g. CMALISAU which stands for *Kyng Alisaunder*[3].

Field E (**Date**) indicates the date of the text, specified as ME1, ME2, ME3 or ME4.

Field F records the geographical dialect.

Field G indicates text type.

Field H incorporates the type of composition (prose vs. verse).

Field I includes syntactic properties of the prepositional phrase. Thus, example 33 has the structure **At-dnC**, that is, the preposition **At** and its noun complement (**nC**) which is preceded by a determiner (**d**). Modifiers, when present, are indicated by (**m**).

Field J (**Sense**) specifies the sense or semantical role of the **at-phrase**. Thus our example is recorded as **Fig**(urative).

In a second database I have included the specific data for each of the 96 texts of the HCME. The database incorporates the characteristics of the text, the prepositions which are present, the number of occurrences of each preposition and the number of instances within the four semantic fields covered by this study: spatial, temporal, figurative and idiomatic (senses). Table 2 shows the structure of this database.

---

3 Ed. G. V. Smithers. London: EETS 227; 1952.

Prepositonal phrases in Middle English 35

Text	Text features		Prep.	Total tokens	Spat.	Temp.	Fig.	Idiom.
			Aboue	1	1	0	0	0
	Date	ME3	After	21	1	15	5	0
			At	31	12	5	6	9
	Dialect	SL	Bi	40	15	0	24	1
			Bifore	1	1	0	0	0
CMALISAU	Text type	Rule	Bihinde	2	2	0	0	0
			Biside	2	2	0	0	0
	Composition type	Prose	In	156	56	9	86	1
		On	96	34	4	35	21	
			Over	11	6	0	4	1
			Þurgh	15	3	0	11	1
	Number of words	3010	Under	15	12	0	3	0

Table 2. CMALISAU data

From a database in which I have counted all prepositional phrases headed by 25 different prepositions (See Appendix) I have chosen those data referring to the 12 prepositions dealt with in this study and exhibited in the following table:

2. 3. The data

Prepositions	aboue	after	at	bi	bifore	bihinde	biside	in	on	over	þurgh	under
CMAELR3	0	5	5	7	0	0	0	60	2	0	3	0
CMAELR4	0	1	1	6	0	0	0	29	2	0	0	0
CMALISAU	1	21	31	40	1	1	2	156	96	11	15	15
CMANCRE	0	16	1	17	0	2	0	32	31	11	36	8
CMASTRO	5	19	7	50	3	0	0	140	23	10	3	18
CMAYENBI	13	2	3	69	2	0	0	234	7	4	0	1
CMBENRUL	0	0	3	0	0	0	0	40	3	0	0	5
CMBESTIA	0	3	4	11	0	0	0	60	34	4	11	2
CMBEVIS	2	10	9	24	0	0	0	81	20	6	10	4
CMBODLEY	0	20	7	19	1	0	0	0	135	0	35	0
CMBOETH	2	4	5	110	3	0	0	81	8	3	0	2
CMBRUT1	0	11	12	23	0	0	2	27	55	13	19	3
CMBRUT3	0	23	37	19	2	1	1	73	11	4	0	0
CMCAPCHR	0	24	40	25	10	0	0	120	37	0	3	0
CMCAPSER	0	2	8	8	0	0	0	4	1	0	1	3
CMCAXPRO	0	16	12	49	1	0	1	35	5	2	1	1
CMCHAULI	5	36	6	43	0	1	0	20	6	9	0	5
CMCLOUD	14	23	19	88	7	1	0	486	48	2	11	10
CMCTPROS	0	9	5	100	7	0	0	187	5	6	8	1
CMCTVERS	1	6	25	38	5	0	1	109	26	6	0	3

CHAPTER TWO

Prepositions	aboue	after	at	bi	bifore	bihinde	biside	in	on	over	þurgh	under
CMCURSOR	1	0	24	9	0	0	1	140	44	6	15	9
CMDIGBY	2	4	4	13	1	0	0	63	12	0	11	2
CMDOCU2	0	0	0	1	0	0	0	4	19	1	6	0
CMDOCU3	0	43	40	102	6	0	0	289	51	1	3	7
CMDOCU4	1	17	46	93	13	0	0	190	16	3	8	10
CMEARLPS	0	1	10	4	0	0	1	442	32	0	6	2
CMEDMUND	1	9	18	15	4	0	0	92	14	5	6	1
CMEQUATO	0	16	8	34	0	0	0	201	37	4	4	5
CMFITZJA	2	18	9	72	1	1	0	141	6	0	1	2
CMFOXWO	0	2	2	5	0	0	0	17	3	1	0	3
CMGAYTRY	1	1	7	5	0	0	0	90	24	6	18	2
CMGOWER	2	11	9	12	0	1	0	57	19	3	12	3
CMGREGOR	1	27	59	25	3	0	0	109	23	0	12	0
CMHALI	0	15	2	11	0	0	0	60	41	16	22	13
CMHANSYN	1	8	31	11	8	2	2	127	31	6	12	1
CMHAVELO	0	4	26	28	1	0	0	69	82	4	0	7
CMHILTON	2	8	1	13	1	0	0	67	82	3	12	6
CMHORN	0	11	23	40	9	0	4	56	53	2	18	0
CMHORSES	3	11	11	18	1	0	0	117	29	11	1	12
CMINNOCE	1	13	3	27	0	0	0	137	3	0	7	0
CMJULIA	1	11	0	7	0	2	0	81	24	6	2	1
CMJULNOR	3	10	3	5	4	0	3	120	4	0	1	1
CMCATHE	0	2	0	3	9	0	0	54	15	2	23	4
CMKEMPE	2	21	23	25	1	0	0	186	31	0	17	0
CMKENTSE	0	2	7	12	1	0	0	40	1	1	17	0
CMLAMBET	0	18	21	15	6	0	0	111	97	12	10	4
CMLAW	15	35	43	151	8	0	0	247	5	1	5	11
CMLUDUS	1	1	14	2	0	0	0	49	15	1	1	0
CMALORY	4	13	40	45	6	4	0	90	57	8	14	4
CMMANDEV	7	11	33	26	4	0	4	90	11	2	1	6
CMMANKIN	1	1	11	20	2	0	0	43	12	1	0	0
CMMARGA	0	3	3	6	0	0	0	43	37	2	11	1
CMMETHAM	0	1	9	0	1	0	0	103	5	7	1	0
CMMIRK	2	7	14	14	3	0	0	38	19	0	0	0
CMMOON	0	0	2	0	0	0	0	5	1	1	0	0
CMNORHOM	1	2	10	16	8	0	2	131	29	1	16	4
CMNTEST	2	17	12	13	10	0	5	207	15	5	0	0
CMOFFIC3	0	8	18	27	2	0	0	97	5	1	1	1
CMOFFIC4	0	11	20	44	6	0	0	71	7	2	0	0
CMORM	2	18	7	4	20	1	0	80	63	0	99	0
CMOTEST	3	14	7	49	22	1	3	185	46	1	4	1
CMPERIDI	0	16	2	2	0	0	0	8	121	0	24	4
CMPETERB	0	7	7	6	2	0	0	22	30	6	5	0
CMPHLEBO	3	22	3	19	0	0	0	82	5	5	0	2
CMPOEMH	1	5	10	17	3	0	1	26	10	1	2	1
CMPOEMS	0	0	4	5	0	0	0	17	14	1	1	0
CMPOLYCH	2	24	41	38	0	0	1	88	6	0	0	3

Prepositonal phrases in Middle English 37

Prepositions	aboue	after	at	bi	bifore	bihinde	biside	in	on	over	þurgh	under
CMPRICK	0	14	9	3	7	0	0	96	17	1	15	0
CMPRIV	2	23	175	95	6	0	0	165	52	9	1	3
CMPURVEY	0	6	9	26	0	0	0	63	9	0	0	0
CMREYNAR	6	8	15	36	1	0	0	111	31	10	7	6
CMREYNES	3	33	48	14	5	1	3	143	28	5	3	1
CMROBGLO	0	11	55	26	4	1	1	151	5	11	29	2
CMROLLBE	0	0	0	0	0	0	0	12	1	2	0	0
CMROLLPS	11	12	12	6	6	0	2	460	6	0	26	0
CMROLLTR	3	7	6	4	0	0	0	164	3	6	6	1
CMROOD	0	11	0	6	3	0	0	13	168	5	45	1
CMROYAL	0	1	11	40	0	0	0	103	23	0	0	0
CMSAWLES	0	12	2	36	4	0	0	103	20	0	3	0
CMSELEG	2	8	29	14	0	0	0	22	17	0	9	4
CMSIEGE	2	12	23	11	7	0	0	105	30	2	0	0
CMSIRITH	0	1	6	4	0	0	0	6	18	4	2	0
CMTHORN	0	7	22	2	0	0	0	114	19	16	16	2
CMTHRUSH	0	0	0	6	0	0	0	14	5	0	2	2
CMTOWNEL	1	1	6	4	1	0	0	58	16	1	1	0
CMTRINIT	1	6	6	11	4	0	0	31	115	2	2	1
CMVESHOM	0	11	0	0	1	0	0	0	128	0	12	2
CMVICES1	0	23	12	2	2	0	0	22	120	7	51	3
CMVICES4	2	0	10	24	0	0	0	114	10	3	3	1
CMWYCSER	1	37	13	71	14	2	2	274	20	5	0	0
CMYORK	0	3	18	5	3	0	0	53	5	2	5	0
TOTAL	**122**	**1001**	**1555**	**2290**	**305**	**24**	**42**	**9437**	**2691**	**371**	**862**	**261**

Table 3. Records for each text and preposition

CHAPTER THREE

OCCURRENCES AND RATES

1. Numbers and rates of p-Phs in Middle English

1. 1. Aboue[1]-Phs

I have only counted 122 phrases headed by *boue(n)/aboue(n)* in the HCME. The total number and percentage, for each of the four subperiods of ME, are shown in Table 4:

Date	N° of words	N° of *aboue-Phs*	Rate ‰
ME1 (1150-1250)	113 010	4	0.03
ME2 (1250-1350)	97 480	9	0.09
ME3 (1350-1420)	184 230	39	0.2
ME4 (1420-1500)	213 850	70	0.3
ME (1150-1500)	**608 570**	**122**	**0.2**

Table 4. Numbers and rates of *aboue-Phs* in ME

Table 4 shows that *aboue-Phs* are scarcely used in ME, particularly in ME1 and ME2, although they did already occur in OE with *a-bufan* with the meanings of "over", "vertically up from", "on the top of". The use of *aboue-Phs* increases progressively during the ME period as its rate rises from 0.03‰ in ME1 to 0.3‰ in ME4.

---

1 Other spelling variants of *above* occurring in the corpus include: *abufe(n), abuue(n), abowve; obove(n), obufe(n); abof, aboyf; aboun(e), abown(e), aboon, oboun(e); abow* and *abo3e* (MED). The preposition *boue(n)* comes from OE *bufan* (< *be* + *ufan*). From the 12th century on *boue(n)* matched with *aboue(n)*. This form with *a-* (from OE *on*) gradually displaced the primitive *boue(n)* which became obsolete by the end of ME period.

Aboue-Phs

	N° of occurrences
ME1	1
ME2	3
ME3	9
ME4	20
	30

Subperiods of ME

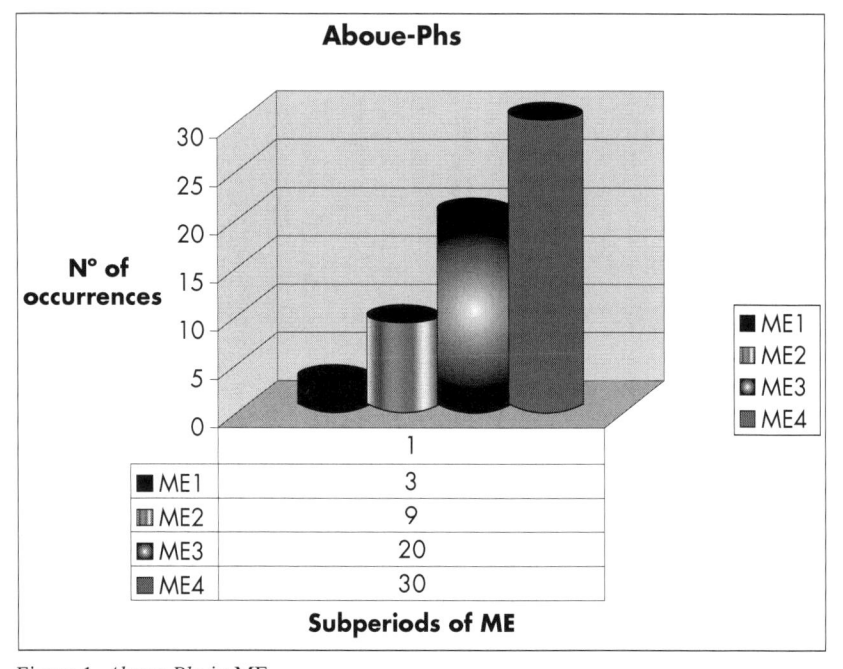

Figure 1. *Aboue-Phs* in ME

1. 2. After[2]-Phs

The survey of the HCME shows that *after-Phs* are very frequent in ME. I have counted 1001 instances in the HCME. Table 5 shows the numbers and rates for the four subperiods of ME:

Date	N° of words	N° of *after-Phs*	Rate ‰
ME1 (1150-1250)	113 010	194	1.71
ME2 (1250-1350)	97 480	84	0.86
ME3 (1350-1420)	184 230	351	1.90
ME4 (1420-1500)	213 850	372	1.73
ME (1150-1500)	**608 570**	**1001**	**1.64**

Table 5. Numbers and rates of *after-Phs* in ME

---

2 Other spelling variants of *after* occurring in the corpus include: *efter, hafter, ofter* and *æfter*(MED). The preposition *after* comes from *OE æfter, efter* which was used as preposition with verbs of motion.

After-Phs

ME1	171
ME2	86
ME3	190
ME4	173

Subperiods of ME

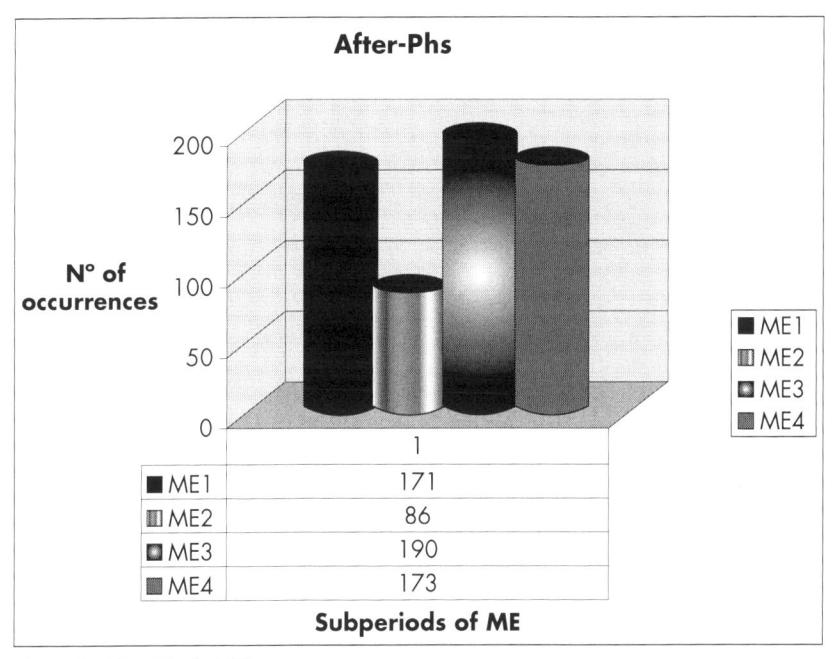

Figure 2. *After-Phs* in ME

According to the data exhibited in Table 5 *after-Phs* have a similar frequency in ME1 (1.71‰), ME3 (1.90‰) and ME4 (1.73‰). This rate, however, diminishes to 0.86‰ in ME2. This decline (in ME2) occurs because the eME spatial uses such as "behind", "moving in the rear of" tend to disappear from 1250 onwards, but from 1350 on, new figurative senses, such as "next to in order or importance" and "in imitation of, like", emerge and therefore the rate of *after-Phs* increases again.

1. 3. At³-Phs

I have counted 1,555 phrases headed by *at* in the 608.570 words of HCME. Their numbers and rates are recorded according to the four subperiods of ME. Consider Table 6:

---

3 Other spelling variants of *at* occurring in the corpus include: *et, ette (et + þet), ed; æt,atte, ætte (at + þat)* (MED). *At*, from OE *æt*, was already used as preposition in OE in locative domains.

Date	N° of words	N° of *at-Phs*	Rate ‰
ME1 (1150-1250)	113 010	62	0.5
ME2 (1250-1350)	97 480	138	1.4
ME3 (1350-1420)	184 230	550	2.9
ME4 (1420-1500)	213 850	805	3.7
ME (1150-1500)	**608 570**	**1555**	**2.5**

Table 6. Numbers and rates of *at-Phs* in ME

The figures in Table 6 show that *at-Phs* are restrictively used in ME1 and ME2. Thus only 62 instances are detected in the first period of ME, and 138 examples are found in ME2. From 1350 on, there is an expansion of *at*-phrases with a varied range of uses.

At-Phs

N° of occurrences

■ ME1	50
▨ ME2	140
◩ ME3	290
▨ ME4	370

Subperiods of ME

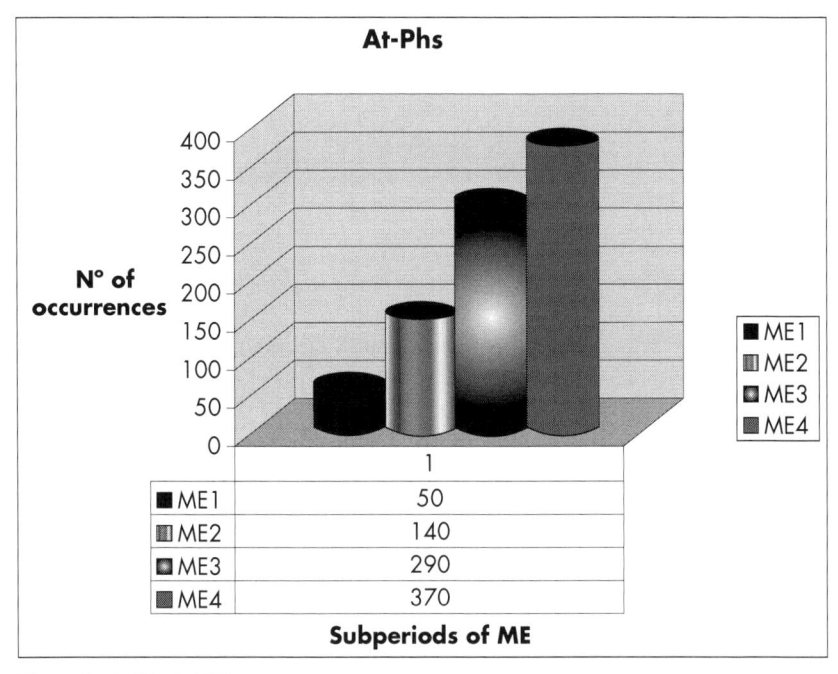

Figure 3. *At-Phs* in ME

1. 4. Bi[4]-Phs

Bi-Phs show a similar tendency as the one exhibited by *in-Phs* (as will be seen in due course), that is, their use increases moderately in ME2 and that increase continues steadily and progressively in the course of ME3, but then their use weakens in the last subperiod. Witness the data of Table 7:

Date	N° of words	N° of *bi-Phs*	Rate ‰
ME1 (1150-1250)	113 010	139	1.2
ME2 (1250-1350)	97 480	299	3.0
ME3 (1350-1420)	184 230	933	5.3
ME4 (1420-1500)	213 850	919	4.2
ME (1150-1500)	**608 570**	**2290**	**3.7**

Table 7. Numbers and rates of *bi-Phs* in ME

Bi-Phs

■ ME1	120
▥ ME2	300
◨ ME3	530
▨ ME4	420

Subperiods of ME

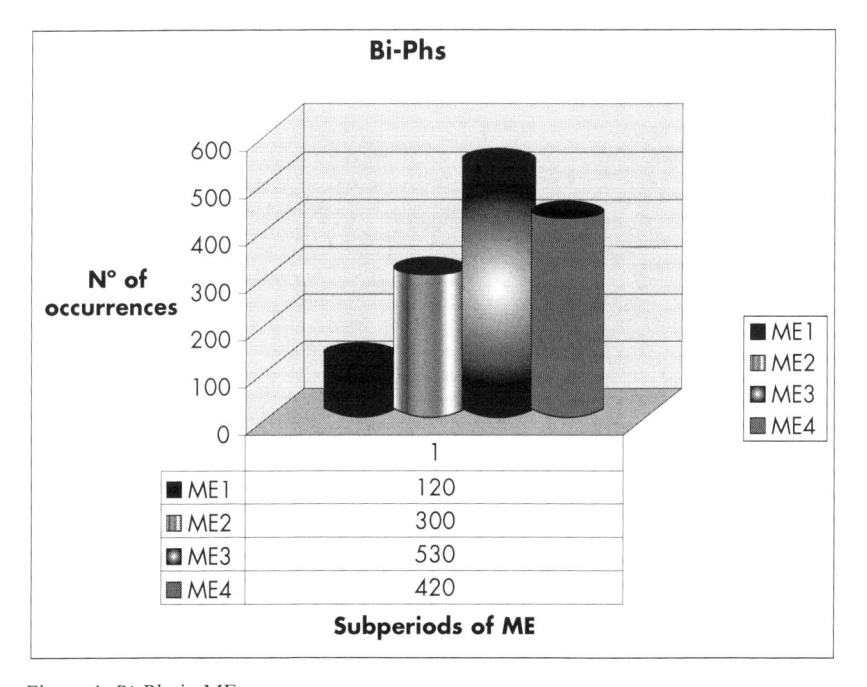

Figure 4. *Bi-Phs* in ME

---

4   Other spelling variants of *bi* occurring in the corpus include: *by* and *be* (MED). This preposition was already used in OE (*be, bi*) with a locative sense, but it aslo indicated temporal relations and instrumentality.

The data shown in Table 7 indicate that only 1.2 examples of *bi-Phs* are found in the corpus for every thousand words in ME1, whereas those figures nearly triple in ME2, reaching their peak in ME3 with 5.3 instances recorded for every thousand words. In the course of the 15th century *bi-Phs* decrease and the rate goes down to 4.2‰.

1. 5. Bifore[5]-Phs
Table 8 displays the data of *bifore-Phs* in ME:

Date	N° of words	N° of *bifore-Phs*	Rate ‰
ME1 (1150-1250)	113 010	78	0.69
ME2 (1250-1350)	97 480	26	0.27
ME3 (1350-1420)	184 230	114	0.61
ME4 (1420-1500)	213 850	87	0.40
ME (1150-1500)	**608 570**	**305**	**0.50**

Table 8. Numbers and rates of *bifore-Phs* in ME

As has been shown in Table 8, *bifore-Phs* are scarcely used in ME. Thus, only 1 instance is found for every two thousand words (0.5‰). This rate varies significantly in the four subperiods. Thus their usage in ME1 (0.6‰) decreases in ME2 (0.2‰), recovers again in ME3 (0.6‰), and falls down again in ME4 (0.4‰). I have not found a coherent explanation for this fluctuation in the course of ME. It is certain that *in front of-Phs* match with *bifore-Phs* in spatial domains in ME, and in the course of eModE "in front of" predominates. However, new figuratives senses of *bifore-Phs* progressively emerge in ME, restoring the balance.

---

5 Other spelling variants of *bifore(n)* occurring in the corpus include: *befor, bifor, biforn, bivore(n)* and *biuore(n)* (MED). *Before(n)*, originally an adverb, comes from OE *be foran* (adv.) > *beforan*, which was already used as preposition in OE in spatial and temporal domains.

Bifore-Phs

■ ME1	69
▥ ME2	27
◨ ME3	61
▨ ME4	40

Subperiods of ME

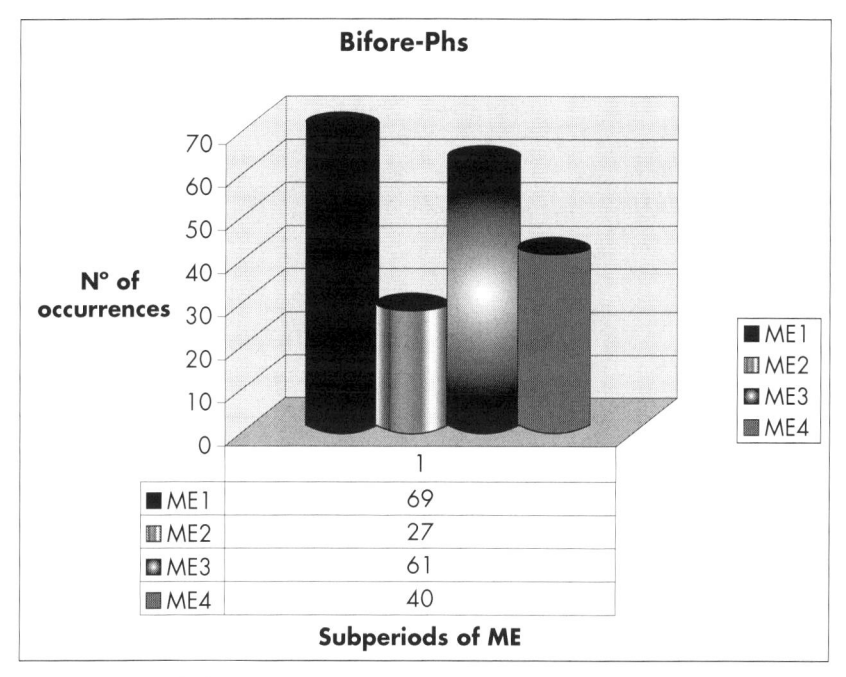

Figure 5. *Bifore-Phs* in ME

1. 6. Bihinde[6]-Phs
The following Table displays the figures for *bihinde-Phs*:

Date	N° of words	N° of *bihinde-Phs*	Rate ‰
ME1 (1150-1250)	113 010	4	0.03
ME2 (1250-1350)	97 480	3	0.03
ME3 (1350-1420)	184 230	11	0.05
ME4 (1420-1500)	213 850	6	0.02
ME (1150-1500)	**608 570**	**24**	**0.03**

Table 9 Numbers and rates of *bihinde-Phs* in ME

Bihinde-Phs were hardly used in the course of ME. I have only detected 24 instances in the corpus. Their use was similar in all the subperiods of ME.

---

6   Other spelling variants of *bihinde* occurring in the corpus include: *behind(e)*, *byhind(e)*, *bihend(e)* and *beheind(e)* (MED). This preposition comes from the OE adverb *be hindan* (dat. sing.) > *behindan*. Its process of grammaticalization must have occurred in early ME because it was not used as preposition until the 13th century.

Bihinde-Phs

	N° of occurrences
■ ME1	3
▨ ME2	3
▢ ME3	5
■ ME4	2

Subperiods of ME

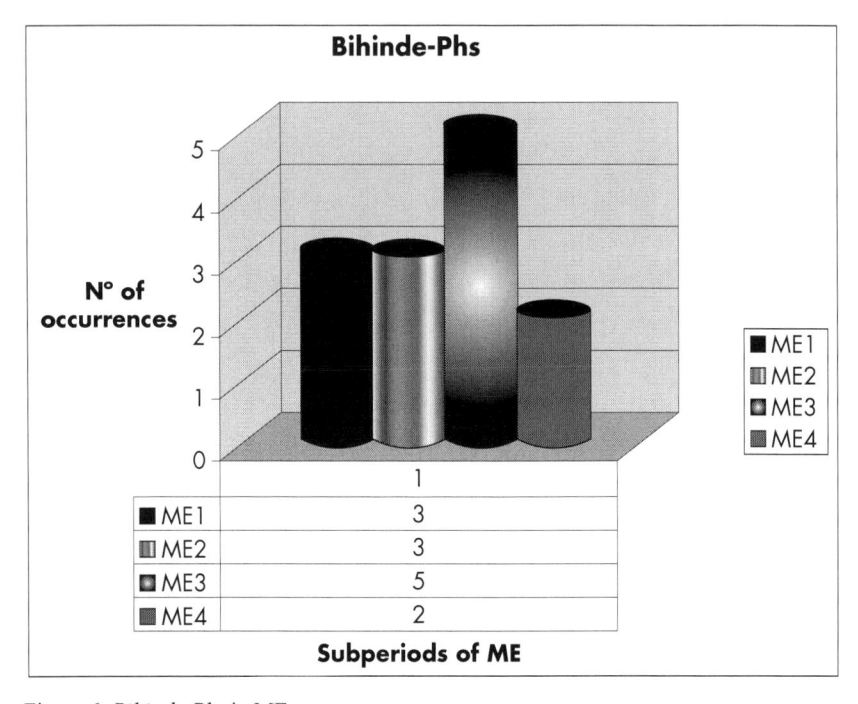

Figure 6. *Bihinde-Phs* in ME

1. 7. Biside[7]-Phs

The following Table shows the data of *biside(s)-Phs* found in the HCME:

Date	N° of words	N° of *biside-Phs*	Rate ‰
ME1 (1150-1250)	113 010	2	0.01
ME2 (1250-1350)	97 480	9	0.09
ME3 (1350-1420)	184 230	22	0.1
ME4 (1420-1500)	213 850	9	0.04
ME (1150-1500)	**608 570**	**42**	**0.06**

Table 10. Numbers and rates of *biside-Phs* in ME

---

[7] Other spelling variants of *biside* occurring in the corpus include: *besides, bisiden, byside(s)* and *besidis* (MED). This preposition comes from the OE adverb *be sidan* (dat. sing.) > *besidan*. Its grammaticalization process must have occurred in early ME because it was not used as preposition until the beginning of the 13th century. In the course of this century the genitival form *besides* also appears for the first time in the North, matching with the form from the dative.

As Table 10 shows, *biside-Phs* are very unusual in ME. Thus ME1 exhibits only 2 examples (both of them in CMBRUT1) and ME2 includes no more than 9 instances. This figure rises to 22 instances in ME3 and falls again in ME4 (9 examples). This decline in lME was produced by the appearance of *near* as a preposition with the meaning of "close to a place, person, thing" after which it was used as an alternative of *biside-Phs*. Thus *bisides þe coste* in *he fonde xxx shippes ful of men and of wymmen bisides þe coste of þe see* (CMBRUT3) could be replaced by *nere to þe coste* in lME.

Biside-Phs

	N° of occurrences
■ ME1	1
▥ ME2	9
◩ ME3	10
▤ ME4	4

Subperiods of ME

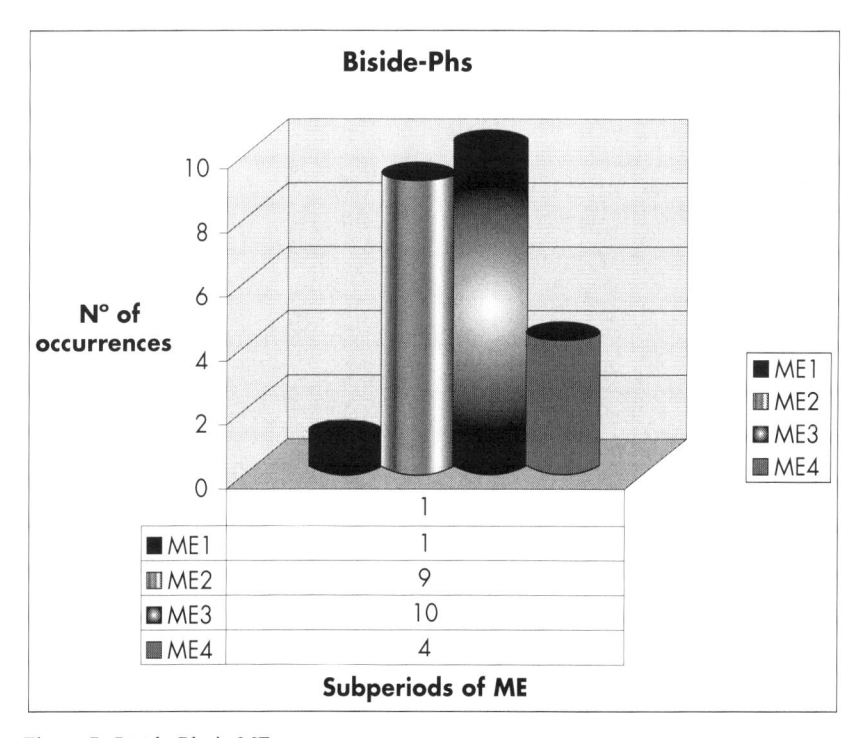

Figure 7. *Biside-Phs* in ME

1. 8. In[8]-Phs

In-Phs show a similar development to *at-Phs*, although their increase slows down in ME4 as the figures in Table 11 indicate:

Date	N° of words	N° of *in-Phs*	Rate ‰
ME1 (1150-1250)	113 010	660	5.6
ME2 (1250-1350)	97 480	1520	15.5
ME3 (1350-1420)	184 230	3570	19.3
ME4 (1420-1500)	213 850	3687	17.2
ME (1150-1500)	**608 570**	**9437**	**15.5**

Table 11. Numbers and rates of *in-Phs* in ME

In-Phs are uncommon in the first period of ME. Thus only 5.6 instances are recorded for every thousand words. However, their use increases significantly in ME2 and ME3 as the rate shifts to 15.5‰ and 19.3‰ respectively. It is worth noting, however, that *in-Phs* become less frequent in the last subperiod of ME.

In-Phs

■ ME1	560
▩ ME2	1550
◨ ME3	1930
▦ ME4	1720

Subperiods of ME

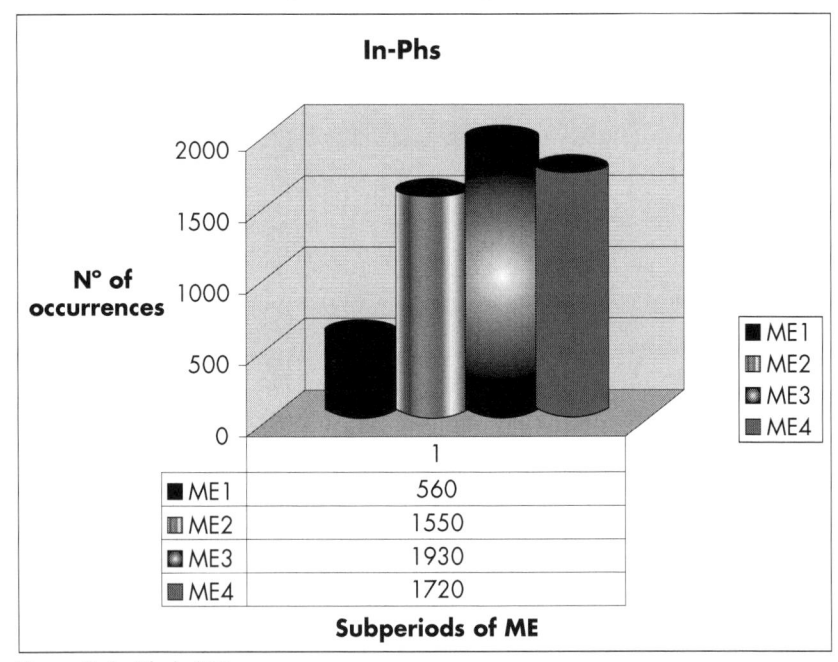

Figure 8. *In-Phs* in ME

---

8 Other spelling variants of *in* occurring in the corpus include: *ine, hin, yn, jn; i, y; en* and *ene* (MED). This preposition was already used in OE as *in*, particularly in the Anglian dialects. In other dialectal areas OE tends to use *on*.

1. 9. On[9]-Phs

On-phrases, with 2,691 instances, are much more frequent than *at*-phrases. My data show the following figures:

Date	N° of words	N° of *on-Phs*	Rate ‰
ME1 (1150-1250)	113 010	1203	10.6
ME2 (1250-1350)	97 480	448	4.5
ME3 (1350-1420)	184 230	491	2.6
ME4 (1420-1500)	213 850	548	2.5
ME (1150-1500)	**608 570**	**2691**	**4.4**

Table 12. Numbers and rates of *on-Phs* in ME

On-Phs

ME1	1060
ME2	450
ME3	260
ME4	250

Subperiods of ME

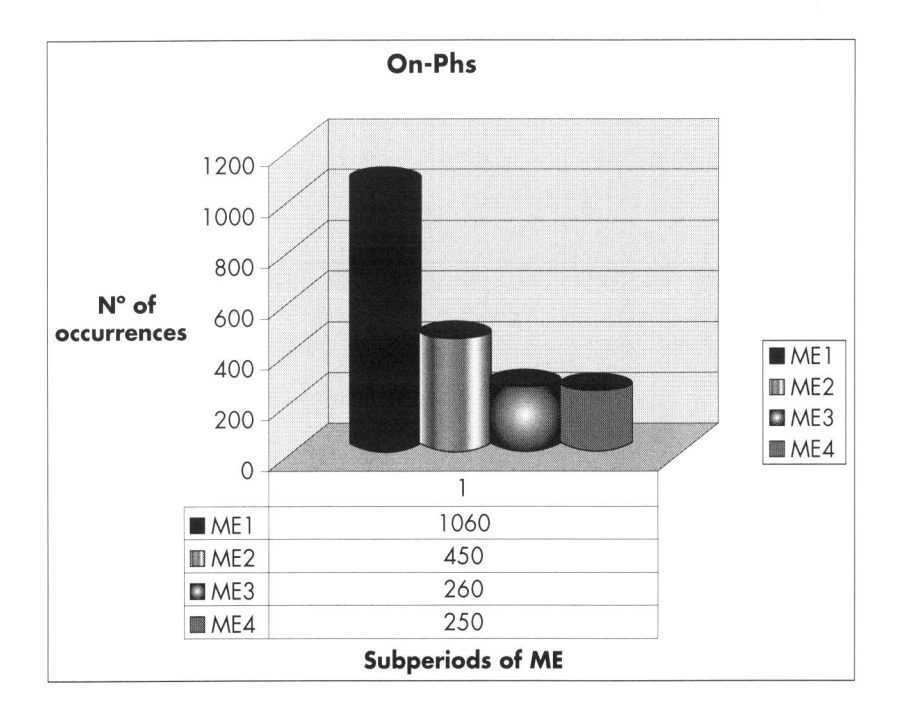

Figure 9. *On-Phs* in ME

---

9 Other spelling variants of *on* occurring in the corpus include: *one, onne, o, a, hon, an, ane* and *un* (MED). This preposition was extensively used in OE (*on*) not only with the meaning "on" (locative-surface), but also with that of "in" (locative-interior) in the South, predominantly in the West Saxon dialect.

I have noticed that *on-Phs* were predominant in ME1 with respect to phrases with other prepositions (*at, in, by*) which contended to cover a similar range of semantic connotations, but their frequency decreased steadily and progressively throughout the ME period, as the figures in Table 12 show. Thus more than 10 *on-Phs* are found for every thousand words in ME1, whereas only 2.5 instances are identified in ME4 for the same number of words.

1. 10. Ouer[10]-Phs

Ouer-Phs are not very frequent in ME. The corpus shows the following figures:

Date	N° of words	N° of *ouer-Phs*	Rate ‰
ME1 (1150-1250)	113 010	91	0.80
ME2 (1250-1350)	97 480	69	0.70
ME3 (1350-1420)	184 230	102	0.55
ME4 (1420-1500)	213 850	109	0.50
ME (1150-1500)	**608 570**	**371**	**0.60**

Table 13. Numbers and rates of *ouer-Phs* in ME

I have only found 371 examples of *ouer-Phs*. Their number declines progressively, although slightly, in the course of the ME period. The rate of 0.8‰ of ME1 falls to 0.5‰ in ME4.

---

10 Other spelling variants of *over* occurring in the corpus include: *ouver, ower, ofer, offr, owr, our(e)* and *nover* (MED). This preposition comes from OE *ofer* in spatial and temporal domains.

Ouer-Phs

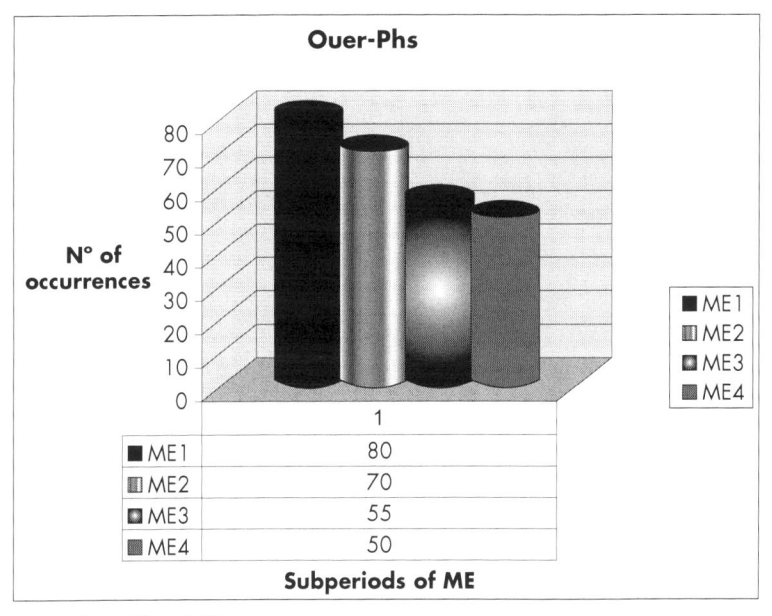

ME1	80
ME2	70
ME3	55
ME4	50

Subperiods of ME

Figure 10. *Ouer-Phs* in ME

1. 11. Þurgh[11]-Phs

The data for *þurgh-Phs* are displayed on the following Table:

Date	N° of words	N° of *þurgh-Phs*	Rate ‰
ME1 (1150-1250)	113 010	464	4.0
ME2 (1250-1350)	97 480	115	1.1
ME3 (1350-1420)	184 230	121	0.6
ME4 (1420-1500)	213 850	162	0.7
ME (1150-1500)	**608 570**	**862**	**1.4**

Table 14. Numbers and rates of *þurgh-Phs* in ME

---

11 Other spelling variants of *þurgh* occurring in the corpus include: *þurghe, þurght, þurg(e), þurʒ(e), þurʒh, purʒgh, þurch; þourghe, þourght, þourg(e), þourʒ(e), þourʒh, þourʒgh, þourch; þorghe, þorght, þorg(e), þorʒ(e), þorʒh, þorʒgh, þorch; þurughe, þurught, þurug(e), þuruʒ(e), þuruʒh, þuruʒgh, þuurch; þorughe, þorught, þorug(e), þoruʒ(e), þoruʒh, þoruʒgh, þoruch; þroghe, þroght, þrog(e), þroʒ(e), þroʒh, þroʒgh, þroch; þrughe, þrught, þrug(e), þruʒ(e), þruʒh, þruʒgh, þruch; þurf, threu, threw, trugh, drogh,* and *dorow* (MED). This preposition was already common in OE (*þurh*, emphatically *þuruh*) to indicate "passage from one side to another". The metathetic form *þruh*, which appears first in the Northern area, was generalised in all dialects by the close of ME.

Þurgh-Ph

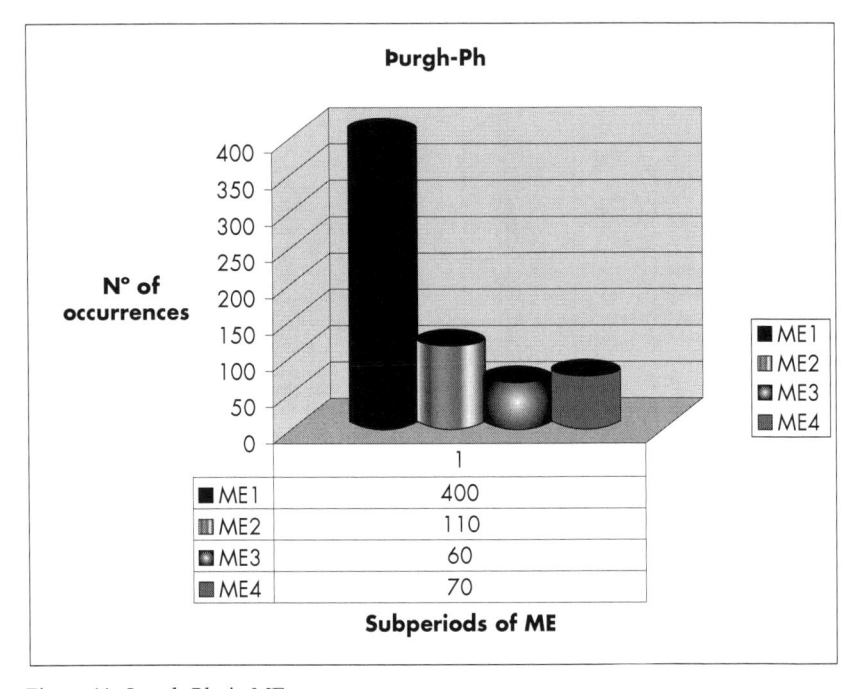

	N° of occurrences
ME1	400
ME2	110
ME3	60
ME4	70

Subperiods of ME

Figure 11. *Þurgh-Phs* in ME

The data shown in Table 14 indicate that *þurgh-Phs* were predominant in ME1, exhibiting a rate of 4 instances for every thousand words. This rate diminishes to 1.1‰ in ME2 and only 0.6‰ were found in ME3, while a similar rate (0.7‰) has been recorded in ME4.

1. 12. Under[12]-Phs

The use of *under-Phs* is very rare in ME. The following table illustrates its frequency:

Date	N° of words	N° of *under-Phs*	Rate ‰
ME1 (1150-1250)	113 010	52	0.46
ME2 (1250-1350)	97 480	61	0.62
ME3 (1350-1420)	184 230	86	0.46
ME4 (1420-1500)	213 850	62	0.28
ME (1150-1500)	**608 570**	**261**	**0.42**

Table 15 Numbers and rates of *under-Phs* in ME

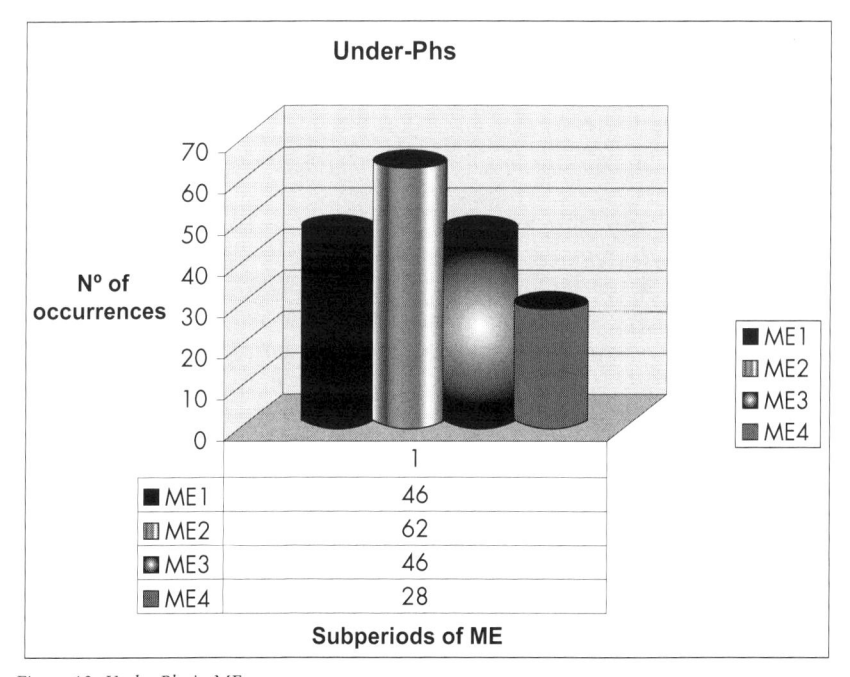

Under-Phs

ME1	46
ME2	62
ME3	46
ME4	28

Subperiods of ME

Figure 12. *Under-Phs* in ME

---

[12] Other spelling variants of *under* occurring in the corpus include: *vnder, ounder, onder, hunder, hounder* and *honder* (OED). This preposition was also used in OE (*under*) in spatial and temporal relations.

I have only found 261 occurrences in the HCME, that is, less than one instance for every two thousand words. It is also noteworthy that its use decreases in late ME. The rate of 0.62‰ recorded for ME2 descends to 0.28‰ in ME4. It is also significant that only 90 instances out of the 261 found in the corpus refer to a position or location in space.

2. COMPILATION AND APPRAISAL OF THE DATA

What follows is a compilation of the data already exhibited for the 12 prepositions examined in this study, so as to compare their figures:

It is worth noting, then, that *in-Phs* predominate in ME with a significant rate of 15.5 instances for every thousand words, whereas the second highest rate, 4.4‰, is represented by *on-Phs*. The usage of *bi-Phs* is limited to 3.7‰, *at-Phs* goes down to 2.5‰. *Þurgh-Phs* follows with a rate of 1.4‰ and the rate diminishes to 0.6‰ in *ouer-Phs* and to 0.42‰ with regard to *under-Phs*.

It should also be noted that this proportion is not homogeneous in all texts. If we examine some of the texts of ME1, we will find, for example, that *Peri Didaxeon. Leechdoms, Wortcunning, and Starcraft of Early England*[13] includes 121 instances of *on-Phs* in the HC extract of 7350 words, and 24 *þurgh*-Phs, whereas only 8 phrases occur preceded by *in* and 2 by *bi*, and not a single instance is found with *at* or *ouer*. Similar figures are found in *Bodley Homilies*[14] where no examples were found with *at, in, ouer* or *under*, whereas *on-Phs* occur on 147 occasions, *þurgh-Phs* 35 and *bi-Phs* 19. On the other hand, other texts such as *St Iuliane* and *St Catherine* show very different data with regard to the previous texts, particularly with regard to the interchange of *on* and *in-Phs*. *St Iuliane* shows 81 instances of *in-Phs* and only 23 *on-Phs* and 19 *þurgh-Phs*. No records were found with *at*, but *bi-Phs* with 7 records, *ouer-Phs* with 6 and *under-Phs* with 3 instances were significantly present. Similar figures are also found in *St Catherine*, which exhibits 54 instances of *in Phs* and only 15 instances were detected preceded by *on-Phs*. *At-Phs* are not spotted, however *bi-Phs, under-Phs* and *ouer-Phs* are slightly represented, 3, 3 and 2, respectively. The following Table illustrate these figures and rates for the six prepositions which are more frequent in these texts:

---

13 Ed. O. Cockayne. Vol. III. London. 1866.
14 Ed. A. O. Belfour. London: EETS, O. S. n° 137.

	Date Text	words	at-Phs Oc. ‰	bi-Phs Oc. ‰	in-Phs Oc. ‰	on-Phs Oc. ‰	ouer-Phs Oc. ‰	þurgh-Phs Oc. ‰
	CM-PERIDI	7350	0 –	2 0.27	8 1.08	121 16.4	0 –	24 3.26
ME1	CM-BODLEY	5880	0 –	19 3.23	0 –	147 25.0	0 –	35 5.95
	CM-JULIA	7180	0 –	7 0.97	81 11.2	23 3.2	6 0.83	19 2.64
	CM-CATHE	4930	0 –	3 0.6	54 10.9	15 3.04	2 0.4	23 4.66

Table 16. The most common prepositions in ME1

Roles		Spatial, temporal, figurative and idiomatic										
Date	N° of words	aboue-Phs	after-Phs	at-Phs	bi-Phs	bifore-Phs	bihinde-Phs	biside-Phs	in-Phs	on-Phs	ouer-Phs	þurgh-Phs	under-Phs
ME1 (1150-1250)	113 010	4 0.03‰	194 1.71‰	62 0.5‰	139 1.2‰	78 0.6‰	4 0.03‰	2 0.01‰	660 5.6‰	1 203 10.6‰	91 0.80‰	464 4.0‰	52 0.46‰
ME2 (1250-1350)	97 480	9 0.09‰	84 0.86‰	138 1.4‰	299 3.0‰	26 0.2‰	3 0.03‰	9 0.09‰	1520 15.5‰	448 4.5‰	69 0.70‰	115 1.1‰	61 0.62‰
ME3 (1350-1420)	184 230	39 0.2‰	351 1.9‰	550 2.9‰	933 5.3‰	114 0.6‰	11 0.05‰	22 0.1‰	3570 19.3‰	491 2.6‰	102 0.55‰	121 0.6‰	86 0.46‰
ME4 (1420-1500)	213 850	70 0.3‰	372 1.73‰	805 3.7‰	919 4.2‰	87 0.4‰	6 0.02‰	9 0.04‰	3687 17.2‰	548 2.5‰	109 0.50‰	162 0.7‰	62 0.28‰
ME (1150-1500)	608 570	122 0.2‰	1001 1.64‰	1555 2.5‰	2290 3.7‰	305 0.5‰	24 0.03‰	42 0.06‰	9437 15.5‰	2691 4.4‰	371 0.60‰	862 1.4‰	261 0.42‰

Table 17. Numbers and rate of all prepositions in ME

Occurrences and rates

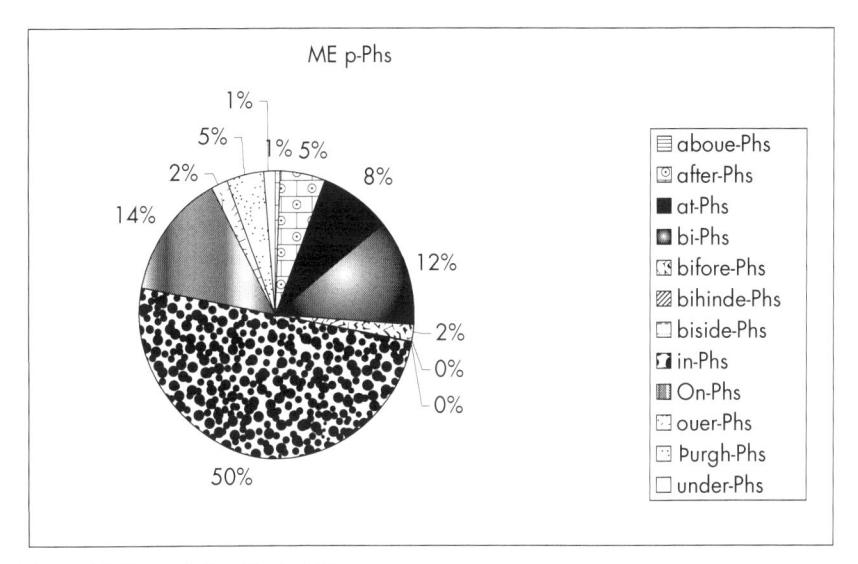

ME p-Phs

- aboue-Phs 5%
- after-Phs 2%
- at-Phs 14%
- bi-Phs 1%
- bifore-Phs 1%
- bihinde-Phs 5%
- biside-Phs 8%
- in-Phs 50%
- On-Phs 12%
- ouer-Phs 2%
- Purgh-Phs 0%
- under-Phs 0%

Figure 13. Rate of all *p-Phs* in ME

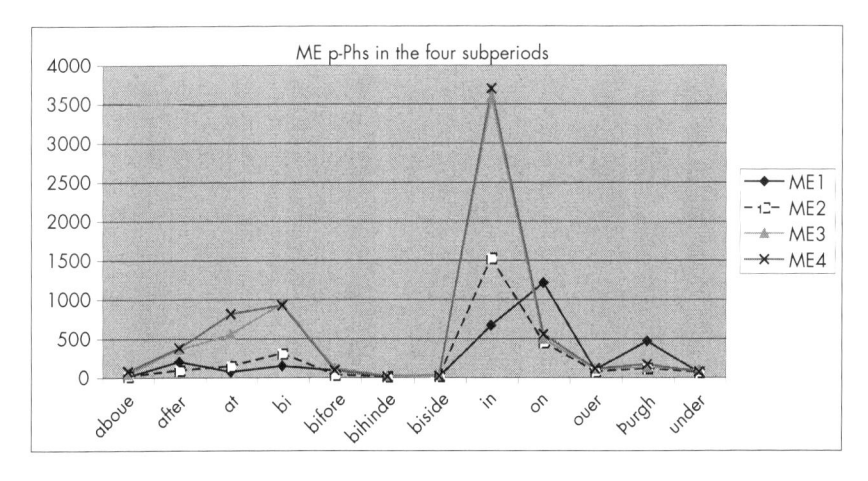

ME p-Phs in the four subperiods

(Graph showing ME1, ME2, ME3, ME4 across: aboue, after, at, bi, bifore, bihinde, biside, in, on, ouer, Purgh, under)

CHAPTER FOUR

DIALECTAL DISTRIBUTION, COMPOSITION TYPE AND TEXT TYPE

1. DIALECTAL DISTRIBUTION

1. 1. Aboue-Phs

The following table records the figures for *aboue-Phs* according to the dialectal area:

Date/Dialect	M1 (1150-1250)			M2 (1250-1350)			M3 (1350-1420)			M4 (1420-1500)		
	Words	Oc.	Rate ‰	Words	Oc	Rate ‰	Words	Oc	Rate ‰	Words	Oc.	Rate ‰
Northern	------	---	-----	----	---	-----	25960	1	0.03	37090	16	0.4
Kentish	5880	-	-	14040	5	0.3	-----	----	------	------	---	------
Southern	20150	-	-	29500	1	0.03	37140	6	0.1	27640	7	0.2
East Mid.	26760	3	0.1	48541	2	0.04	83680	31	0.3	108690	44	0.4
West Mid.	60220	1	0.01	4260	1	0.2	8160	2	0.2	22260	2	0.08

Table 18. Dialectal distribution of *aboue-Phs* in ME

As has been displayed in Table 18, there are some variations with respect to the dialectal occurrences of *aboue-Phs*. Thus, the East Midland dialect includes more examples than the other dialects in the course of ME. It is also interesting to point out that the southern and eastern parts of England do not show any examples in early Middle English (ME1), but the small number of instances found in other areas in this period indicates that there is not sufficient evidence to conclude that *aboue-Phs* were predominant in the Midlands in ME1. In ME2, the Kentish dialect seems to be well in the lead in the use of these phrases; however, the fact that all instances are found in the same text (CMAYENBI) shows that these figures are not relevant. It is worth noting that regardless of the low figures for *aboue-Phs* detected in the corpus, all dialects include this type of prepositional phrase, which proves that they were present all over the country.

1. 2. After-Phs

Table 19 exhibits the figures for *after-Phs* according to the dialectal area:

Date/Dialect	M1 (1150-1250)			M2 (1250-1350)			M3 (1350-1420)			M4 (1420-1500)		
	Words	Oc.	Rate ‰	Words	Oc	Rate ‰	Words	Oc	Rate ‰	Words	Oc.	Rate ‰
Northern	------	---	-----	----	---	-----	25960	16	0.6	37090	30	0.8
Kentish	5880	11	1.8	14040	4	0.2	-----	----	------	------	---	------
Southern	20150	42	2.0	29500	34	1.1	37140	71	1.9	27640	56	2.0
East Mid.	26760	54	2.0	48541	30	0.6	83680	212	2.5	108690	270	2.4
West Mid.	60220	87	1.4	4260	5	1.1	8160	36	4.4	22260	19	0.8

Table 19. Dialectal distribution of *after-Phs* in ME

As Table 19 shows, frequency of occurrence of *after-Phs* varies considerably from one dialect to another. In broad terms, the East Midland dialect incorporates more *after-Phs* than the other dialects in the course of ME. It is also worth pointing out that all dialects show a similar rate in early Middle English (ME1) ranging from 2.0‰ in the East Midland dialect to 1.4‰ in the West Midlands. The small number of examples detected in all dialects for ME2 do not allow us to reach reliable conclusions about the deviations shown among dialects. Thus the rate of 0.2‰ for the Kentish dialect in ME2 seems to be unpredicted, particularly because in ME1 that rate had been 1.8‰ and there is no reason to explain such a remarkable decline. When considering the subperiod ME3 we detect surprising variations among dialects. Thus the rate of *after-Phs* is very small in the Northern dialect (0.6‰) and amazingly prominent in the West Midlands (4.4‰), that is, whereas in the Northern dialect we come across one *after-Ph* for approximately every two thousand words, we find eight instances in the West Midlands for the same number of words, and nearly five in the East Midlands and four in Southern dialects. The data for ME4 indicate that *after-Phs* consolidate their incidence in the East Midland and the Southern dialect, whereas in the West Midlands the rate variations in the course of ME confirm that the use of *after-Phs* is basically ruled by author preferences rather than linguistic usage. It is noteworthy that (regardless of the low figures for *after-Phs* found in the Northern dialect), all dialects include these prepositional phrases, which proves that they were commonly used in all dialects.

1. 3. At-Phs
The following table records the figures for *at-Phs* according to the dialectal area:

Date/Dialect	M1 (1150-1250) Words Oc. Rate ‰	M2 (1250-1350) Words Oc Rate ‰	M3 (1350-1420) Words Oc Rate ‰	M4 (1420-1500) Words Oc. Rate ‰
Northern	------ --- -----	---- --- -----	25960 99 3.8	37090 166 4.4
Kentish	5880 3 0.5	14040 13 0.9	----- ---- ------	------ --- ------
Southern	20150 29 1.4	29500 67 2.2	37140 149 4.0	27640 147 5.4
East Mid.	26760 18 0.6	48541 53 1.0	83680 228 2.7	108690 466 4.2
West Mid.	60220 12 0.1	4260 5 1.1	8160 22 2.6	22260 78 3.5

Table 20. Dialectal distribution of *at-Phs* in ME

As shown in Table 20, there are significant variations with regard to the dialectal distribution of *at-Phs*. Thus, on the one hand, the Southern dialect includes more examples than the other dialects in all the subperiods of ME, while on the other hand the Kentish one scarcely contains any *at-Phs*. The rest of the dialects do not present considerable differences among them. It is also noteworthy that all dialects show a progressive and steady increase in the course of ME. Thus, for example, the Southern dialect contains only 1.4 instances for every thousand words in ME1, whereas it includes 5.4 in ME4. In like manner, East Midlands begins with 0.6‰ in ME1 and ends with to 4.2‰ in ME4. A similar tendency is recorded for the West Midland and the Northern dialects.

1. 4. Bi-Phs
Table 21 shows the data for *bi-Phs*:

Date/Dialect	M1 (1150-1250) Words Oc. Rate ‰	M2 (1250-1350) Words Oc Rate ‰	M3 (1350-1420) Words Oc Rate ‰	M4 (1420-1500) Words Oc. Rate ‰
Northern	------ --- -----	---- --- -----	25960 28 1.0	37090 26 0.7
Kentish	5880 0 0	14040 81 5.7	----- ---- ------	------ --- -----
Southern	20150 27 1.3	29500 95 3.2	37140 113 3.0	27640 156 5.6
East Mid.	26760 24 0.8	48541 110 2.2	83680 731 8.7	108690 699 6.4
West Mid.	60220 88 1.4	4260 23 5.3	8124 64 7.8	22298 25 1.1

Table 21. Dialectal distribution of *bi-Phs* in ME

The data exhibited in Table 21 illustrate that there are noteworthy differences according to the dialectal area. The 5880 words of the *Vespasian Homilies* (the only text recorded in the corpus for Kentish dialect) do not include a single instance of *bi-Ph* in early Middle English. There are no data for the Northern dialect. East Midlands scarcely records one example for every thousand words (0.8‰), whereas the Southern and West Midland areas raise their rate to 1.3‰ and 1.4‰, respectively in ME1. The figures for ME2 exhibit a considerable increase of *bi-Phs* with regard to the earlier period. This increase is mostly noticeable in the Kentish and West Midland dialects, whose rates rise to 5.7‰ and 5.3‰, respectively. There are no data for the Northern dialect in this subperiod. The other dialects maintain a similar rate, varying from 3.2‰ *bi-Phs* to 2.2‰. This rise persists in ME3, particularly in the East and West Midland areas with 8.7 and 7.8 occurrences for every thousand words. The Southern dialect maintains its rate in ME3, whereas the Northern dialect hardly includes a single instance for every thousand words. This rate even diminishes in this area in the following subperiod (ME4). The Southern and the East Midland dialects do not show significant variations with regard to ME3. However, the West Midland areas exhibit an important decrease in late Middle English.

In broad terms, the increase of *bi-Phs* in the course of ME is not homogeneous. In fact, there is significant variation within each region, except in the North where the use of *bi-Phs* is very rare in the two subperiods for which we have data (ME3 and ME4). West Midlands shows great variation, starting with a rate of 1.4‰ in ME1, then the rate rises to 5.3‰ in ME2 and 7.8‰ in ME3, but then it diminishes to 1.1‰ in ME4. However, the increase of *bi-Phs* seems to be steady in East Midlands and in the South, with a moderate upsurge in ME3. The data we have for the Kentish area in ME1 and ME2 show that no examples were found for the earliest period, but there is a noticeable presence in the following subperiod (5.7‰).

1. 5. Bifore-Phs

Table 22 exhibits the figures for *bifore-Phs* according to the dialectal area:

Date/Dialect	M1 (1150-1250)			M2 (1250-1350)			M3 (1350-1420)			M4 (1420-1500)		
	Words	Oc.	Rate ‰	Words	Oc	Rate ‰	Words	Oc	Rate ‰	Words	Oc.	Rate ‰
Northern	------	---	-----	----	---	-----	25960	15	0.5	37090	8	0.2
Kentish	5880	1	0.1	14040	2	0.1	-----	----	------	------	---	------
Southern	20150	4	0.1	29500	13	0.4	37140	20	0.5	27640	8	0.2
East Mid.	26760	30	1.1	48541	11	0.2	83680	71	0.8	108690	59	0.5
West Mid.	60220	42	0.6	4260	3	0.7	8160	8	0.9	22260	10	0.4

Table 22. Dialectal distribution of *bifore-Phs* in ME

The figures shown in Table 22 indicate that there is a great deal of fluctuation within each dialect in the course of ME. The West Midland dialect exhibits some uniformity, as the rate ranges from 0.6‰ in ME1 to 0.4‰ in ME4. East Midlands displays a great incidence in ME1 (1.1‰), but that rate falls to 0.2‰ in ME2, basically because some texts such as CMBESTIA, CMDOCU3, CMALISAU hardly use any *bifore-Phs*. The Southern and the Northern dialects show great variability and the Kentish dialect seems not to favour these prepositional phrases. In broad terms, both the low number of examples and the great variability shown within each dialect do not allow us to draw reliable conclusions so as to estimate significant divergences among dialects.

1. 6. Bihinde-Phs

The number of *behinde-Phs* found in the corpus are not sufficiently indicative so as to measure their dialectal distribution.

1. 7. Biside-Phs

The above observation regarding *bihinde-Phs* also applies to *biside-Phs*.

1. 8. In-Phs

We shall now see the dialectal distribution of *in-Phs* in Middle English. Our survey of the HCME shows in the four sub-periods the following figures:

Date/Dialect	M1 (1150-1250)			M2 (1250-1350)			M3 (1350-1420)			M4 (1420-1500)		
	Words	Oc.	Rate ‰	Words	Oc	Rate ‰	Words	Oc	Rate ‰	Words	Oc.	Rate ‰
Northern	------	---	-----	----	---	-----	25960	517	19.9	37090	867	23.3
Kentish	5880	0	0	14040	271	19.3	-----	----	------	------	---	------
Southern	20150	21	1.0	29500	396	13.4	37140	682	18.3	27640	387	14.0
East Mid.	26760	161	6.0	48541	830	17.0	83680	2187	26.1	108690	2301	2.11
West Mid.	60220	455	7.5	4260	48	11.2	8124	111	13.6	22298	203	9.1

Table 23. Dialectal distribution of *in-Phs* in ME

The figures in Table 23 show that there are noteworthy variations depending on the dialectal area. Kentish and Southern areas hardly include any *in-Phs* in ME1. The 5880 words of the *Vespasian Homilies* (the only text recorded in the corpus for Kentish dialect) do not contain any *in-Ph* and the Southern dialect records only 1 *in-Ph* for every thousand words. The East Midland dialect, however, records 6 *in-Phs* for every thousand words and the West Midland 7.5. There is no material to measure this variable in the Northern dialect. The tabulated figures for ME2 show an important increase of *in-Phs* with regard to the earlier period. This increase is mainly detected in the Kentish dialect, which shows 19.4 *in-Phs* for every thousand words. The rest of the dialects maintain a similar rate, varying from 11.2 *in-Phs* to 17. This increase continues in ME3 as the rate rises to figures between 1.36% and 2.61% (the *in*-occurrences found in the West Midlands are not relevant because there are not sufficient data to measure a tendency). The data for ME4 show significant differences with regard to ME3. There is a decline which is attested in all dialects, except in the Northern dialect. The use of *in-Phs* falls to rates that vary between 0.91% in the West Midland area and 2.33% in the Northern area. The assessment of *in-Phs* in the course of the ME period proves that the West Midland dialect keeps a similar rate of usage, from ME1 (0.75%) to ME4 (0.91%) with a moderate increase during ME2 and ME3, whereas the Southern dialect increases from 0.1% in ME1 to 1.83% in ME3, falling to 1.40% in ME4. The East Midlands have the most notable increase, from 0.6% to 2.61% in ME3, declining to 2.11% in ME4.

1. 9. On-Phs

We shall now see the dialectal distribution of *on-Phs* in Middle English. The survey of the HCME shows in the four sub-periods the following figures:

Date/Dialect	M1 (1150-1250)			M2 (1250-1350)			M3 (1350-1420)			M4 (1420-1500)		
	Words	Oc.	Rate ‰	Words	Oc	Rate ‰	Words	Oc	Rate ‰	Words	Oc.	Rate ‰
Northern	------	---	-----	----	---	-----	25960	90	3.4	37090	68	1.8
Kentish	5880	129	21.9	14040	1	0.01	-----	----	-----	------	---	----
Southern	20150	438	21.7	29500	113	3.8	37140	89	2.3	27640	93	3.3
East Mid.	26760	296	11.0	48541	287	5.9	83680	275	3.2	108690	247	2.2
West Mid.	60220	310	5.1	4260	25	5.8	8160	7	0.8	22260	119	5.3

Table 24. Dialectal distribution of *on-Phs* in ME

The figures in Table 24 show that there are significant variations according to dialect. Kentish and Southern areas include more than 2 *on-Phs* in ME1 for every hundred words (2.19% and 2.17%, respectively), whereas the East Midland dialect records 1.10% and the West Midland area falls to 0.15%. There is no material to measure this variable in the Northern dialect, and it is worth noting that the figures for Kentish are not sufficiently conclusive because the corpus contains only 5880 words of a single text (*Vespasian Homilies*). The tabulated figures for ME2 show a huge decline in *on-Phs* with regard to the earlier period. Thus, only one instance is found in Kentish. Equally, the Southern dialect undergoes an enormous decline. In fact the 2.17 *on-Phs* for every hundred words in ME1 drop to 0.38% in ME2. In like manner, the number of examples in the Midlands amounts to half those found in ME1, 0.59% in East Midlands and 0.58% in West Midlands. This decline continues in ME3 as the rate drops to figures between 0.23% and 0.34% (the *on*-occurrences found in the West Midlands are not relevant because there are not sufficient data to measure a tendency). The data for ME4 show no significant variation with regard to ME3. The assessment of *on-Phs* in the course of the ME period proves that the West Midland dialect keeps the same rate of usage, from ME1 (0.51%) to ME4 (0.53%), whereas the Southern dialect diminishes from 2.17% in ME1 to 0.33% in ME4, and the East Midlands drops from 1.10% to 0.22%.

1. 10. Ouer-Phs

The data for the dialectal distribution of *ouer-Phs* are shown in the following Table:

Date/Dialect	M1 (1150-1250)			M2 (1250-1350)			M3 (1350-1420)			M4 (1420-1500)		
	Words	Oc.	Rate ‰	Words	Oc	Rate ‰	Words	Oc	Rate ‰	Words	Oc.	Rate ‰
Northern	------	---	-----	----	---	-----	25960	8	0.03	37090	33	0.08
Kentish	5880	4	0.06	14040	5	0.03	-----	----	------	------	---	-----
Southern	20150	5	0.02	29500	30	0.10	37140	22	0.05	27640	9	0.03
East Mid.	26760	15	0.05	48541	21	0.04	83680	52	0.06	108690	52	0.04
West Mid.	60220	62	0.10	4260	3	0.07	8124	12	0.14	22298	8	0.03

Table 25. Dialectal distribution of *ouer-Phs* in ME

The data shown in Table 25 prove that all dialects include *ouer-Phs* in all subperiods of ME. It is also noteworthy that there are no significant variations in the dialectal distribution of these phrases. Furthermore, the oscillation within each dialect in the course of the whole period of Middle English shows that we cannot establish indicative tendencies. Thus West Midlands presents a quotient of one occurrence for every thousand words in ME1. This rate diminishes to 0.7‰ in ME2, but then it rises again to 1.4‰ in ME3. This upsurge is reversed again as the rate falls to 0.3‰ in ME4. This proves that there are no indicative trends and the data must be analysed in terms of author preferences, rather than in terms of regular use in common speech.

1. 11. Þurgh-Phs.

The following table records the figures for *þurgh-Phs* according to the dialectal area:

Date/Dialect	M1 (1150-1250)			M2 (1250-1350)			M3 (1350-1420)			M4 (1420-1500)		
	Words	Oc.	Rate ‰	Words	Oc	Rate ‰	Words	Oc	Rate ‰	Words	Oc.	Rate ‰
Northern	------	---	-----	----	---	-----	25960	44	1.6	37090	51	1.3
Kentish	5880	14	2.3	14040	17	2.8	-----	----	------	------	---	------
Southern	20150	108	5.3	29500	42	1.4	37140	22	0.5	27640	16	0.5
East Mid.	26760	188	7.0	48541	53	1.0	83680	43	0.5	108690	90	0.8
West Mid.	60220	154	2.5	4260	3	0.7	8160	14	1.7	22260	5	0.2

Table 26. Dialectal distribution of *þurgh-Phs* in ME

The data shown in Table 26 indicate that East Midland dialect favours the presence of *þurgh-Phs* in ME1, as 7 instances were detected for every thousand words, whereas the Kentish dialect with a rate of 2.3‰ does not give preference to these phrases in this subperiod of ME. It is worth noting, however, that the Kentish dialect is well in the lead in ME2, rising its rate to 2.8‰. West Midland lags behind all dialects, with a rate of 0.7‰. The dialectal differences are still visible in ME3, as the Northern and West Midland dialects include more *þurgh-Phs* than Southern and East Midland dialects. The dialectal variation shown for ME4 is not significant.

In broad terms, except for the Southern dialect which shows a progressive tendency to reduce *þurgh-Phs* in the course of ME, the other dialects present a great deal of oscillation in their figures.

1. 12. Under-Phs

The figures for *under-Phs* are as follows:

Date/Dialect	M1 (1150-1250)			M2 (1250-1350)			M3 (1350-1420)			M4 (1420-1500)		
	Words	Oc.	Rate ‰	Words	Oc	Rate ‰	Words	Oc	Rate ‰	Words	Oc.	Rate ‰
Northern	------	---	-----	----	---	-----	25960	22	0.08	37090	9	0.02
Kentish	5880	1	0.01	14040	2	0.01	-----	----	------	------	---	-----
Southern	20150	9	0.04	29500	11	0.03	37140	5	0.01	27640	11	0.03
East Mid.	26760	7	0.02	48541	30	0.06	83680	53	0.06	108690	55	0.05
West Mid.	60220	30	0.04	4260	4	0.04	8124	4	0.04	22298	7	0.03

Table 27. Dialectal distribution of *under-Phs* in ME

The figures exhibited in Table 27 show that *under-Phs* are used in all dialects and in all sub-periods recorded in the HCME. There are, however, significant variations in the dialectal distribution of *under-Phs*. Thus, the Kentish dialect hardly includes the preposition *under*. In fact, we have to check about six thousand words to find a single instance of *under-Phs* in the subperiods (ME1 and ME2) recorded in the HCME. However, it seems to be clear that East Midland areas tend to include more *under-Phs* than other dialectal areas. Thus, apart from ME1 with 0.2‰, the other sub-periods show a rate of 0.6‰ (ME3) and 0.5‰ (ME4). West Midlands has a rate of 0.4‰ in ME and maintains a similar quotient throughout the Middle English period. In the Southern dialect there is a great deal of oscillation in the course of ME. The rate varies from 0.4‰ in ME1 to 0.1‰ in ME3. In like manner, the Northern dialect fluctuates from 0.8‰ in ME3 to 0.2‰ in ME4. So the variations shown within each dialect in the course of the whole period of Middle English proves it to be difficult to provide an indicative tendency in the dialectal distribution of *under-Phs*.

2. Type of composition (prose vs. poetry)

In this study I intend to appraise whether composition type affects or not the presence of *p-Phs*. The data are grouped into two sub-periods: ME1 + ME2 and ME3 + ME4, and the total numbers for the whole period of ME are also provided.

2. 1. Aboue-Phs
The following Table shows the figures for *aboue-Phs* both in prose and poetry:

Date	M1 & M2		M3 & M4		Middle English	
Composition type	Prose	Poetry	Prose	Poetry	Prose	Poetry
N° of words	105.570	104.920	334120	63960	439690	168880
N° of *aboue-Phs*	6	7	88	20	94	28
Rate ‰	0.05	0.05	0.2	0.3	0.21	0.16

Table 28. *Aboue-Phs* in prose and poetry in ME

The data given in Table 28 show that there are no noteworthy variations in the use of *aboue-Phs* when comparing prose and poetry, although in the later period the figure for prose is slightly higher.

2. 2. After-Phs
These are the data for *After-Phs*:

Date	M1 & M2		M3 & M4		Middle English	
Composition type	Prose	Poetry	Prose	Poetry	Prose	Poetry
N° of words	105.570	104.920	334120	63960	439690	168880
N° of *after-Phs*	196	103	636	66	832	169
Rate ‰	1.8	0.9	1.8	1.0	1.8	1.0

Table 29. *After-Phs* in prose and poetry in ME

Table 29 shows that *after-Phs* are much more common in prose (1.8‰) than in poetry (1.0‰) in ME. Certainly, these phrases were regularly used in the account of events which are typically narrated in prose. Thus, widely used expressions such as "after that" "after the death of", etc. occur predominantly in prose.

2. 3. At-Phs
Table 30 shows the figures for *at-Phs* in prose and poetry recorded in the HCME:

Date	M1 & M2		M3 & M4		Middle English	
Composition type	Prose	Poetry	Prose	Poetry	Prose	Poetry
N° of words	105.570	104.920	334120	63960	439690	168880
N° of *on-Phs*	89	111	1064	291	1153	402
Rate ‰	0.8	1.0	3.1	4.5	2.6	2.3

Table 30. *At-Phs* in prose and poetry in ME

The data exhibited in Table 30 prove that there are no important differences in the use of *at-Phs* between prose and poetry, although the rate seems to be higher in poetry, in early Middle English. However, on comparing the data for the whole period the rates (2.6‰ vs 2.3‰) are similar.

2. 4. Bi-Phs

The following table exhibits the figures for *bi-Phs* in prose and poetry:

Date	M1 & M2		M3 & M4		Middle English	
Composition type	Prose	Poetry	Prose	Poetry	Prose	Poetry
N° of words	105.570	104.920	334120	63960	439690	168880
N° of *bi-Phs*	198	246	1709	137	1907	383
Rate ‰	1.8	2.3	5.1	2.1	4.3	2.2

Table 31. *Bi-Phs* in prose and poetry in ME

The data shown in Table 31 show that prose duplicates the number of *bi-Phs* with regard to poetry throughout the Middle English period. Thus the rate of 2.2‰ found in poetry rises to 4.3‰ in prose, although for the period extending from 1150 to 1350 (ME1 and ME2) the use of *bi-Phs* in poetry is more common than in prose.

2. 5. Bifore-Phs

These are the data for *bifore-Phs*:

Date	M1 & M2			M3 & M4		Middle English	
Composition type	Prose	Poetry		Prose	Poetry	Prose	Poetry
N° of words	105.570	104.920		334120	63960	439690	168880
N° of *bifore-Phs*	51	61	147	46	198	107	
Rate ‰	0.4	0.5	0.4	0.7	0.4	0.6	

Table 32. *Bifore-Phs* in prose and poetry in ME

The data shown in Table 32 indicate that there are no noteworthy differences in the use of *bifore-Phs* between prose and poetry, although the rate seems to be higher in poetry in both early and late Middle English. However, on comparing the data for the whole period the rates (0.4‰ vs 0.6‰) are alike.

2. 6. Bihinde-Phs

There are not sufficient data to determine whether prose or poetry favours the use of *bihinde-Phs*, although they predominate in prose for the data provided in the corpus.

2. 7. Biside-Phs

Biside-Phs are more frequent in prose according to the data exhibited in the HCME, but the low figures provided by the corpus do not allow us to measure this variable.

2. 8. In-Phs

The following table shows the differences in frequency of *in-Phs* between prose and poetry, according to the data exhibited in the HCME. Consider the data shown in Table 33:

Date	M1 & M2		M3 & M4		Middle English	
Composition type	Prose	Poetry	Prose	Poetry	Prose	Poetry
N° of words	105.570	104.920	334120	63960	439690	168880
N° of *in-Phs*	1298	897	6271	971	7569	1868
Rate ‰	12.2	8.5	18.7	15.1	17.2	11.0

Table 33. *In-Phs* in prose and poetry in ME

The data shown in Table 33 confirm that prose includes more *in-Phs* than poetry in the ME period. Thus 17.2 instances were found for every thousand words in prose, whereas this rate falls to 11.0‰ in poetry. It is worth noting that the figures in Table 33 show that the difference in the usage of *in-Phs* between prose and poetry is kept stable in the course of the ME period.

2.9. On-Phs

The following table shows the variation of *on-Phs* between prose and poetry, from the data obtained in the HCME:

Date	M1 & M2		M3 & M4		Middle English	
Composition type	Prose	Poetry	Prose	Poetry	Prose	Poetry
N° of words	105.570	104.920	334120	63960	439690	168880
N° of *on-Phs*	1160	491	797242	1957	773	
Rate ‰	10.9	4.6	2.33.7	4.4	4.3	

Table 34. *On-Phs* in prose and poetry in ME

The figures given in Table 34 show that prose duplicates the number of occurrences of *on-Phs* with regard to poetry in the material provided for the period extending from 1150 to 1350 (ME1 and ME2). In fact, 10.9 examples were found for every thousand words in prose, whereas this rate falls to 4.6 in poetry. It is, however, striking that *on-Phs* predominate in poetry (3.7‰) for the period ranging from 1350 to 1500 (ME3 and M4), as prose includes only 2.3‰ of *on-Phs*. It is worth noting, however, that the assessment of the whole period of ME shows that there is virtually no variation in the usage of *on-Phs* between prose and poetry as both of them show a similar rate of usage, 4.4‰ and 4.3‰ respectively.

2. 10. Ouer-Phs

The following Table show the data of *ouer-Phs* in prose and poetry:

Date	M1 & M2		M3 & M4		Middle English	
Composition type	Prose	Poetry	Prose	Poetry	Prose	Poetry
N° of words	105.570	104.920	334120	63960	439690	168880
N° of *ouer-Phs*	82	73	182	34	264	107
Rate ‰	0.7	0.5	0.5	0.5	0.6	0.5

Table 35. *Ouer-Phs* in prose and poetry in ME

The data exhibited in Table 35 show that *ouer-Phs* are slightly more frequent in prose (0.6‰) than in poetry (0.5‰) in all the subperiods of Middle English. The variations depending on composition type are, thus, not significant. This co-occurrence implies that *ouer-Phs* are not avoided in poetic form.

2. 11. Þurgh

Table 36 exhibits the data for *þurg-Phs* in prose and poetry:

Date	M1 & M2		M3 & M4		Middle English	
Composition type	Prose	Poetry	Prose	Poetry	Prose	Poetry
N° of words	105.570	104.920	334120	63960	439690	168880
N° of *þurgh-Phs*	262	276	232	92	494	368
Rate ‰	2.4	2.6	0.6	1.4	1.1	2.1

Table 36. *Þurgh-Phs* in prose and poetry

The figures shown in Table 36 indicate that *þurgh-Phs* are more frequent in poetry (2.1‰) than in prose (1.1‰). However, it should be noted that this difference is basically due to the great number of instances (122) found in the *Ormulum*. Thus the average rate of 1.4‰ of *þurgh-Phs* in ME rises to 13.78‰ in the *Ormulum*.

2. 12. Under-Phs

The following table shows the data for *under-Phs* in prose and poetry:

Date	M1 & M2		M3 & M4		Middle English	
Composition type	Prose	Poetry	Prose	Poetry	Prose	Poetry
N° of words	105.570	104.920	334120	63960	439690	168880
N° of *under-Phs*	55	59	122	25	177	84
Rate ‰	0.5	0.5	0.3	0.3	0.4	0.4

Table 37. *Under-Phs* in prose and poetry in ME

The numbers displayed in Table 37 show that *under-Phs* are slightly more frequent in poetry (0.49‰) than in prose (0.4‰).

3. TEXT TYPE

What follows is an assessment of the use of *p-Phs* according to the type of text. The data are also grouped into two sub-periods: M1 + ME2 and ME3 + ME4 and the total number for the whole period of ME are also included.

3. 1. Aboue-Phs

The data provided in the corpus for *aboue-Phs* show that there are no significant differences in the use of these phrases according to the type of text, although technical texts (Law, Historical Documents, Handbooks, Philosophy, Science, Medicine, Travelogue) show a certain predominance. However, the small number of *aboue-Phs* detected in the corpus are not sufficient to draw valid conclusions.

3. 2. After-Phs

Table 38 displays the data of *after-Phs* exhibiting the differences attested in the corpus according to the type of text.

Date	M1 & M2 (1150-1350)			M3 & M4 (1350-1500)			Middle English		
Text type	N° of words	N° of *after-Phs*	Rate‰	N° of words	N° of *after-Phs*	Rate‰	N° of words	N° of *after-Phs*	Rate‰
Religion (Homily, Bible, Rel. Treat., Life of Saint, & Sermon, Rule).	154396	186	1.2	124428	261	2.0	278824	447	1.6
History	39650	32	0.8	26930	27	1.0	66580	64	0.9
Technical (Law, Docum., Handb., Philosophy, Science, Medicine, Travelogue)	10850	16	1.4	115933	287	2.4	126783	303	1.7
Letters				29050	45	1.5	29050	45	1.5
Drama				25670	41	1.5	25670	41	1.5
Romance & Fiction	41434	75	1.8	50112	26	0.5	91546	101	1.1

Table 38. *After-Phs* and text type in ME

The data exhibited in Table 38 show that there are noteworthy variations in the use of *after-Phs* according the type of text. Thus, religious texts (Homilies, Bible, Religious Treatises, Life of Saints, Sermon, Rule) include more *after-Phs* than some other types of text (with an average of 1.6 examples for every thousand words), whereas history (0.9‰) and romance and fiction (1.1‰) exhibit the smallest number of instances.

3. 3. At-Phs
The following table shows the frequency of *at-Phs* according to the type of text.

Date	M1 & M2 (1150-1350)			M3 & M4 (1350-1500)			Middle English		
Text type	N° of words	N° of at-Phs	Rate‰	N° of words	N° of at-Phs	Rate‰	N° of words	N° of at-Phs	Rate‰
Religion (Homily, Bible, Rel. Treat., Life of Saint, & Sermon, Rule).	154396	126	0.8	124428	386	3.1	278824	512	1.8
History	39650	24	0.6	26930	148	5.4	66580	172	2.5
Technical (Law, Docum., Handb., Philosophy, Science, Medicine, Travelogue)	10850	4	0.3	115933	367	3.1	126783	371	2.9
Letters				29050	152	5.2	29050	152	5.2
Drama				25670	121	4.7	25670	121	4.7
Romance & Fiction	41434	46	1.1	50112	181	3.6	91546	227	2.4

Table 39. *At-Phs* and text type in ME

The data shown in Table 39 indicate that there are significant variations in the use of *at-Phs* according the type of text. Certainly, religious texts exhibit the smallest number of instances with an average of 1.8 examples for every thousand words, whereas letters and drama show the greatest rates (5.2‰ and 4.7‰ respectively). The other text types do not show considerable differences and their rate varies from 2.4‰ to 2.9‰.

3. 4. Bi-Phs

I have recorded the following figures for *bi-Phs* with regard to text type:

Date	M1 & M2 (1150-1350)			M3 & M4 (1350-1500)			Middle English		
Text type	N° of words	N° of bi-Phs	Rate‰	N° of words	N° of bi-Phs	Rate‰	N° of words	N° of bi-Phs	Rate‰
Religion (Homily, Bible, Rel. Treat., Life of Saint, & Sermon, Rule).	154396	217	1.4	124428	486	3.9	278824	703	2.5
History	39650	72	1.8	26930	232	8.6	66580	304	4.5
Technical (Law, Docum., Handb., Philosophy, Science, Medicine, Travelogue)	10850	3	0.2	115933	821	7.0	126783	824	6.4
Letters				29050	166	5.7	29050	166	5.7
Drama				25670	44	1.7	25670	44	1.7
Romance & Fiction	41434	179	4.3	50112	142	2.8	91546	321	3.5

Table 40. *Bi-Phs* and text type in ME

The figures displayed in Table 40 do not indicate significant variations with regard to the type of text, although we notice the infrequent use of *bi-Phs* in drama (1.7 instances for every thousand words). On the other hand, scientific and technical language uses 6.4 *bi-Phs* for every thousand words, particularly due to the descriptive character of this type of text.

3. 5. Bifore-Phs

The following table exhibits the data for *bifore-Phs* according to the type of text:

Date	M1 & M2 (1150-1350)			M3 & M4 (1350-1500)			Middle English		
Text type	N° of words	N° of *bifore-Phs*	Rate‰	N° of words	N° of *bifore-Phs*	Rate‰	N° of words	N° of *bifore-Phs*	Rate‰
Religion (Homily, Bible, Rel. Treat., Life of Saint, & Sermon, Rule).	154396	74	0.4	124428	95	0.7	278824	169	0.6
History	39650	12	0.3	26930	14	0.5	66580	26	0.3
Technical (Law, Docum., Handb., Philosophy, Science, Medicine, Travelogue)	10850	0	0.0	115933	50	0.4	126783	50	0.3
Letters				29050	14	0.4	29050	14	0.4
Drama				25670	8	0.3	25670	8	0.3
Romance & Fiction	41434	18	0.4	50112	18	0.3	91546	36	0.3

Table 41. *Bifore-Phs* and text type in ME

The data shown in Table 41 confirm that religious texts tend to use more *bifore-Phs* than the other types of texts. They include about 0.6 instances for every thousand words in ME, whereas all other texts vary from 3‰ to 4‰.

3. 6. Bihinde-Phs

The data found in the corpus for *bihinde-Phs* indicate that there are no noteworthy differences in the use of these phrases according to the type of text, although they are slightly more frequent in religious texts. However, the small number of *bihinde-Phs* exhibited in the corpus are not sufficient to indicate a certain predominance in a particular type of text.

3. 7. Biside-Phs

The above observation regarding *bihinde-Phs* also applies to *biside-Phs*.

3. 8. In-Phs

Table 42 gives the frequencies of *in-Phs* according to the type of text:

Date	M1 & M2 (1150-1350)			M3 & M4 (1350-1500)			Middle English		
Text type	N° of words	N° of *in-Phs*	Rate‰	N° of words	N° of *in-Phs*	Rate‰	N° of words	N° of *in-Phs*	Rate‰
Religion (Homily, Bible, Rel. Treat., Life of Saint, & Sermon, Rule).	154396	1305	8.4	124428	3658	29.3	278824	4963	17.7
History	39650	263	0.66	26930	410	1.52	66580	673	10.1
Technical (Law, Docum., Handb., Philosophy, Science, Medicine, Travelogue)	10850	15	1.3	115933	2217	19.1	126783	2232	17.6
Letters				29050	343	11.8	29050	343	11.8
Drama				25670	276	10.7	25670	276	10.7
Romance & Fiction	41434	461	11.1	50112	489	9.7	91546	950	10.3

Table 42. *In-Phs* and text type in ME

Bearing in mind that the average ME rate of *in-Phs* is 15.5‰, the data shown in Table 42 do not show relevant deviations from that rate. Religious texts and technical works show a slightly higher rate (17.7‰). However, history texts offer a lower frequency as they only show one *in-Ph* for every hundred words. An equal rate is also provided by drama, and romance and fiction works (10.3‰ and 10.7‰, respectively). The figures for letters (11.8‰) are also below average. It is worth noting, however, that religious texts show a great variety of frequency. The rate of 8.4‰ for ME1 and ME2 triplicates in ME3 and ME4 (29.3‰).

3. 9. On-Phs

Table 43 gives the frequency of *on-Phs* according to the type of text. I have recorded the following figures:

Date	M1 & M2 (1150-1350)			M3 & M4 (1350-1500)			Middle English		
Text type	N° of words	N° of *on-Phs*	Rate‰	N° of words	N° of *on-Phs*	Rate‰	N° of words	N° of *on-Phs*	Rate‰
Religion (Homily, Bible, Rel. Treat., Life of Saint, & Sermon, Rule).	154396	1073	6.9	124428	317	2.5	278824	1390	4.9
History	39650	118	2.9	26930	180	6.6	66580	298	4.4
Technical (Law, Docum., Handb., Philosophy, Science, Medicine, Travelogue)	10850	121	11.1	115933	175	1.5	126783	296	2.3
Letters				29050	62	2.1	29050	62	2.1
Drama				25670	78	3.0	25670	78	3.0
Romance & Fiction	41434	288	6.9	50112	177	3.5	91546	465	5.0

Table 43. *On-Phs* and text type in ME

Taking into account that the average ME rate of *on-Phs* is 4.4‰, the figures shown in Table 43 do not provide significant deviations from that rate. Religious texts are very close to that average with a rate of 4.9‰. History texts (4.4‰) Romance and Fiction works (5.0‰) show a similar rate. The figures for Letters (2.1‰) and Drama (3.0‰) are coherent with the rate of usage found in ME3 and ME4, as is shown in Table 43. It is worth noting, however, that technical texts show a great variety of frequency. The rate of 11.1‰ for ME1 and ME2 seems to be high with regard to other text type; however this proportion should be expected because that figure is taken from *Peri Didaxeon*, a text dated in ME1, whose average rate is 10.6‰, as shown in Table 43. What is striking, however, is the low rate (1.5‰) found in technical texts for ME3 and ME4 compared with the rates for other text types for the same period.

3. 10. Ouer-Phs

Concerning text type, I have recorded the following figures for *ouer-Phs*:

Date	M1 & M2 (1150-1350)			M3 & M4 (1350-1500)			Middle English		
Text type	N° of words	N° of *ouer-Phs*	Rate‰	N° of words	N° of *ouer-Phs*	Rate‰	N° of words	N° of *ouer-Phs*	Rate‰
Religion (Homily, Bible, Rel. Treat., Life of Saint, & Sermon, Rule).	154396	73	0.4	124428	62	0.4	278824	135	0.4
History	39650	43	1.0	26930	13	0.4	66580	47	0.7
Technical (Law, Docum., Handb., Philosophy, Science, Medicine, Travelogue)	10850	3	0.2	115933	89	0.7	126783	93	0.6
Letters				29050	21	0.7	29050	21	0.7
Drama				25670	7	0.2	25670	7	0.2
Romance & Fiction	41434	27	0.6	50112	41	0.8	91546	68	0.7

Table 44. *Ouer-Phs* and text type in ME

The data shown in in Table 44 evince that the rates of *ouer-Phs* do not vary greatly according to the text type, as the quotient basically oscillates between 0.6‰ and 0.7‰ during the whole ME period. However, the drama texts present a very small number of *ouer-Phs* (0.2‰). This scarceness may be due to the fact that all drama texts are written in poetry. As mentioned earlier, poetic texts include less *ouer-Phs* than texts written in prose.

3. 11. Þurgh
The following records show text type assessment of *þurgh-Phs*:

Date	M1 & M2 (1150-1350)			M3 & M4 (1350-1500)			Middle English		
Text type	N° of words	N° of *þurgh-Phs*	Rate‰	N° of words	N° of *þurgh-Phs*	Rate‰	N° of words	N° of *þurgh-Phs*	Rate‰
Religion (Homily, Bible, Rel. Treat., Life of Saint, & Sermon, Rule).	154396	438	2.8	124428	154	1.2	278824	592	2.1
History	39650	56	1.4	26930	30	1.1	66580	86	1.2
Technical (Law, Docum., Handb., Philosophy, Science, Medicine, Travelogue)	10850	31	2.8	115933	59	0.5	126783	90	0.7
Letters				29050	2	0.06	29050	2	0.06
Drama				25670	17	0.6	25670	17	0.6
Romance & Fiction	41434	42	1.0	50112	33	0.6	91546	75	0.8

Table 45. *Þurgh-Phs* and text type in ME

The data shown in Table 45 corroborate that letters hardly include any *þurgh-Phs*, as only two instances were found in this type of texts. Drama texts also exhibit a restricted use of the preposition *þurgh* (0.6‰). The uncommon use of this preposition in letters and drama confirms that it was not very much accepted in colloquial speech. The data also indicate that religious texts duplicate the number of *þurgh-Phs* with regard to all the other texts, particularly due to their descriptive and formal character.

3.12. Under-Phs
The following records show text type assessment of *under-Phs*:

Date	M1 & M2 (1150-1350)			M3 & M4 (1350-1500)			Middle English		
Text type	N° of words	N° of *under-Phs*	Rate‰	N° of words	N° of *under-Phs*	Rate‰	N° of words	N° of *under-Phs*	Rate‰
Religion (Homily, Bible, Rel. Treat., Life of Saint, & Sermon, Rule).	154396	51	0.3	124428	33	0.2	278824	84	0.3
History	39650	6	0.1	26930	10	0.3	66580	16	0.2
Technical (Law, Docum., Handb., Philosophy, Science, Medicine, Travelogue)	10850	4	0.3	115933	72	0.6	126783	76	0.5
Letters				29050	4	0.1	29050	4	0.1
Drama				25670	2	0.1	25670	2	0.07
Romance & Fiction	41434	43	1.0	50112	16	0.3	91546	59	0.6

Table 46. *Under-Phs* and text type in ME

The figures displayed in Table 46 substantiate the idea that the rates of *under-Phs* do not differ clearly according to the type of text. However, technical texts present more occurrences of *under-Phs* than the others, basically due to the descriptive character of the texts.

CHAPTER FIVE

SPATIAL AND TEMPORAL SENSES

1. SPATIAL ROLES. THE TERM "SPATIAL" REFERS TO PHYSICAL LOCATION, POSITION OR MOVEMENT IN SPACE.

1. 1. Aboue-Phs

The preposition *above* exhibits mainly locative, source and goal uses in PDE. Path expression uses, if they occur, are very rare (Bennett: 57). *Above* has been used in the history of English as a spatial reference which expresses a physical position of an object which appears in an area adjacent to the top of another object. Lakoff (1987: 425) posits that the Higher-than Sense of *over* is "roughly equivalent" in meaning to *above*. However, Tyler and Evans (2003: 111) state that "it is the functional element that distinguishes these two particles". Thus, the trajector, in the case of *over*, is within potential reach of the landmark producing a "conceptual connectedness between the TR and the LM". However, "the functional element associated with *above* emphasizes an unbridgeable distance between the TR and the LM, such that the TR is not within potential reach of the LM". Tyler and Evans (2003: 115ff) develop the semantic network for *above* in four distinct senses: The More Sense ("the proto-scene can in some contexts implicate more"), the Superior Sense ("being superior in one way"), the Next-one-up Sense ("the next element above the one currently in focus is identified") and the Topographical-distance Sense. Thus, in *the partie of the hevene above the erthe* (CMASTRO), the landmark indicates a topographical distance or an orientation point of the trajector. It is worth noting, however, that spatial *aboue-Phs* are not frequent in ME and when they occur they usually express the notions of being "resting upon" and "directly over" without touching.

The following Table shows the spatial domain of *aboue-Phs*:

Sense		Spatial	
Semantic fields	Position resting upon; covering; lying on	Position vertically up from, directly over	Position beyond, past or further than a point
Oc.	13	10	4
Rate % (with regard to all *aboue-Phs)*	10.65	8.19	3.27
Reference	S-1	S-2	S-3

Table 47. Spatial *aboue-Phs* in ME

The HCME shows only 27 instances of *aboue-Phs* which express a spatial reference, representing a ratio of 22.13% of all *oboue-Phs* found in the corpus. These 27 instances basically indicate one of the following spatial connotations: S-1) a position resting upon the top of earth or sea, e.g. *Narpeles his hors was good, And keuered vp abouen þe flood, And swam to þe oþer syde,*(CMALISAU); *as þou makest lye & helde aboue see-water* (CMHORSES); S-2) a position vertically up from or directly over, e.g. *alle his payns as heuen es abouen erthe* (CMJULNOR); and S-3) a position beyond, past or further than a point, e.g. *And it sytt abouen toward the desert of Syrye a lytill abouen the ryuere aboueseyd* (CMMANDEV); *beʒonde Babyloyne aboue the Flode of Nile* (CMMANDEV).

1. 2. After-Phs

The preposition *after* is typified as "locative posterior time" in PDE (Bennett, 1975: 119). In particular, Tyler and Evans state that the "proto-scene" of *after* is associated "to a spatial relation in which both TR and LM are inherently oriented, and are related by virtue of an in tandem alignment. A consequence of this configuration is that the functional element associated with *after* is one in which the TR is following or pursuing the LM". This functional element provides the basis to develop a "Sequential Sense" as it relates "two entities in a sequence" (2003: 169-175),

In contrast to *behind*, which mostly contains the component "place", *after* integrates the component "time" in PDE. However, *after-Phs* have a significant incidence in spatial uses in ME, particularly with verbs, adjectives and nouns of action to indicate that an activity is involved in pursuit of or in search of somebody or something, e.g. *I woll ryde aftir hym and assay hym* (CMMALORY). Thus we characterize the preposition *after* as "spatial or temporal locative posterior" in ME. This means that *after*-complements (physical objects, states, periods of time, points of time, etc.) are prone to have a front and a back. As Bennett (1975:119) states, the "front is the leading end or side, according to the metaphor that sees time as a kind of conveyor-belt moving past a stationary observer. Or it is the side that the observer first reaches, according to the metaphor that sees time as stationary and the observer is moving through it. The other side is of course the back".

The following Table shows the basic spatial sense in which *after-Phs* were used in ME:

Sense	Spatial			Total
Semantic fields	Locative posterior position ("behind")	Moving in the rear	In pursuit of, in search of (with verbs, adjectives and of nouns of action)	
Oc.	5	2	57	64
Rate % (with regard to all *after-Phs)*	0.49	0.19	5.69	6.39
Reference	S-1	S-2	S-3	

Table 48. Spatial *after-Phs* in ME

I have detected only 44 *after-Phs* used as spatial references. Thus only 6.39% of all instances found in the HCME have a spatial sense, although the meaning involved in a spatial role also implies a temporal reference, as one action is subsequent to another. I have found only five examples of *after-Phs* which indicate a locative posterior position "behind" (S-1), e.g. *Make faste þe dore aftur þe : and ne lat þou no man in gon* (CMSELEG). Only two instances exhibit the meaning of "moving in the rear of" (S-2) e.g. *Y schal make my couenaunt with ȝou, and with ȝour seed after ȝou, and to ech lyuynge soule which is with ȝou* (CMOTEST). The remaining 57 examples are used with verbs, adjectives and nouns which express an action involved "in pursuit of, in search of" somebody or something (S-3), e.g. *I woll ryde aftir hym and assay hym* (CMMALORY); *he wente aftir hym on foote*, cryyng (CMMALORY); *te king sende efter him* CMPETERB).

1. 3. At-Phs

The preposition *at* basically denotes an orientation point either in space or time for a given trajector in PDE (Dirven 1993: 74). Thus the *at-Ph*, *at the station* (landmark), in *the queen is at the station,* indicates an orientation point for *the queen* (trajector) without further implications such as the physical appearance or shape of the landmark (station), or the particular location (near, inside, on the top, above) of the trajector. Although the spatial meaning of the preposition *at* is conceptually unbiased or neutral, Dirven (1993:76) maintains that PDE *at* moves from an "orientation-point" in space to a radial network of other extensions such a time (time-point orientation, e.g. *at six o'clock*); state (metaphorical orientation, e.g. *at rest*); manner (point on scale, e.g. *at full speed*); and area ("thematic context", e.g. *good at guessing*). In its turn, from time point orientation it might extend to a circumstantial sphere [e.g. *at these words* (*he left*)].

In broad terms, we may suggest that the landmark construed by *at* is thought as one-dimensional point or reference location, that is, a "co-location between a TR and a LM, in which the location is conceptualized as a point" (Tyler and Evans 2003: 178).

Spatial *at-Phs* show a wide range of senses in Middle English and some of them are not present in PDE. Table 49 shows the occurrences of at-phrases for each spatial sense and the rate of their usage with regard to all at-phrases found in the HC and to the number of words of the HC.

Sense	Spatial					
Semantic fields	Location in a city or town	Location at part of/ within a building	To be in a given position	Location within a region or country	To be at a person	Arrival to/in a place
Oc.	496	91	78	6	31	26
Rate % (within spatial)	68.13	12.5	10.71	0.82	4.25	3.57
Rate % (with regard to all *at-Phs*)	31.89	5.85	5.01	0.38	1.99	1.66
Reference	S1	S2	S3	S4	S5	S6
Total of occurrences 728 Rate ‰ (with regard to the corpus words): 1.1						

Table 49. Spatial *at-Phs* in ME

S-1. *At-Phs* which indicate a location in a city or town are predominant as they are found on 496 occasions which represent a rate of 68.13% of all spatial *at-Phs* and 31.89% with regard to all *at*-Phs, e.g.*At ʒour forsayde cite of London* (CMOFFIC3).

S-2. The second highest number of *at-Phs* are found in the category "to be located at part of/within a building", e. g. *at chirche dore* (CMTVERS); *at scole* (CMEDMUND), as 91 examples were found, which represents 12.5% with respect to all spatial *at-Phs*.

S-3. In this category, to be in a given position, 78 occurrences were found with a rate of 10.71% within spatial sense.

S-4, to be located within a region or country is rarely found with *at-Phs*. In fact, only 6 instances were detected. Other usages such as "to be at a person" (S-5), e.g.*Y sat at my fadir* (CMNTEST) and "the arrival to/in a place" (S-6) were also recorded in the corpus, although the frequences of these types is not significant.

1. 4. Bi-Phs

The preposition *by* indicates four basic spatial senses in PDE: locative, source, path and goal. Thus, in *my house is by the river bank* (locative); *they stole the car by the farm* (source); *we went down by the seaside* (path); and *I'll put it by your arms* (goal), it seems clear that *by* is associated with the idea of "proximity" or the space that is neighbouring some side of a thing. Bennett (1975: 61) states that the component "proximity" might be "decomposed into more elementary components of meaning, one of which would be the notion "side"". Leech (1969:170) considers that *by* indicates not only a general idea of proximity, but also horizontal or lateral proximity. It is worth noting however, that Coriston-Oliver (2001) states that the spatial role of *by* embodies only 10% of its uses.

Table 50 records the number of occurrences for spatial sense and sub-senses which *bi-Phs* cover in ME as well as the ratio within spatial domain and with regard to all *by-Phs*.

Sense	Spatial			
	S1	S2	S3	S4
Semantic fields	Location or position: near, close to, at (*bi hond*)	Location: within an area: over, in, on (*bi water, bi lond, bi northe*)	Movement, direction: across, along, through (*bi se, bi the weie, bi gate*)	Seize sb. at, by or hang sb. by hand, neck (*bi fet, bi hed*)
Oc..	35	38	102	64
Rate % (within spatial)	14.64	15.89	42.67	26.77
Rate % (with regard to all *bi-Phs)*	1.52	1.65	4.45	2.79
Total of occurrences 239				
Rate ‰ (with regard to the corpus words) 3.7				

Table 50. Spatial *bi-Phs* in ME

The figures shown in Table 50 record 239 spatial *bi-Phs* which represent a ratio of 3.7 spatial *bi-Phs* for every thousand words in ME, and this number also represents 26.77% of the total number of *bi-Phs* found in the corpus. Let us see the spatial semantic fields in detail:

S-1) The data exhibited in Table 50 show that *bi-Phs* were scarcely used to express a location or position that is near, close to, next to, at. I have only recorded 35 instances. These include: *A-doun bi þe putte he sat* (CMFOXWO; *by þe watersyde* (CMALISAU); *slepeð bi ðe tre in ðe sadue* (CMBESTIA); *by the Towne Wallys* (CMDOCU4). Apart from *syde* which occurs on 9 occasions, there are no prepositional complements repeated more than 3 times.

S-2) *Bi-Phs* expressing location or position within an area are not frequent either. I have only found 38 examples such as *By wodes, by dales, and by douns* (CMALISAU); *By this cercle equinoxiall* (CMASTRO); *bi ðe sunne and bi ðe mone* (CMBESTIA); *assyse of our lord þe Kyng be generally by all Ynglond* (CMREYNES); *Bi hor londes her & þer* (CMEROBLO). No prepositional complement is found more than twice, with the exception of *land, sea, valley* which occur four times each. This confirms that there is no tendency to idiomaticity in this spatial sub-sense.

S-3) There are 102 *bi-Phs* which express movement or direction across, along, through an area. Examples of this semantic field include: *And by a ryuer tourned west* (CMALISAU); *and so rode by a foreste* (CMMALORY); *Ne with no wood man walke by the weye* (CMTVERS); *Nouth bi þe gate but ouer þe falwes* (CMHAVELO); *wolde cownselyn hym to comyn be lond er be watyr* (CMKEMPE). The prepositional complement *weye*, with 31 instances, although 7 of these are figurative rather than spatial, is well in the lead. It should be noted that there is a great tendency towards idiomatization of *by weye* as in *by wey of goodnesse* (CMMALORY); *other portes yaim lust by waye of marchandise* CMOFFIC3; *þo me tolde him bi þe wei* (CMEROBLO); *"ne sholde men nat by no weye seken blisfulnesse* (CMBOETH). *Bi-land* is found on 12 occasions, *bi-sea* 11 times, and *bi-water* 15.

S-4 There are 64 prepositional complements which refer to a part of the body. To seize somebody by his/her hand(s) is found on 19 occasions, to hang or seize somebody by the neck or feet occurs 4 times each, as in *Me henged up be the fet* (CMPETERB); *þus er þai bunden by hend and fete* (CMPRICK), *He sholden hange bi þe necke* (CMHAVELO).

1. 5. Bifore-Phs

The preposition *before* is basically defined as "locative anterior" in PDE (Bennett 1975: 119) with both "place" and "time" components. In temporal uses, *before* indicates a relationship of time between two events. However, the component "place" as in *he was ordered to appear before the Magistrate* (*ibid*) is very unusual in PDE as it is not interchangeable with "in front of". According to Tyler and Evans, two senses matched together in the early history of English: "the Location Sense (involving a TR and an oriented LM) and the In Advance Of Sense (involving an in tandem configuration)". In the course of history a network of senses develop: Location, Priority, Preceding, Temporal, Access To, Rather Than (2003: 164-165).

Our data, however, confirm that its historical ("located at the front of") meaning is predominant in ME.

The following Table exhibits the spatial senses in which *bifore-Phs* occur in ME:

Sense	Spatial	
Semantic fields	Of motion: ahead of, brought to the presence of	Of position: to be in front of, in the sight of or under the presence of
Oc.	44	95
Rate % (with regard to all *bifore-Phs)*	14.42	31.14
Reference	S-1	S2

Table 51. Spatial *bifore-Phs* in ME

I have found 139 *bifore-Phs* (45.56%) which are involved in a spatial reference, whereas temporal occurrences are only 84 (27.54%). As has been mentioned, the spatial role of *before-Phs* in PDE is very rare.

S-1. In this category I have gathered 44 occurrences (14.42% with regard to all *bifore-Phs*) which indicate an active or passive motion of the trajector so as to be in the sight of the landmark, *he cam to þe halle before þe lord ffaunhop* (CMDOCU4); *Before þe pore men hyt was broght* (CMHANSYN); *þat he was ladde to þe barr bifore þe Kynges Iustice3* (CMBRUT3).

S-2. Most spatial occurrences (95, 31.14% with regard to all *bifore-Phs*) indicate a position of the trajector "in the sight of" or in the presence of the landmark, e.g. *Horn in halle fond he þo, Bifore þe kyng on benche* (CMHORN); or a location "in front of" as in *he stode byfore his dore without lyke a pylgryme* (CMREYNAR); *and þai buriede hit bifor þe hye auter in the right side* (CMBRUT3).

1. 6. Bihinde-Phs

Behind-Phs involve source, path and goal expressions in PDE. The preposition *behind* usually indicates a locative posterior position or roughly located at the back. According to Tyler and Evans, the proto-scene "locates the TR at the back of the LM, that is, the TR is understood to be located such that the front of the LM is directed away from the TR" (2003: 170). The semantic connotation of locative posterior place may refer not only to physical entities but also to events, states and temporal references (Bennett: 83). The speaker's location point may have an intrinsic front and back. Thus in *Behynde the hygh awter lyeth many kyngis and qwenys* (CMREYNES), *awter* is seen as a physical body which has an inherent front and back. But we sometimes refer to entities which do not have an intrinsic front and back, e.g. a tree, and we refer to them as a "point of observation" (Leech 1969: 180-2). Thus we may choose as the front of a given physical object the part which is near us, and its back as the opposite, i.e. behind. Tyler and Evans, however, state that the "functional element denoted by *behind* relates to lack of perceptual access and lack of surety about the location of the TR" (2003: 169)

Behinde-Phs are very rare in ME. I have only found 24 instances in the HCME. They mainly express source and goal and only 9 examples are used to indicate a position in the rear of, or on the back side of, e.g. *Riht so behinde his brother bak* (CMGOWER); *and on the ryght syde he saw a pew closed with iron, and behynde the awter he saw a ryche bedde* CMMALORY).

1. 7. Biside-Phs

ME *biside* comes from OE *be* + *sidan* (dat sing). By c.1200 both words are fossilized into an adverbial form with the meaning "by the side". This adverbial form grammaticalized as a preposition governing a noun with the meaning "by the side of" a place, person, thing, state or condition.

It should be noted that 37 out of 42 *beside-Phs* detected in the corpus are used with a spatial reference with the meaning "by the side of" such as *the body and corps lieth buried in thabbay of Westmestre beside london* (CMCAXPRO); *And Joon was baptisinge in Ennon, bisidis Salym, for many watris weren there* (CMNTEST).

1. 8. In-Phs

On the semantic level, *in-Phs* were associated with a spatial or temporal sense in OE. However, many instances of *in-Phs* found in ME lost much of their original referential meaning as they developed from a spatial or temporal sense to a figurative or abstract one. There are two contending theories about the semantic roles of topological prepositions (*at, in, on*) in PDE. Thus Bennet (1975: 116) considers that the meaning (locative interior *vs.* locative surface, etc.) resides in the terms of the relationship rather than in the preposition itself. By specifying the roles of the preposition *in*, Bennet states that "the componential definition of *in* as locative-interior covers not only its spatial uses but also its temporal uses" (*ibid.*). Following Bennet's perspective, the topological prepositions *at, on* and *in* are not semantically distributed, and therefore the choice of one rather than another depends on the nature of the NP that follows. If so, we may state that the prepositional complements monitor the preposition. Thus, a large city, for example, will require *in*, a village, *at*, and a small island, *on*[1]. Leech (1969:3), however,

---

1 Bennet (1975: 65) insists on the fact that "what matters is the way an object is thought of on a particular occasion". Thus, one may think of Coventry, for example, as an enclosed area

considers that the topological prepositions *at, on* and *in* indicate that they "ascribe" to the following NP a particular dimensionality. Thus, the NP that functions as complement of the preposition *in* is seen as an area or volume, that is, as two-or-three dimensional[2]. A similar approach is defended by Dirven (1993: 78-9) as he indicates that English *in* "conceptualises space as an enclosure or volume" and following this notional category he outlines a radial network of extensions of *in*: spatial enclosure is the centre from which other branches develop: time-span, state as enclosure, area, manner or means, circumstance and cause. The notion of physical enclosure is expanded to psychological states such as *in despair*. Similarly, other types of enclosing experiences such as manner or means, circumstance or cause denote an "enveloping" state. Bennet (1975: 71) conceptualises *in* as A [locative [interior of B]], that is, the interior of B is the location of A. So in the example "the key is in the drawer", the message is, "the interior of the drawer is where the key is located". Cuyckens (1993: 32-33) considers that the notion of "interior" of English *in* is neither necessary nor sufficient. Indeed, the notion of "interior" is not detected in all cases, such as "he got a kick *in* the stomach". Besides, not all cases classified as "interior" are expressed with *in*, as in "the pear is *under* the cheese-cover", in which the pear being inside is not expressed with *in*. Zelinsky-Wibbelt (1993: 7) considers that English *in* is prototypically used in topological relations, either positional or static[3]. Tyler and Evans (2003: 178ff) also consider that the preposition *in* construes a three-dimensional (bounded) LM typically thought of as possessing an interior. They maintain that the location cluster of senses gave rise to a range of closely related senses: the In Situ Sense, the State Sense, the Activity Sense and the Means Sense.

In broad terms, prepositions may be viewed either as words that limit themselves to providing a given relation and marking a specific function, or as words that have their own semantic connotations such as spatial or temporal; locative interior or locative surface, etc. For practical purposes, my analysis follows the latter approach[4]

---

surrounded by the city boundaries (*x lives in Coventry*), as a given point on an itinerary (*you have to change trains at Coventry*) or as a surface (*more bombs were dropped on Coventry*).

2 Leech's interpretation implies that an example such as "the key is in the drawer" includes: a) the drawer is where the key is located; and b) it ascribes to the drawer the property of being 3-dimensional.

3 From a syntactical point of view, Fillmore (1968), Dirven (1982) and Radden (1982) argue that prepositions are a manifestation of underlying verb and noun phrase relations. Thus a preposition shows a given relation and marks a given function in the framework of Case Grammar. Fillmore (1968: 367) considers prepositions as variants of inflectional units and therefore as markers on noun phrases. This view is contended by Jackendoff (1973, 1977). He posits that although "diachronically the reduction of prepositions to case markers is undeniable, it is not clear that such a process plays a role in synchronic grammar" (1977: 80).

4 Lindkvist (1950) differentiates seven senses of *in* in PDE. Sandhagen (1965: 86-150) goes further and distinguishes five different senses of the preposition *in* in its temporal relationship alone.

in line with the semantic classification provided by the MED for the preposition *in*.
Table 52 shows the figures for spatial sense and sub-senses expressed by *in-Phs* in ME as well as the number of occurrences of each semantic field.

Sense	Semantic fields	Oc.	Rate % (within spatial sense)	Rate % (with regard to all *in-Phs*)	Field
	Inside a solid object or immersed in a fluid substance. Enclosed in (fire, air) or into (a solid, liquid). Within a building, ship, bed, bag.	667	21.42	7.06	S-1
	In a book, document, poem, etc.	245	7.87	2.59	S-2
	In or into sb., in one's body, in one's heart, mind, memory, thought.	389	12.49	4.12	S-3
Spatial	In the hand(s), arm(s). Also fig. in someone's hand (= in someone's possession). In chains, ropes, fetters, tied with, bound in.	167	5.36	1.76	S-4
	On or onto the surface of sth. and surrounded by its parts: in or into a city, town, wood, forest. Also on the surface of sth. which extends in all directions: heaven, hell, earth, world, sea, field, island, country.	1327	42.62	14.06	S-5
	At a place or position; at, beside.	198	6.36	2.09	S-6
With regard to quantity, dimension, number.		120	3.85	1.27	S-7
ME/Total		3113	Rate % (with regard to the corpus words): 0.51.		

Table 52. Spatial *in-Phs* in ME

The data extracted from the HCME show 3113 spatial *in-Phs*. The average rate of usage is 0.51 spatial *in-Phs* for every hundred words in ME, and this represents 32.98% of the total number of *in-Phs* found in the corpus. Let us see the spatial semantic fields in detail:

S-1) The corpus contains 667 occurrences of *in-Phs* expressing a static local position of sb. or sth. situated inside a solid object or immersed in a fluid substance; enclosed in (fire, air) or into (a solid, liquid) or within a building, ship, bed, bag, e.g. *in the nonry of Catysby* (CMEDMUND) The data show that only 7.06 % of *in-Phs* have this semantic connotation in ME and cover 21.42% of all instances found for spatial sense. The complements *prisun*, with 47 instances, and *chirche/kirke*, with

46, are the most frequent for this semantic category. The third highest number of *in- Phs*, with 40 instances, occur with *house*. Being on the surface of or immersed in *water* is found on 31 occasions. Staying, dwelling or being enclosed in a *halle*, with 30 examples, a *castel* (18), *the Parliament-(house)* (16), or *tower* (10) are also frequently expressed with *in-Phs*. Thus, the preposition *in* predominates in contexts in which sb. or sth. is placed inside a solid object, immersed in a fluid substance, or enclosed in a building, but this semantic field is also covered by *at-* and *on-Phs*, although with a much lower rate.

S-2) *In-Phs* expressing the appearance of certain contents in a book, document, poem, etc. account for 245 instances, that is, a rate of 7.87% within the spatial sense and 2.59% with regard to all *in-Phs* detected in the corpus. The complement *boke/book* predominates with 51 examples e.g. *In þese same bokes* (CMCAXPRO). The second highest number of *in-Phs* in this category is found with the complement *gospel* (25). There is a stable tendency to use the preposition *in* and not *on* or *at* for this semantic category.

S-3) The corpus includes 389 instances of *in-Phs* to denote that sth. is located in or put into sb. Such phrases referring to location in one's heart, mind and thought are frequently used. Thus the complement *herte* is the most common and occurs on 126 occasions, e.g. *Jn herte he gynneþ fecche mood* (CMALISAU). In one's *mynde* is found on 47 occasions, e.g. *And conceyve in your myndes* (CMDIGBY), and in one's *þouhte* 36 times, e.g. *þan ani man mai thing in thoght* (CMCURSOR). The second highest number of examples found in this category occurs with *soule*, with 76 instances such as *vertuous diuersete fourme in þy soule* (CMAELR3). Location in one's body or flesh (very often opposed to soul) tends to be expressed with *in-Phs*. Thus the complement *bodi/body* appears 49 times, e.g. *þe find he sal in bodi ber* (CMCURSOR) and *flesh* 18 times. *In-Phs* appear on 61 occasions to express position poised on part of one's body such as head, breast, nose, etc. On one's *hed* appears 23 times, e.g. *His eyen stepe, and rollynge in his heed* (CMTVERS); in one's breast 13, in one's nose 6, and in one's forehead 6. It is worth noting that **in fot, *in fet, *in kne, *in leg* are not found. The number of occurrences in this semantic field shows a ratio of 12.49% when compared with all spatial examples and 4.12% within the whole number of *in-Phs* found in the corpus.

S-4) *In-Phs* appear on 167 occasions to express position in one's hand(s), arm(s); also figuratively in someone's hand (= in someone's possession). Being bound in, or tied with chains, ropes, fetters is also expressed with *in-Phs*. In this category, most instances occur with the prepositional complements *hande*, with 127 instances, e.g. *and in the hand of oure Lord God Almyghty* (CMECTPROS) and *arme* which appears 23 times, e.g *Take hym in your armys* (CMDIGBY). Other prepositional complements include *pyte, cage*, etc. e.g. *For thei be as fers as a lyon in a cage* (CMDIGBY). The small number of examples in this category corresponds to a rate of 5.36% within the spatial location and 1.76% when related to all *in-Phs* of the corpus.

S-5) This is the category which expresses a position on the surface of sth. and surrounded by its parts: in or into a city, town, wood, forest. Also the situation of sth. in or on a place which extends in all directions: heaven, hell, earth, world, sea, field, country, etc. This category includes 1327 examples, that is, a rate of 42.62% within the spatial location and 14.06% when related to all *in-Phs* of the corpus. The prepositional phrase *in heuen* predominates in this category. It has been detected on 162 occasions, e.g *þet he is ine heuene* (CMAYENBI). Likewise *in þe/þis werold/ world* is highly represented and there are 131 examples, e.g. *Nis in þis werlde so fair quene* (CMALISAU). Each of the prepositional complements *eorþe/erþe* and *place* is found on 96 occasions, e.g. *Alle men leuyng in erþe* (CMCLOUD); *in a place beside your Castell* (CMDOCU4). The location of sth. or sb. *in land/lond* (of) has been found on 72 occasions, e.g. *in þe londe of Ermonie* (CMBEVIS). *In helle* follows with 71 instances, e.g. *in helle shame and confusioun* (CMECTPROS); The complements *toune, contry,* and *felde* are also extensively used as they appear on 57, 46, and 43 occasions respectively. Examples include: *Kni3ttes hem armen in court and tounes* (CMALISAU); *in euery contre þai hade grete werre and stryfe* (CMBRUT3); *Most strong and myghty in feld for to fyght* (CMDIGBY). 36 examples are found with *see*, e.g. *trauailede half 3ere and more in þe see* (CMBRUT3). With regard to countries and cities, *in Engeland* predominates with 26 instances and *in London* follows, with 17 examples, e.g. *in london as elles where in the rewme* (CMDOCU3). This spatial category includes many other prepositional complements that occur less than ten times, such as *wode, stret, forest*, etc. One may conclusively state that *in-Phs* still cover the roles that *at-* and *on-Phs* came to fill later on.

S-6) The 198 occurrences, with a rate of 6.36% when compared with other spatial instances and 2.09% with regard to all examples in the corpus, were also found to denote a position at or beside a place, e.g.. *in þat oþer syde of þe cros* (CMAELR3); *equaciouns in the bordure of thin Astralabie* (CMASTRO); *and in the botme of the ship* (CMECTPROS); *sitte bitwene bothe alras in his right place* (CMASTRO). The prepositional complements *line*, with 36 instances, *centre*, with 34, *border* with 15, and *circle* with 11, predominate in this category. The remaining instances occur less than five times for each type. Some prepositional complements in this category are less typical than these figures imply as many instances occur in the same text. Thus the corpus shows 36 instances of *in line* (19 of them in CMQUATO), 34 of *in center* (26 of them also in CMQUATO), 15 of *in border* (11 of them in CMASTRO).

S-7) This category includes 120 *in-Phs*, that is, a rate of 3.85% within the spatial reference and 1.27% when related to all *in-Phs* of the corpus. They denote a specification with regard to quantity, dimension or number such as *in which fifthe partie shalt thou fynden* (CMASTRO); *Was twenti fote in lengþe be tale* (CMBEVIS). *In part* (66), in *lengþe*, (21), *in depnesse* (12), *in heiht* (7), and *in wydness* (4) are the most common.

In conclusion, the most significant feature of spatial *in-Phs* is the absence of idiomatic constructions. In fact, on the semantic level the preposition *in* and its complement constitute a conceptual unit with an informative content in our corpus. However, I have already found that many *at-*[5] and *on*[6]*-Phs* develop from a spatial or temporal sense to a figurative or abstract meaning, initiating a process of idiomatisation. My data, for the ME period, show similar results to those given by Lundskær-Nielsen (1993) with regard to the use of *in-, at-* and *on-Phs* in OE. Lundskær-Nielsen compared the range of uses of these prepositions and found that in the *Anglo-Saxon Chronicle* (years 892-900) only *on*, with 9 occurrences, has a figurative or abstract sense (1993:88). His study of the *Peterborough Chronicle* for the years 1122-54 also shows that the preposition *on* is found 25 times with a figurative or abstract sense, whereas *in* presents no instances of this and there is only one example with *æt* (1993: 96). Lundskær-Nielsen's data are not so conclusive for the ME period, partly because his corpus is limited to three ME texts (*Ancrene Wise*, parts six and seven, *Vices and Virtues* and Chaucer's *A Treatise on the Astrolobe*).

1. 9. On-Phs

In broad terms, the spatial meaning of *on* in PDE is "locative surface", including both "on the top of" and "at the surface of" (cf. Bennett, 1975: 69). It should be noted, however, that many spatial references defined as "locative" (*at*, in PDE) and "locative interior" (*in*, in PDE) are expressed in ME with *on*-Phs. It is well-known that the ME prepositions *at, on, in* and *bi* are very often interchanged in either spatial or temporal references. It is still arguable whether or not all spatial and temporal uses of each of these prepositions might be analysed in terms of a single sense. In other words, should the differences be substantiated in the context of the terms of the preposition rather than in the preposition itself? Leech (1969: 249), when accounting for the spatial distinctions between these prepositions in PDE, refers to "ascription features of dimensionality". In Leech's terms, *on* is said to imply that the prepositional complement is seen as a line or surface/area, i.e. as one- or two-dimensional, whereas *in* is perceived as an area or volume, *i.e.* two- or three-dimensional. In like manner, Tyler and Evans consider that *on* "mediates a relation of contact between a TR and a LM, which is a a two-dimensional planar surface" (2003:179). This approach does not resolve the problems we have found with the preposition *on* in ME, because examples such as *on þe French side were but fraude* (CMCAPCHR) cannot be analysed as if the preposition *on* ascribed to the prepositional complement a particular dimensionality. Dirven (1993: 78) expands the notion of "contact" for the preposition *on* with a radial network which includes a central notion of "contact with line/surface": from there it expands to "time", which, in its turn, expands to "circumstance". The central notion also expands to

---

5 See Chapter VI.
6 See Chapter VI.

"state", to "area", to "means" and "reason". This notional development in chains of meaning from physical into mental may seem more appropriate for our study. However, theoretical discussion of the meaning of the preposition on, whether in PDE or in ME, is not one of the aims of the present study. For practical purposes then, I basically propose for this preposition the classification of "senses" and "sub-senses" which appears in the MED. Table 53 shows the figures for spatial sense and sub-senses[7] covered by *on-Phs* in ME as well as the number of occurrences of each semantic field.

Sense	Semantic fields	Oc.	Rate % (within spatial sense)	Rate % (with regard to all *on-Phs*)	Field
Spatial	Sb. or sth. is placed on the top of or in a close contact with a surface, e.g. on (a) table, wall, stone; head, etc.	161	22.11	5.98	S1
	Sb. or sth. is riding on horseback, on an ass, etc., (carried) on the back, on the wind, (walking) on foot, etc. or motion towards a position, e.g. *on sa* "onto the sea."	128	17.58	4.75	S2
	Sb. or sth. is located in an open place (sea, river, ground, field, road, street, way, hill) or within the boundaries of earth, heaven, hell, kingdom, country, region, city, town, etc.).	296	40.65	10.99	S3
	Position indicating the part of the body which supports sth., e.g. poised on one's feet, legs, knees, shoulder, back, etc.	19	2.60	0.70	S4
	Sb. or sth. is placed above (not touching); around, surrounding (clothes, armour, garment, cape) or supended from, hung on; fixed to, etc.; in proximity to, near, by, at.	87	11.95	3.23	S5
	Clasped in, enclosed in, got into (sb's) possession, power or control: on *(the) hand, fot, castle, prison*, etc. ruling over: bishop, lord on (= of) a place.	31	4.25	1.15	S6
	With regard to a dimension: *on brede, on heigh, height, on lengthe, on long, on brod.*	6	0.82	0.22	S7
ME/Total		728	Rate % (with regard to the corpus words): 0.14		

Table 53. Spatial *on-Phs* in ME

---

7 Cf. OED and MED.

The data extracted from the HCME show 728 spatial *on-Phs*. The average rate of usage is 0.14 spatial *on-Phs* for every hundred words in ME, and this represents 27.05% of the total number of *on-Phs* found in the corpus. Let us see the spatial semantic fields in detail:

S-1) The corpus contains 161 occurrences of *on-Phs* expressing a static local position of sb. or sth. placed on the top of an object or in close contact with a surface, e.g. *Bi Crist þat wolde on rode blede!* (CMHAVELO). The figures show that only 5.98 % of *on-Phs* have this semantic connotation in ME and cover 22.11% of all instances found for spatial sense. The expression *(Christ) on (the) rode/cross/ tre* is the most frequent for this semantic category.

S-2) *On-Phs* expressing movement on or onto a position account for 128 instances, that is, a rate of 17.58% within the spatial sense and 4.75% with regard to all *on-Phs* detected in the corpus. Thus 32 examples were found referring to somebody riding on horseback, on an ass, etc., e.g. *Quyklich and on hors wende* (CMASTRO). Movement *on fot/fet* has been detected on 13 occasions, e.g. *he wente aftir hym on foote* (CMMALORY). It is worth noting that 91 *on-Phs* out of 128, which belong to this semantic field, occur with only six nouns *(fot, stede, horse, bac, sa* and *land)*. No other noun is recorded more than twice.

S-3) The corpus includes 296 instances of *on-Phs* to denote the location of sth. or sb. in an open place (sea, river, ground, field, road, street, way, hill*)*, e.g. *ðe leun stant on hille* (CMBESTIA).

The prepositional complement, *(þe) e(o)rþe* is the most common and occurs on 74 occasions. Location within the boundaries of a country (including England) or region is referred to 60 times. *On werold/world* is found 31 times. The location *on water* (sometimes referring to the sea) appears on 28 occasions whereas *on se/sea*, 12. Location *on lond/land*, as opposed to sea, includes 16 instances. *On heuen/heven* is represented with 17 instances, whereas *on hell* is found only on 4 occasions. In broad terms, the number of occurrences in this category occount for a rate of 40.65% within the spatial sphere and becomes 10.99% when related to all instances found in the HCME.

S-4) *On-Phs* appear on 19 occasions to express the position poised on part of one's body such as feet, legs, knees, e.g. *And braided hym doune on knee to grounde*. (CMANCRE). In this category, all instances occur with the prepositional complements *cnes/knees*, with 11 instances, or *fot/fet/feet* which is registered on 9 occasions. The small number of occurrences in this semantic field shows a ratio of 2.60% when compared with all spatial examples and 0.70% within the whole number of *on-Phs* found in the corpus.

S-5) This category expresses a position above (not touching) or around (surrounding), suspended from or fixed to, in proximity to, close to, near, by or at, includes 87 examples, that is, a rate of 11.95% within the spatial location and 3.23% when related to all *on-Phs* of the corpus. Examples include: *Peres and apples hongeþ on bou3* (CMALISAU). Christ hung *on cross/crois* is found 11 times, and *on tre/tree* 5. This prepositional complement has also been featured under the heading S-1. Some nouns are overrated as most of the instances occur in the same text. Thus the corpus shows 12 instances of *on centre* (10 of them in CMQUATO) and 19 of *on ende* (13 of them also in CMQUATO), and the location on a zodiac sign such as *on Cancer* is found in 5 times in the corpus, but all of them in CMQUATO. The indication of a position *on þe cherch-dores/gates* seems to be significant as it occurs on 5 occasions. An equal number of instances is recorded to indicate that sth. is placed or hung on one's neck.

S-6) The 31 occurrences, with a rate of 4.25% when compared with other spatial instances and 1.15% with regard to all examples in the corpus, were also found to denote that sth. or sb. is clamped in, enclosed in or got into (sb's) possession, power or control (on one's hand, feet, prison, castle, etc.), e.g.. *He took on honde a styf launce* (CMALISAU). The prepositional complements *hond/hand*, with 16 instances, *armes*, with 8, and *poer/miht* with 5, predominate in this category. The remaining instances do not occur more than once each.

It is worth mentioning that *on*, instead of *of* or *at*, is used to denote somebody's ruling over a place such as *bishop, lord on* (county, town, etc.) is used only in CMDOC2, which includes 17 instances such as e.g. *Duk on Normandi* (CMDOCU2). No other text of the corpus includes this structure.

S-7) Under this heading I include only 6 *on-Phs* (0.82% within the spatial area and 0.22% in relation to all the other instances) which express a certain dimension such as *on brede/brod, on heigh, height, on lengthe, on long*, etc. e.g. *Als has þe cros on lang and brade*.

1. 10. Ouer-Phs

The preposition *over* plays many different roles in PDE, the most common being locative (LOCATION) and directional (SOURCE, PATH, and GOAL). Wood (1967: 67-69) distinguishes fifteen senses of over in PDE. On the one hand, Bennett (1975: 50ff) glosses a componential definition of the meanings of *over* in PDE as follows:
 a) Directional
  – Path locative superior of: "passing directly above" (via)
  – Goal locative superior of: "to a position directly above" (to)
 b) Locative
  –Locative superior of: "directly above"
  –Locative path locative superior of: "on the other side of"

On the other hand, Zelinsky-Wibbelt (1993: 371) proposes a "relation of nearness in the vertical dimension" as a spatial schematization type for *over*. Dirven (1993: 95) says that *over* indicates a "path in its back and forth directions" and implies a two-way or repeated movement. Kreitzer (1997) suggests the TR is in the same vertical axis as the LM, whereas Tyler and Evans (2003:111) posit that the TR is "within potential reach of the LM".

The following table exhibits the spatial occurrences and rates of *ouer-Phs* in ME:

Sense	Spatial			
Semantic fields	From one side to the other of (sea, lake)	Throughout (a land, city)	Directly above without touching	Lying on; upon the outer surface
Oc.	41	22	8	28
Rate % (within spatial)	41.41	22.22	8.08	28.28
Rate % (with regard to all *ouer-Phs)*	11.05	5.92	2.15	7.53
Fields	S1	S2	S3	S4

Table 54. Spatial *ouer-Phs* in ME

I have identified 99 *ouer-Phs* with spatial connotations. What follows is a survey of the various senses:

S-1. This category includes the passage from one side to the other of a sea, lake, river, field, valley, bridge or fire. This is the most common semantic field within spatial sense. I have found 41 instances, most of them with the noun complement *see*. Thus, passage from one side of the sea to the other or from one country to another via the sea is found on 17 occasions, e.g. *Ich fley ouer þe salte se Til Engeland* (CMHAVELO). The complement *water* has been also recorded five times, e.g. *(Jesus) passe ouer the water of Jordan* (CMFITZJA). Crossing from one side of a bridge to the other and from one side of a river to the other, are recorded 5 times each, e.g. *So sir Launcelot rode over that brydge that was olde and feble* (CMMALORY); *with his host he scholde ride Over Danubie thilke flod* (CMGOWER). No other prepositional complements occur more than once.

S-2. Everywhere around or throughout the earth, the world, a land or city or throughout a book, is not very frequent as only 22 instances were found. *Ouver (al) land* ("all over the world") is the most frequent *ouer-Ph* with 5 instances, e.g. *þa þestrede þe dæi ouer al landes* (CMPETERB). All other complements do not occur more than twice, such as "valley", "country" and "kingdom", eg. *rode thorow many stronge contrayes over mores and valeis* (CMMALORY).

S-3. *Ouer-Phs* espressing a movement directly above without touching, such as "jump over the fence" in PDE, are not common in ME. In fact only 8 instances are included in the corpus to express the action of up, over and to the other side of a wall or bridge, e.g. *Horn þreu him ouer þe brigge* (CMHORN); *a full fair brigge to passen ouer the dyches* (CMMANDEV).

S-4. The action of lying on or resting upon something or somebody, expressed by means of *ouer-Phs*, is usually preceded by the notion of movement up and over as in *Ouer þe table he lep* (CMALISAU); *he lete breke þe suerde ouer his heuede* (CMBRUT3). My data include 17 examples which combine these two actions: up and over the top of a table, horse, etc. On 11 occasions *ouer-Phs* are used to express location upon the outer surface of somebody or something, e.g. *ymagined to ben the verrey point over the crowne of thin heved* CMASTRO), although the meaning of something lying on or affecting the whole outer surface is usually implied, as in *ouer al his bodi*.

1. 11. Þurgh-Phs

Tyler and Evans (2003:217-227) have accounted a detailed study of the proto-scene and the network of senses for *through*. According to them, this preposition construes a "bounded LM" with multiple elements, some structural (interior, boundary, exterior) and some other additional structural (entrance point, exit point and the contiguous locations between the entrance point and the exit point). Thus, it "designates a spatial relation in which the TR is held to occupy a contiguous series of spatial points with respect to a LM, which has an interior structural element" (2003:217). Consequently, the functional notion of path and motion is evoked. Tyler and Evans have proposed a semantic network of seven distinct senses for *through* derived from the proto-scene: the Extended Action Sense, the Temporal Sense, the On-the-other-side Sense, the Completion Sense, the Transmission Sense, the Means Sense and the Cause Sense.

The semantic fields we have found in ME are the following:

Sense		Spatial	
Semantic fields	Go across/along a place in a single direction (country, region, county, city, town, street; field, wood); from one position or location to another	Go across (all directions) all over/throughout the world, sea, country, region, county, town, field, wood)	Go through a book, the gospel
Oc	15	62	4
Rate % (within spatial)	18.51	76.54	4.93
Rate % (with regard to all þurgh-Phs)	1.74	7.19	0.46
Reference	S1	S2	S3
Total of occurrences 81			

Table 55. Spatial *þurgh-Phs* in ME

The data displayed in Table 55 show that only 81 examples (9.39% with respect to all þurgh-Phs) were shown with a spatial sense, out of the 862 instances exhibited in the whole corpus. It is also noteworthy that only 15 instances (18.51%, with regard to all spatial *þurgh-Phs*) were recorded with the general sense of going through an alleyway or path, that is, passing from one spatial position or location to another, (S-1), e.g. *Of france to þe holi lond . wende & þoru paris* (CMEROBLO); *ande so forthe thorowe the cytte of London* (CMGREGOR).

In category S-2 I have included 62 instances which express a movement from one spatial point to others, that is, movement in many/all directions as in *So sir Launcelot rode many wylde wayes thorowoute morys and mares* (CMMALORY); *and kepe watche thrugh this towne withinne the boundys* (CMREYNES); *durst go þorw all þe þik wodis in þat cuntre* (CMCAPCHR); *That ye make serche thurghout alle my region* CMDIGBY).

In field S-3 I have found 4 instances which refers to some evidence which may be found in a book, such as *hwuch-se he mei preouin þurh his boc* (CMSAWLES); *þurrh hallʒhe goddspellwrihhtess* (CMORM).

1. 12. Under-Phs

The preposition *under* implies that the TR is conceptualized as being "lower than and yet proximal to", and hence in "potential contact with" the LM (Tyler and Evans: 2003: 121-123). The network of senses is developed by Tyler and Evans

(2003: 123ff) as follows: a) the Down Cluster, that is, a TR that is lower than, or lower than and within the potential reach of. The LM implies either "less" or "control" (subject to the control of the LM) respectively; b) the Covering Sense (the spatial configuration between the TR and the LM is mostly a horizontal one, although an interpretation of occlusion is implied); and c) the Non-existence Sense (there is a correlation between located under and non-existence or no longer being alive).

Spatial roles of *under-Phs* in ME are distributed as follows:

Sense		Spatial		
Semantic fields	Indicating position beneath or below sth.	With reference to sth. which covers, envelops or conceals ("within")	All over the world ("under heaven, under moon")	
Oc.	25	55	10	
Rate % (within spatial)	27.77	61.11	11.11	
Rate % (with regard to all *under-Phs*)	12.90	21.07	3.83	
Fields	S1	S2	S3	

Table 56. Spatial *under-Phs* in ME

The data for *under-Phs* show that only 90 examples (34.48%) were found with a spatial sense out of the 261 instances detected in the whole corpus. It is also noteworthy that only 25 instances (12.90%, with regard to all *under-Phs*) were recorded with the general sense of indicating a position beneath or below something (S-1), e.g. *And vnder the Emperoures table sitten .iiij.clerkes þat writen all þat the Emperour seyth* (CMMANDEV); *vnder the costes of Irland at the feste of Michelmasse* (CMDOCU4). Within this category I include noun complements of *under* denoting natural or artificial means of shelter, e.g. *went allone into a medowe vnder an hedge saying his devocions* (CMEDMUND). The most common spatial use of *under-Phs* involves noun complements that indicate the notion of covering, enveloping or concealing within boundaries (S-2). I have found 55 instances which represent a ratio of 61.11% of all spatial instances and 21.07 with regard to all *under-Phs*. In this category I include references to something that covers or clothes, e.g. *And gouþlich vnder gore* (CMSIRITH); *Iarmed vnder clope* (CMHORN); or something that protects, e.g. *Wel y-armed vnder sheld* (CMALISAU); or something located within boundaries, e.g. *the names of the monthes writen under the same cercle* (CMASTRO). The other ten instances include *heuen* and *moon* as complements, and indicate the idea of "all around the world" (S-3), e.g. *That oonly man of creatures vnder heuen dyrectyth & ordereth his actes* (CMFITZJA); *þe fayrest wymman under mone* (CMHAVELO). No idiomatic spatial instances were found (S-4).

2. TEMPORAL ROLES
2. 1. Aboue-Phs
The survey of the data found in the corpus concerning *aboue-Phs* shows that only a single instance is found with a temporal role with the meaning of "beyond, further than": *and chylde that was above xij yere age* (CMGREGOR).

2. 2. After-Phs
The temporal role of *after-Phs* predominates, by comparison with other senses. The corpus includes 437 instances which express time, and this figure represents a ratio of 43.65% with regard to all *after-Phs* detected in the corpus. The following Table exhibits the data:

Sense	After a point in time	Following in time, in succession to; next to, subsequent to	Total
Oc.	148	289	437
Rate % (within temporal sense)	33.86	66.13	Rate % (with regard to the corpus words): 0.05
Rate % (with regard to all *after-Phs*)	14.78	28.87	
Field	T-1	T-2	

Table 57. Temporal *after-Phs* in ME

All temporal *after-Phs* express a similar sense: the occurrence of an action that either comes about after a point in time (T1) or follows another in time or occurs in succession to another (T2). From this latter semantic connotation, "next to" and consequently "subsequent to" develop. I have detected 148 instances (33.86% with regard to all temporal *after-Phs*) which express that something occurs or is expected to occur after a given point in time, e.g. *The kyng was in þe feld sone aftir mydnyte* (CMCAPCHR); *þe sonday next after Micheles day* (CMDOCU3). In 211 examples (66.13% with regard to all temporal instances), *after-Phs* indicate that an action follows another in time. Examples include: *aftur speche of oon may come speche of anoþur* (CMWYCSER); *After þis Ryuallo, regnede Gorbodyan his sone xv ʒere* (CMBRUT3).

2. 3. At-Phs

Only 359 *at-Phs* out of the 1555 found in the HCME express a temporal relationship. This figure represents a rate of 23.08% of all *at-Phs* found in the corpus. It is also worth noting that nearly half of them indicate the time at which an event happens. Consider the following Table:

Sense	Part of day	Calendar	A point in time; within, for, during a period of time	Total
Oc.	76	31	239	346
Rate % (within temporal sense)	21.96	8.95	69.07	Rate % (with regard to the corpus words): 0.05
Rate % (with regard to all *at-Phs*)	4.88	1.99	15.36	
Field	T-1	T-2	T-3	

Table 58. Temporal *At-Phs* in ME

T-1 field includes 76 occurrences which express an action or process that occurs at a given time (hour) of the day such as *at middai, at noon, at vij of clock* etc. This category represents the second highest rate (21.96%) within temporal uses. Examples include *at brekefaste* (CMPRIV); *at diner* (CMDOCU4), *at iiij aftyrnone* (CMMETHAM).

In field T-2 I have only found 31 instances which refer to the calendar such as *at sonday, at mai, at þe feste of saint Ioane*, etc.

Category T-3 comprises 239 instances with a rate of 69.07 % within the temporal senses and 15.36% with regard to all *at-Phs* found in the corpus. Examples include *At the comyng of Criste* (CMROLLTR), *at such tyme* (CMNTEST), *at min ende day* (CMSELEG), etc.

2. 4. Bi-Phs

The review of the HCME shows that out of the 2290 *bi-Phs* found in the corpus, only 105 have a temporal sense. The following Table shows the data:

Sense	Part of a day	Calendar	At a point in time; within, for or during a period of time	Total
Oc.	11	6	81	98
Rate % (within temporal sense)	10.22	6.12	82.65	Rate % (with regard to the corpus words): 0.017
Rate % (with regard to all *bi-Phs*)	0.48	0.26	3.53	
Field	T-1	T-2	T-3	

Table 59. Temporal *bi-Phs* in ME

T-1. In this semantic field I have included only 11 temporal *bi-Phs* which refer to actions or processes which occur at a certain part of the day, e.g. *he that cam to hym bi ny3t* (CMNTEST); *And so hi seghen þo þet bi þe Morghen waren icomen* (CMKENTSE). Only 6 instances were spotted for the calendar (T-2).

T-3. In this category 81 instances were found (82.65% within temporal sense, and 3.53% with regard to all *bi-Phs*). They all express an action which takes place within, for or during a period of time, e.g. *walkeris aboute in the deseert bi fourti geer* (CMOTEST); e.g. *þe kyng of Frauns cam not be þat tyme* (CMBRUT3). *Bi-Phs* are also used to indicate that sth. occurs at a point in time as in *by vij of þe clokke* (CMDOCU3) or the number of times sth. occurs in a period, e.g. *twelfe penyes by þe 3er* (CMDOCU3).

2. 5. Bifore-Phs

The corpus shows 82 instances which express time and this figure represents a ratio of 26.88% with respect to all *bifore-Phs* found in the corpus. The following Table shows the data:

Sense	Preceding in order of time (reigned before)	Earlier than a date or event (before Monday, Pentecostes)	Total
Oc.	18	64	82
Rate % (within temporal sense)	21.95	78.04	Rate % (with regard to the corpus words): 0.01
Rate % (with regard to all *bifore-Phs*)	5.90	20.98	
Field	T-1	T-2	

Table 60. Temporal *bifore-Phs* in ME

All temporal *bifore-Phs* indicate a similar role: the occurrence of an action that either precedes another in time (T1) or takes place earlier than a point in time or event (T2). I have only found 18 examples (21.95% with regard to all temporal *bifore-Phs*) which indicate that an action or event precedes another in time, e.g. *iudas sett the deuyls werkis bifor the werkis of crist* (CMROLLPS); *byfore þat he seruede oþur þing* (CMWYCSER). In 64 instances (78.04% with regard to all temporal instances) *bifore-Phs* indicate that an action occurs earlier than a date or event. Examples include: *the thorsday Befor the feste of seint laurence*, (CMDOCU3); *I mene from xi of the clokke before the houre of noon* (CMASTRO); *þe Sunday befor Myhilmesse* (CMCAPCHR).

2. 6. Bihinde-Phs
No temporal *bihinde-Phs* were detected in the corpus.

2. 7. Biside-Phs
No temporal *biside-Phs* were found in the corpus.

2. 8. In-Phs
The survey of the HCME reveals 487 *in-Phs* with a temporal sense. The occurrences are much fewer than those found in spatial categories. For each 6.46 spatial occurrences a single instance is found with a temporal sense. So the average rate of usage falls to 0.08 *in-Phs* for every hundred words in ME and covers only 5.16% of the total number of *in-Phs* found in the corpus. The following is a detailed account of temporal categories:

Sense	Part of a day	Calendar	At a point in time; within, for, during a period of time	Total
Oc.	40	101	315	456
Rate % (within temporal sense)	8.77	22.14	69.07	Rate % (with regard to the corpus words): 0.08
Rate % (with regard to all *in-Phs*)	0.42	1.07	3.33	
Field	T-1	T2	T-3	

Table 61. Temporal *in-Phs* in ME

T-1) In this category I have included parts of a day such as *in þe morowenyng* (22 times), *in þe nihte* (15), and *in þe euenyng* (3), e.g. *Many ben jolyf in þe morowenyng.. And þolen deþ in þe euenyng* (CMALISAU); *in al þe niȝte* (CMFOXWO).

T-2. In this semantic field (calendar) I have counted 101 *in-Phs* (22.14% within temporal sense) such as *in the 13 day of Decembre* (CMASTRO); *in the ȝere of our Lord God M=l=CCC & xxij* (CMBRUT3); *In Mai, in þe formeste dai* (CMBEVIS).

T-3. Most temporal instances (198 instances) were found to indicate that an action either takes place during a period of time or occupies the whole of a period, e.g. *In þe tyme of þe bataile* (CMCAPCHR), although they are also used to indicate that sth. occurs at a point in time (117 examples) as in *in þe fest of Seyn Jerom* (CMCAPCHR). The rate of *in-Phs* found under this category rises to 69.07% within temporal uses.

2. 9. On-Phs

Our survey of the HCME reveals for 307 *on-Phs* with a temporal sense. The number of occurrences is less than half the frequency found in spatial categories. So the average rate of usage falls to 0.05 *on-Phs* for every hundred words in ME and covers only 11.40% of the total number of *on-Phs* found in the corpus. The following Table is a detailed account of temporal roles:

106 CHAPTER FIVE

Sense	At a point in time; within, for, during a period of time	Calendar	Part of day	Total
Oc.	145	86	57	288
Rate % (within temporal sense)	50.34	29.86	19.79	Rate % (with regard to the corpus words): 0.05
Rate % (with regard to all *on-Phs*)	5.38	3.19	2.11	
Field	T-1	T-2	T-3	

Table 62. Temporal *on-Phs* in ME

T-1) The analysis of the corpus has shown that 145 instances (50.34% within temporal senses and 5.38% with regard to all *on-Phs*) are used either to indicate the time (a point in time; within, for, during a period of time) when an event occurs, such as *Thus was he crowned on Seynt Edward day* (CMCAPCHR), *and there they came ynne on seynt lukes Even* (CMDOCU4), or to refer to an event that occurs at an unspecified time, e.g. *And on a daye he came to an ymage of oure Lady* (CMEDMUND), *Seynt Edmond and his felowys on a daye came* (CMEDMUND), *And on a tyme was he taken bi pirates* (CMFITZJA). Just over half the instances in this category (125) use the prepositional complement *dai/day*, whereas *tyme/time* appears on 24 occasions.

T-2) Within this category I have included the 86 instances which refer to the calendar. In more than half (52), a day of the week is mentioned, e.g. *And on þe Wednesday, erly* (CMCAPCHR), *on Saterday at nygh* (CMPRIV). The examples that belong in this category represent a rate of 29.86% within the temporal sense and 5.38% when related to all *on-Phs* in the corpus.

T-3) Within this category I have classified 57 o*n-Phs* (that is, a rate of 19.79% of all temporal instances and 2.11% of all examples in the corpus) which are used to indicate the parts of the day (in the morning, in the afternoon or at night), e.g. *On the morn, wen it was dai* (CMCURSOR), *ða on þære nihte com* (CMROOD).

2. 10. Ouer-Phs
The following Table exhibits the data for *ouer-Phs*:

Sense	Calendar	Within, for or during a period of time
Oc.	2	5
Rate % (within temporal)	28.57	71.42
Rate % (with regard to all *ouver-Phs*)	0.53	1.34
Fields	T-2	T-3

Table 63. Temporal *ouer-Phs* in ME

The temporal use of *ouer-Phs* is very unusual in ME. In fact, I have only found 7 instances. Only two *ouer-Phs* were found in the corpus indicating that an event occurs at a given time (T-1) as in *Tho leyde I my reule over this foreseide day* (CMASTRO). The other examples refer to an action which occurs within or for a period of time: day, night, year (T-2), e.g. *holden ouer a ʒer* (CMDOCU3); *ouer-nyʒt* (CMHORSES); *ouer .xii. monþe* (CMLAMBET); *ouer a day* (CMPHLEBO).

2. 11. Þurgh
No temporal *þurgh-Phs* were detected in the corpus.

2. 12. Under-Phs
No temporal *under-Phs* were found in the corpus.

INTERCHANGEABILITY OF ME TEMPORAL PREPOSITIONS (CONCLUSIONS)
By comparing the temporal uses of the prepositions analysed in this study (Table 64) we observe that *at* (359 oc.), *on* (307 oc.) and *in* (487 oc.) maintain a similar frequency, although *in-Phs* predominate; *bi-Phs*, with 105 instances, are more restricted for temporal domains, whereas *ouer-Phs* (7 oc..) are extremely rare.

Sense	Part of day	Calendar	A point in time; within, for or during a period of time	Idiomatic phrases (cf. Chapter VI)	Total
At	76	31	239	13	359
On	57	86	145	19	307
In	40	101	315	31	487
Bi	11	6	81	7	105
Ouer	0	2	5	0	7
Total	184	226	785	70	1265

Table 64. Temporal uses *p-Phs*

We also observe that 184 *p-Phs* headed by *at, on, in* and *bi* are used to refer to the parts of the day (morning, noon, afternoon, evening, night). The preposition *at* is predominant, with 76 instances (41.30%). The prepositions *on* (57 oc.) and *in* (40 oc.) are also frequent, whereas *bi* with 11 examples is uncommon and *ouer* is not found. There are 226 *p-Phs* which refer to the calendar. The prepositions *in* (101 oc.; 44.69%) and *on* (86 oc..; 38.05%) clearly stand in the lead, whereas the other prepositions show a much lower frequency. Both the indication of a point in time and within (for, during) a period of time are expressed by all the prepositions involved. The most frequent is *in* with 315 examples (40.12%) followed by *at* (239 oc.; 30.44%). *On-Phs* are also common for this category including 145 instances (18.47%). Finally, 81 instances occur in this domain with the preposition *bi*, and 5 with *ouer*.

CHAPTER SIX

FIGURATIVE SENSES: SEMANTIC EROSION

Prepositions initially have a specific meaning for a specific context, but they gradually tend to lose much of their specificities shifting from concreteness to abstractness ("semantic generalization"/erosion: Hopper and Traugott 2003 :96ff; Heine and Reh (1984). Then, the primary meaning (the "proto-scene sense": Tyler and Evans 2003) develop a semantic network of distinct figurative or abstract senses. Let us consider the figurative senses of the prepositions involved in this study in detail.

1. ABOVE-PHS

Above originally expressed a physical position of something which is located in an area adjacent to the top of another thing. This notion of something or somebody placed in a higher/upper position developed into a varied range of figurative senses. In fact, 94 instances (77.04%) out of the 122 found in the HC of ME have a figurative connotation. The following Table exhibits the figurative subsenses of *aboue-Phs* in ME:

Sense	Semantic fields			Total
Semantic fields	Superior to (with influence over somebody)	Higher in degree or quality (above all)	Higher in rank or position than	
Occ	32	49	12	94
Rate % (within figurative)	34.04	52.12	12.76	100
Rate % (with regard to all *aboue-Phs*)	26.22	40.16	9.83	77.04
Reference	F1	F2	F3	

Table 65. Figurative *aboue*-phrases

F-1. The survey of the corpus shows 32 *aboue-Phs* which express the idea of being in a superior position or with influence over somebody, e.g. *With a prerogative aboue eche creature!* (CMDIGBY); *þei maken hem-silf aboue þe lawe of Holy Chirche* (CMHILTON); *blessed be þou abowen all wommen* (CMROYAL).

F-2. In this category I have detected 49 instances which show a state which turns up as higher in degree or quality, e.g. *Ther nys no thyng in gree superlatyf, As seith Senek, above an humble wyf* (CMCTVERS); *your seid realme shall be sold above iiij l~i. sterling* (CMLAW); *And also by fayth as a pryncypall above naturall knowlege* (CMINNOCE). Only 12 instances were found with the meaning of being higher in rank or position (F-3). These instances include: *Bot hey coround kynge abowne all His angells* (CMGAYTRY); *aboven þe hiest ordere of angels* (CMROYAL).

2. AFTER-PHS

The preposition *after* is defined as "spatial or temporal locative posterior" in ME. However, from this locative (spatial or temporal) sense, new figurative subsenses developed in the course of ME. Table 66 presents the basic figurative senses detected in the corpus:

Semantic fields	Subsequent to and in consequence of (also in OE)	Next to in order or importance (ME)	According to, in harmony with (also in OE)	In imitation of, like (ME)	Total
Occ	223	36	189	52	500
Rate % (within figurative)	44.6	7.2	37.8	10.4	100
Rate % (with regard to all *after-Phs*)	22.27	3.59	18.88	5.19	49.95
Reference	F1	F2	F3	F4	

Table 66. Figurative *after*-phrases

The figurative meanings of *after-Phs* include 500 instances, which represent a ratio of 49.95% with regard to all *after-Phs* found in the corpus (1001). Table 66 exhibits these figures classified in the following semantic fields:

F-1. The notion that a state or an event is "subsequent to and in consequence of" is detected on 223 occasions. This figure represents a ratio of 44.6% with regard to all figurative instances and 22.27% on comparing with all *after-Phs* found in the corpus. Examples include: *com to him efter help his flescliche broðer* (CMANCRE); *after a trewe feling comeþ a trewe knowing* (CMCLOUD); *after socour of scotlond longe he mowe prye* (CMPOEMH).

F-2. In this category I have identified 36 instances which indicate that a state or event is "next to in order or importance", which represent a rate of 7.2% with regard to all figurative occurrences and 3.59% with respect to all instances found in the corpus. Thus CMFITZJA includes examples like these: *Prudence after him is a wisdom to lede man; And Sapyence after hym stondeth; after him restyth mannys felycyte*.

F-3. In this semantic field I have included 189 examples which indicate that an action is performed "according to, in harmony with" (law, one's advice or will). This semantic domain is highly represented (37.8%, within figurative senses) and includes examples such as *after the laws of the lond* (CMDOCU3); *aftyr þe custom of þe place* (CMKEMPE); *Aftur þat ore swete louerd* (CMSELEG).

Field F-4 includes 52 examples (10.4%, within figurative senses) which indicate that an action is performed "in imitation of, like" e.g. *After Ercules hij weren ymad* (CMALISAU); *namyd Josue Be~nun after saynt Jerom* (CMFITZJA); *and Augustus Cesar clepid the month of August after his name* (CMASTRO).

3. At-Phs

Originally, the preposition *at* denoted an orientation point either in space or time. This basic notion developed in the course of time into a radial network of other semantic connotations such as metaphorical orientation, e.g. *at rest* (state), a point on a scale, (manner), e.g. *at full speed* thematic context, e.g. *good at guessing*, etc. This radial network of subsenses are shown in Table 67.

At-Phs were mainly restricted to spatial and temporal senses in Old English. In Middle English, however, there is an expansion of these prepositional phrases with an abstract and figurative meaning. The widespread usage of figurative *At*-phrases in ME must have been fostered by French *à*-phrases which have a similar sense in this language. The following is a detailed account of the figurative domains which emerge in ME:

F-1. The corpus shows 13 *at-Phs* which appear for the first time in ME expressing some type of attitude or emotial reaction, such as *At tin herte* (CMBESTIA). In category F-2, the object or action which acts as the instrument or cause of a certain activity, I have found 23 instances, e.g. *at his writyng* (CMTVERS). Field F-3 shows 47 instances which indicate an action in which sb. participates or is engaged, e.g. *euer ilk day at drinc* (CMCURSOR). This is the first semantic field in which figurative *at-Phs* appear in Middle English. For the semantic domain F-4, I have counted 23 instances which refer to price or value, e.g. *at xx s.* (price) (CMREYNES). For F-5, state or situation, I have found 21 instances such as *at your reste* (CMREYNAR), *at ese* (CMTOWNEL). In category F-6, mutual relations, I

Sense	Semantic fields	Occ.	% of all *at*-hrases found in the HC	% of the number of words of the HC	Field
	Expressions of attitude and emotional reactions, e.g. *at herte, at laZht*, etc.	13	3.12	0.83	F1
	The object or action which acts as the instrument or cause of a certain activity, *at hand, at laug*, etc.	23	5.52	1.47	F2
	The action in which one participates or is engaged, e.g. *at drinc, at fihte*, etc.	47	11.29	3.02	F3
	Price or value *at price, at xx d., at iii s.*, etc.	23	5.52	1.47	F4
	State or situation, e.g. *at ese, at pes*, etc.	21	5.04	1.35	F5
	Mutual relations, e.g. *at accord, at asent*, etc.	16	3.84	1.02	F6
Figurative	Manner of acting, *at gre, at nede, at devis*, etc.	72	17.30	4.63	F7
	The conditioning circumstance, e.g. *at reste, at leiser* etc.	17	4.08	1.09	F8
	Relation to someone's will or disposition, e.g. *at will, at bydding*, etc.	57	13.70	3.66	F9
	Extent, amount, degree, e.g. *at þe fulle, at myght, at al*, etc.	62	14.90	3.98	F10
	Action subject to the control, will, commandment, request of sb., e.g. *at will, at conmmandyng, at requeste*, etc.	65	15.62	4.18	F11
	Total	416	Rate % (with regard to the corpus words): 0.06		

Table 67. Figurative *at-Phs* in ME

have included 16 examples such as *at accord* (CMCAXPRO), *at asent* (CMYORK). The most frequent figurative domain (72 occurrences) expresses some kind or manner of acting (F-7). Examples include: *at my degre* (CMLUDUS); *at your most nede* (CMMANKIN). 17 examples express a conditioning circumstance (F-8) as in *at hys makyng* (CMYORK); *at sume leysire* (CMPRIV). In field F-9, I have counted 57 instances which express a relation to someone's will or disposition, e.g. *at my biddyng* (CMYORK); *at thair will* (CMROLLPS). Extent, amount and degree (F-10) are frequently expressed with *at-Phs*. 62 instances were found, such as *at þe fulle* (CMCLOUD); *at þy might* (CMCURSOR). An action subject to the control, will, commandment or request of sb. (F-11) has been found on 65 occasions, such as *at their special request and desire* (CMLAW); *at þe commanding of God* (CMKEMPE).

4. BI-PHS

The preposition *by* is basically related to the notion of "proximity". This primitive sense developed into more sophisticated figurative subsenses, as shown in the following Table:

Sense	Semantic fields	Occ.	Rate % (within fig./abstr. sense)	Rate % (with regard to all *in-Phs*)	Field
Figurative	By means of (reasoning, learning), motivation: *bi force, bi grace, bi drede*, etc.	620	36.34	27.07	F-1
	Agency and mediation: *bi me*; *bi hyre eʒene*; *bi bote*; *bi ensaumple*; *bi mowthe*; *bi vertu* ("by authority of").	667	39.09	29.12	F-2
	In accordance with: *bi assent* "by agreement"; *bi rede* "in accordance with one's advice".	262	15.35	11.44	F-3
	In a certain manner: *bi herte* "by heart"; *bi craft* "craftly".	74	4.33	3.23	F-4
	With respect to: *bi God* (oaths).	39	2.28	1.70	F-5
	Number, amount, extent, degree. *bi two* "in pairs"; *bi thre times* "thrice"; *bi michel* "by much".	44	2.57	1.92	F-6
	Total	1706	Rate % (with regard to the corpus words): 0.30		

Table 68. Figurative *bi-Phs* in ME

The figurative meaning of *bi-Phs* is predominat. Thus, 1706 instances out of 2290 found in the corpus have no spatial or temporal meaning, but an abstract or figurative one. Table 68 exhibits these figures classified in the following semantic fields:

F-1. An indication that an action or activity is performed by means of or motivated by *grace, force, drede, evidence, counseil*, etc. is found on 662 occasions. This figure represents a ratio of 36.34% with regard to all figurative instances and 27.07% on comparing with all *bi-Phs* found in the corpus. Examples include *by cours of the lawe* (CMLAW); *he schulde come in safte be þe grace of God* (CMKEMPE); *by his Infinyte wysdom* (CMFITZJA). It is worth indicating that some of these *bi-Phs* also occur as agent complements of passive constructions.

F-2. The use of *bi-Phs* to express agency or mediation is very frequent in ME. The survey of the corpus shows 667 examples which either indicate an action performed by an agent, e.g. *Bi þe kyng*, particularly in passive constructions; or else imply mediation, as in *bi hyre eʒene* "with their eyes"; *bi bote* "by boat"; *bi ensaumple* "for example"; *bi mowthe* "by word of mouth"; *bi vertu* "by authority of". Examples include: *A laumpe he let doun be a cord* (CMBEVIS); *Gloys can tell yow by mouthe* (CMPRIV); *Summe bi þa fet; summe bi þa honden; summe bi þe tunge; summe bi þe eȝen, summe bi þe hefede; summe bi þer heorte* (CMLAMBET). The figures represented for this semantic domain correspond to a ratio of 39.09% within figurative sense and 29.12 with respect to all *bi-Phs*.

F-3. In this category I have included 262 instances which indicate that an action is performed in accordance with one's advice or will, or simply by agreement. This semantic domain is fairly well represented (15.35%, within figurative senses) and includes examples such as *þe kyng of þe londe dude by rede* (CMALISAU); *by the auys of hise wise lordes* (CMDOCU3). Field F-4 incorporates 74 examples which indicate that an action occurs in a certain manner, e.g. *we schal holde hym by manere of his leuynge* (CMPOLYCH). In domain F-5 I have included 39 examples which indicate that an action is viewed with regard to sth. or sb. This domain is very frequent in oaths, particularly *bi god!* (18 occurences), *bi christ* (11 occurrences), e.g. *Jch ȝou sigge, by Goddes ore* (CMALISAU). 44 instances were found indicating number, amount or extent, and also the parts into which a whole is divided, e.g. *ben compowned ...somme by two, and somme by thre* (CMASTRO); *in a signe departed by two degrees* (CMASTRO).

5. BIFORE-PHS

The primary meaning of the preposition *before* is characterized as "locative anterior" (spatial and temporal). I have already stated that the component "place" with the meaning "in front of" is very common in OE and ME. However, this physical sense developed into new abstract subsenses. Table 69 displays them, with their figures and rates:

Semantic fields	In the mental view of; in the knowledge of	In preference to	Total
Occ.	80	6	86
Rate % (within figurative)	93.02	6.97	100
Rate % (with regard to all *bifore-Phs)*	26.22	1.96	28.19
Reference	F1	F2	

Table 69. Figurative *bifore*-phrases

F-1. In this category I have included 80 instances (93.02%, within the figurative sense) which express the notion that something or somebody is either in the mental view of (God, the Lord, world, country) or in the knowledge of (God, man). Examples include: *at alle þe times þet þou zayst þi pater noster beuore god*

(CMAYENBI); *whiche synnes openly been shewed biforn God and biforn every creature* (CMCTPROS); *al þt fulðe schaweð him.* & *wringeð ut þt wursum biuoren al þe wide worlt* (CMANCRE). In the course of ME *bifore-Phs* are also used to indicate that an action or state occurs "in preference to another" (F-2) such as *I behote ʒow ʒe schal haue it before any oþer man ʒyf ʒow lyke it* (CMKEMPE).

6. Bihinde-Phs

The preposition *behind* initiated its role as a preposition in the course of the 13th century with the meaning of "locative posterior position". This physical semantic connotation was gradually extended to refer to abstract entities such as events, states and manner. The following table records the 12 figurative instances found in the corpus referring to a single semantic field:

Semantic fields	Behind somebody: in the absence/departure of a person	Total
Occ.	12	12
Rate % (within figurative)	100	100
Rate % (with regard to all *bihinde-Phs)*	57.14	
Reference	F1	

Table 70. Figurative *bihinde*-phrases

F-1. Within this semantic field I have recorded 12 instances in which *bihinde-Phs* indicate a figurative or abstract locative posterior event or state, e.g. following somebody's departure or in their absence. Examples include: *When þise ij breþerne were so dede, þai nade Lefte bihynde ham noo sone ne doughter* (CMBRUT3); *by reason of his laudable wysdom left behynde hym in wrytyng in the boke of wysdom callyd Ecclesiasticus* (CMFITZJA); *Aʒʒ follʒhenn rihhtwisnesse Biforenn menn, bihinndenn menn* (CMORM). Sometimes the preposition *bihinde* is followed by *of*, as in *And so monye men in þis world ben byhynde of dette of loue* (CMWYCSER). Other figurative categories such as "in imitation of" (MED) are not recorded in the corpus.

7. Biside-Phs

By 1200, the preposition *biside* started governing a noun with the meaning "by the side of" a place, person or thing. From this physical sense developed the figurative meanings shown in Table 71:

Semantic fields	In the mental view of or on the knowledge of	As well as, in addition to	Total
Occ.	3	2	5
Rate % (with regard to all *biside-Phs)*	7.14	4.76	11.90
Reference	F1	F2	

Table 71. Figurative *biside*-phrases

I have gathered only 5 figurative instances, out of the 41 examples of *biside-Phs* detected in the HCME. Three of these (F-1) indicate not a physical location, but a state or a location that is true in the "mental view of or in the knowledge of" (God, devil), e.g. *alle that is besyde oure saluacion* (CMJULNOR); *and he wonnys noght bysyd god, bot bysyd the deuel* (CMROLLPS). The other two instances (F-2) express the subsense "as well as, in addition to", e.g. *so lustful lyf of men þat schulden florischen in vertewis brynguþ in syche lawes bysyde wordis of byleue* (CMWYCSER); *rewle þat þei han foundon, bysyde þe rewle þat Crist ʒaf* (CMWYCSER).

8. IN-PHS

The notion of physical enclosure primarily associated with the preposition *in* extends to psychological states such as *in pain*. Similarly, other forms of enclosing experiences such as manner or means, circumstance or cause denote an "enveloping" condition. The following table records the figurative uses of *in-Phs*:

I have recorded 5372 *in-Phs* which express a figurative sense. The number of occurrences is surprisingly high as it exceeds, for example, the figures found in both spatial and temporal categories. Thus, 0.88 instances were found for every hundred words in the corpus. Let us consider them in detail:

F-1. In the survey of the data in this category I have found 609 examples of *in-Phs* indicating that sb. or sth. is engaged in an action. They are basically used with prepositional complements implying an action: battle, war, quarrel, fight. The examples found in this section represent a rate of 11.33% in relation to all figurative instances and 6.45% when compared with all *in-Phs* found in the corpus. The prepositional complement *thing* (= action, activity) predominates with 74 instances, e.g. *But [in] this thing hath ben discoveryd* (CMBOETH). 21 instances of *in bataile* are recorded, e.g. *a strong man in bataile he was* (CMCAPCHR), and 7 of *in fiht/ fihting*, e.g. *in þan fihte* (CMBRUT1). Another 7 instances were found including the prepositional complement *werre*, e.g. *Lesen her lorde in þat werre* (CMALISAU). Other prepositional complements occur less than five times each.

Sense	Semantic fields	Occ.	Rate % (within fig./abstr. sense)	Rate % (with regard to all *in-Phs*)	Field
In the course of an action	In an action or in a course of action, engaged in sth., during an action or process. With a noun implying an action: arms, battle, war, quarrel, works, things.	609	11.33	6.45	F-1
Manner	In two parts, divisions, pieces; in a form, shape or manner; in the presence, sight, or hearing of sb.; in a language.	1811	33.71	19.19	F-2
State or condition	With a noun implying a state: faith, truth, haste, right; purpose, will, hope, point. Subject to sth. or sb. (under God, law, vow) e.g. in god, grace, mercy, pain, accordance.	2776	51.67	29.41	F-3
As sth.	As sth. or in the shape of sth. e.g. conclusion, example. (as sign, token) sign, cause, token, witness.	47	0.87	0.49	F-4
Benefit	On behalf of: half (behalf), name, honour, worship.	129	2.40	1.36	F-5
	Total	5372	Rate % (with regard to the corpus words): 0.88		

Table 72. Figurative *in-Phs* in ME

F-2. I have identified 1811 occurrences which denote a certain form, shape or manner. In this category I have also include "in the presence or sight, of sb. or sth", and "in a language". The instances for this section represent the high rate of 33.71% in relation to all figurative instances and 19.19% when compared with all *in-Phs* found in the corpus. The survey reveals many examples which express a certain manner -*in (no, al, this, ani, mani) manner* (162 instances), *wise* (126), e.g. *in a ful gastfull maner* (CMEDMUND); *and seyde in this wise: "My lord," quod she, "as..* (CMECTPROS). *In degre* is found on 33 occasions, e.g. *leuyng in þe comoun degree of Cristen* (CMCLOUD). Within this category are 53 *in-Phs* which indicate the language in which somebody speaks or writes *in Latyn* is found 22 times, *in Englisch* 12 times, *on the godspelle* 26 times-, e.g. *"bestes" in Latyn tunge* (CMASTRO), *And God seyd in þe gospel* (CMAELR3). There are a great number of *in-Phs* whose complement occurs less than 10 times, e.g. *in blod, in red, in clops,* etc.

F-3. There are 2776 instances expressing a certain state or condition. This number represents nearly half of all figurative examples (51.67%) and 29.41% within the whole number of *in-Phs*. They usually occur with a noun implying a state: faith, truth, haste, pain, peace, will, hope. They also occur to indicate that sb. or sth. is subject to sth. or sb. (God, law, vow) e.g. in god, grace, mercy, etc. *In lyfe* with 96 instances predominates in this category. Being under the rule or protection of God is expressed as *in god* on 49 occasions; *in lawe* (under law) is also expressed 36 times. *In service* follows, with 35 instances. Each of the following is found more than twenty times: *in peyne* (32 occasions.), *in pes* (31), *in loue* (31) *in sorou* (24), *in grace* (24) *in joie* (24), *in will* (24), *in bliss* (23), *in spirit* (22). Examples include: *in my lyf* (CMEARLPS); *He was ydo in gode warde* (CMALISAU); *In þe ald lagh was be-for þe neu* (CMCURSOR); *and in greet peyne* (CMECTPROS); *Jn mychel loue is grete mournynge* (CMALISAU); *in þe blisse of heuen* (CMCLOUD); *he is oon in spirit wit hym* (CMAELR3).

F-4. In this category I have included 47 instances of *in-Phs* which indicate that sth. appears in the form of sth. e.g. *in conclusioun, in ensaumple, in signe, in cause, in token, in witnesse*. The phrase *in signe* predominates with 16 examples, e.g. *A cros was mad in signe o rode* (CMCURSOR), while all other phrases are recorded less than ten times each. The small number of instances found in this category represent a ratio of only 0.87% with regard to the figures found in the figurative roles and 0.49% within the whole number of *in-Phs* of the corpus.

F-5. I have found 129 *in-Phs* with the sense "for the benefit of sb., on behalf of sb., for the service of sb, etc. These phrases represent a ratio of 2.40% with regard to all figurative *in-Phs* and 1.36% taking into account all *in-Phs* in the corpus. The most common prepositional complement is *name* with 56 examples, e.g. *Jn þe name of þe kyng* (CMALISAU). *Worscipe* follows with 35 instances, *e.g. In whos worshippe this fest we honoure* (CMDIGBY). Other prepositional phrases such as *in honour, in behalf*, etc. are recorded less than 10 times each.

9. ON-PHS

The primary notion of "contact with line/surface" conveyed by the preposition *on* has extended to states, events, circumstances, means, reason, etc. This physical notion develops to figurative and is summarised in the following table:

Sense	Semantic fields	Occ.	Rate % (within figurat. sense)	Rate % (with regard to all *on-Phs*)	Field
Order or manner	Indicating a certain physical arrangement in a group, company, sequence (*on hepe, on lump, on roue*); a certain manner, e.g. *on (no, al, this, ani, mani) wise, manner*; a certain language (*on English*); dressed or covered with, e.g. *on blod*.	244	66.30	9.06	F-1
State or condition	Expressing a certain state or condition e.g. *on loue, on live, on slep, on witnesse, on fir, on thirst, on game*, and also *on cas, on happes, on fer, on god, on egge, on haste, on hed, on heigh, on loft, on mis, on rest, on rune, on (the) strai, on warantise, on blod*.	124	33.69	4.60	F-2
	Total	368	Rate % (with regard to the corpus words): 0.06		

Table 73. Figurative *on-Phs* in ME

The survey of *on-Phs* shows 368 instances which are no longer associated with a spatial or temporal sense. The number of occurrences is relatively high as it exceeds, for example, the figures found in temporal categories. Thus, 0.6 instances were found for every thousand words in the HCME. Let us consider them in detail:

F-1. The analysis of the data exhixbits 244 examples of *on-Phs* expressing some type of order or manner. These instances represent a rate of 66.30% in relation to all figurative instances and 9.06% when compared with all *on-Phs* found in the corpus. The survey reveals 98 occurrences which express a certain manner -*on (no, al, this, ani, mani) wise* (70 instances), *manner* (28 instances), e.g. *Y-armed wel on knī ttes wise* (CMALISAU), *þi beyng may on no wise be distroyed* (CMCLOUD), *on alle maner opes þat heo me wulleþ awe* (CPOEMS). Within this category are 30 *on-Phs* which indicate the language in which somebody speaks or writes –*on English* is found 18 times, *on Latin* 3 times, *on the godspelle* 12 times-, e.g. *Forr he ne maȝȝ nohht elless Onn Ennglissh writtenn* (CMORM), *hire nome seið ihud on englische* (CMANCRE).

In this category I have included *on he(o)rte*, the meaning of which may be considered to be at an intermediate stage between spatial location and figurative. This type of *on-Ph* occurs in 31 cases, e.g. *þe fule gost on his heorte* (CMTRINIT). Finally, I have come across 6 *on-Phs* indicating a certain physical arrangement in a group, company or sequence, e.g. *on hepe, on a lump, on rou*-, e.g. *þa heo weoren þer on hepe* (CMBRUT1), *þer hy sitteþ on rowe* (CMTRUSH).

F-2. There are 124 *on-Phs* expressing a certain state or condition. This number represents a rate of 33.69% of all figurative examples and 4.60% within the whole number of *on-Phs*. Most instances have already acquired an idiomatic sense, such as *on life/liue* occurring 41 times (e.g. *wa is me on liue* (CMBRUT1)), *on fer* (9) *(*e.g. *Bath on fer and ner he soght* (CMCURSOR)), *on slep* (5) (e.g. *Fal men sone on slepe* (CMHANSYN))*, on rest* (4) (e.g. *of þe deore rode þt he on reste* (CMMARGA)), *on death* (4) (e.g. *he schal not deye on no sodeyn deth* (CMREYNES)), *on flood* (4) (e.g. *Tambre wes on flode* (CMBRUT1)), *on loue (of)* with 4 instances, 3 of them in the phrase *on luue godes* (e.g. *wallinde on soðere luue godes* (CMTRINIT)), *on cas* (4) (e.g. *3if he mi3th come on cas* (CMALISAU)), *on blod/blood* (4) (e.g. *the bedde alle on blode* (CMJULNOR)), *on haste* (3) (e.g. *He slo3 þer on haste* (CMHORN)) and some others such as *on witnesse, on thirst, on game, on happes, on god, on egge, on mis, on rune, on (the) strai, on warantise,* etc.

10. OVER-PHS

The basic meaning "locative superior" (passing directly above, position directly above) of the preposition *ouer* gradually extends to the figurative fields expressed in Table 74:

Sense	Figurative		
Semantic fields	To a greater degree or extent: above all else, more than anything (all things)	Circumstance or human experience over sb. or sth.)	Action above sb. or sth. (power, might, lordship
Occ.	102	11	38
Rate % (within spatial)	67.54	7.33	25.16%
Rate % (with regard to all *ouer-Phs)*	27.49	2.96	10.24
Fields	F1	F2	F3

Table 74. Figurative *ouer-Phs* in ME

Out of the 371 *ouer-Phs* found in the corpus, I have counted 151 which show a figurative or abstract meaning. Most of them (102 occurrences, 67.54% within figurative sense) indicate that sth. is performed to a greater degree or extent, that is, above all else, more than anything or all things (F-1). Examples include: *tat we luffe Godd ouer all thynges* (CMGAYTRY); *ouer al present* (CMVICES4). It is worth noting that 63 instances within this semantic domain occur as *ouer all*, and 24 as *ouer allþhing(s)*. Certainly, these two phrases had already initiated a process of idiomatization.

Only 11 *ouer-Phs* were detected expressing a type of circumstance or human experience (F-2) such as *þey are enuyous ouer outrage* (CMHANSYN); *and yit over al his wikkidnesse* (CMBOETH). This semantic field is, then, very restricted (7.33% within figurative sense) in ME. Finally, semantic field F-3 includes 38 examples (25.16% within figurative sense) which indicate some type of action imposed on or over sb. as in *And mad him lauerd ouer all his kin* (CMCURSOR); '*and the deuyll shall haue no power ouer the*' (CMEDMUND); *Quen and leuedi ouer me?* (CMHAVELO).

11. Þurgh-Phs
The basic meaning of "going across/along" of *þurgh-Phs* developed into the following figurative semantic fields:

Semantic fields	Through the mediation of a holy being or person	Go through one's body, heart	Sth. occurs by means of virtue, grace, violence, etc.	Expressing reference to something already mentioned	By means of sth. used as instrument
Occ.	155	27	429	104	61
Rate % within figurative	19.97	3.47	55.28	13.40	7.86
Rate % (with regard to all *þurgh-Phs*)	17.98	3.13	49.76	12.06	7.07
Fields	F1	F2	F3	F4	F5

Table 75. Figurative *þurgh-Phs* in ME

Out of the 862 *þurgh-Phs* detected in the corpus, I have identified 776 which exhibit a figurative or abstract meaning.

F-1. In this category I have found 155 examples (19.97% within figurative sense) which indicate the mediation or intercession of a holy being or person, e.g. *þurh þene halie gast* (CMLAMBET); *hit is i-writen þus þurh þe prophete* (CMHALI); *Remued þoru seint edmund out of þe court* (CMEROBLO). In field F-2 I have found 27 instances which indicate that a physical or intangible entity (sword vs. grief, sorrow) goes through one's body or heart, e.g. *thurgh your bodies shalle goon* (CMDIGBY); *He smyt hym þorouȝ body and shelde And cast hym ded in þe felde* (CMALISAU)*, He smot him þureȝ þe herte* (CMHORN).

In field F-3 the corpus exhibits 429 occurrences (55.28% within figurative sense) which indicate that sth. occurs by means of a given manner of acting/behaviour, e.g. *thorow hir falsehode and trechory* (CMMALORY); *tak heede of hem þat beþ oppressed poruӡ greet meschyef* (CMAELR3) or "under the protection of" e.g. *pouɾӡ þe grace of god almiӡt* (CMBEVIS); *Thurgh vertu of þe haly gaste* (CMNORHOM), or in consequence of, by reason of, on account of, e.g. *pouɾӡ king Ermines gile* (CMBEVIS); *thurghe þe myghte and þe strenghe of þe Haly Gaste* (CMGAYTRY). In F-4 I have included 104 *þurgh-Phs* which refer to something (it, that, which, all, all things) which has usually been already mentioned or known, e.g. *þurh-ut alle cunnes þinge* (CMBRUT1); *þorow þe whiche we loue God* (CMCLOUD). For field F-5 I have counted 61 examples (7.86% within figurative figures) which express medium, means, or instrument, e.g. *þu schalt swelten þurh sweord* (CMMARGA); *Thurgh þe ensampel of þe ryche man in helle* (CMPRICK).

12. UNDER-PHS

The primary role of *under-Phs* indicating a position beneath or below, developed into a varied range of figurative meanings. The following were detected in the HCME:

Semantic fields	Subordination or subjection to a person. Beneath the rule of, during the reign of	Denoting protection or care of	Denoting that a thing is presented or observed in a certain form	Below, less than a specified number or amount	Denoting authoritative or confirmatory effect of a seal, signature, etc.
Occ.	65	29	56	6	15
Rate % (within figurative)	38.01	16.95	32.74	3.5	8.77
Rate % (with regard to all *under-Phs*)	24.9	11.11	21.45	2.29	5.74
Fields	F1	F2	F3	F4	F5

Table 76. Figurative *under-Phs* in ME

F-1. The semantic connotations of "subordination or subjection to a person", "beneath the rule of", "during the reign of" have been recorded on 65 occasions (38.01%, within figurative senses). Examples include: *Oxeatre, wiþ mychel wonder, Antiochun hadde hym vnder* (CMALISAU); *and referr hem to dyuers religions whech lyue vndir Seynt Austyn reule* (CMCAPSER); *vnder subieccioun of man* (CMMANDEV); *þei hadde under þe olde kyng schulde be wiþdrawe* (CMPOLYCH).

F-2. In this category I have included 29 instances which express the notion of being under the "protection or care of". This figure represents a rate of 16.95% within the figurative range of meanings. Examples include: *ye sal be meke vnder yure abbes and do godis seruise* (CMBENRUL); *þe ordr of Premonstracenses, whech be-gan in Fraunce vndir a holy man þei cleped Norbertus, who was her foundor* (CMCAPSER); *for wit is hire scheld under godes grace* (CMHALI).

F-3. *Under-Phs* are also figuratively used to denote that a thing is presented or observed in a certain form or manner The corpus shows 56 instances (32.74%, within figurative senses) and includes examples like these: *under the correccion and punysshment of the cite* (CMPRIV); *But some thinges ben put undir purveaunce* (CMBOETH); *ðai couer sin vnder wordes faire* (CMNORHOM).

F-4. In this field I have classified 6 instances which denote a certain degree, number or amount which appears as below or less than previously specified, e.g. *that is under the seid prises* (CMLAW); *for all the Hattes and Cappes under that value to be sold at such a price* (CMLAW).

F-5. I have found 15 instances (8.77%, within figurative senses) which express authoritative or confirmatory effect of a seal, signature, etc. Examples include: *under the King~ grete Seale* (CMLAW); *she com undir my sauffconduyghte* (CMMALORY).

CHAPTER SEVEN

COLLOCATIONAL FRAMEWORK

The recurrent use in modern languages of set phrases whose meaning is not to be interpreted on a word-by-word basis, has recently attracted the attention of many scholars. The reasons why some words tend to associate with others in a given order and at a given time of the history of a language is still a matter of conjecture. However, it is generally assumed that, whatever the circumstances of mental organisation turns out to be for speakers to associate some words, word-combinations must have eventually developed in a cultural framework and more dependent on linguo-cultural domains than on a statistical probability of co-occurrence. The study of set phrases in the earlier periods of languages has incited less interest as there are no clear applications in modern intercultural communication (natural language generation, machine translation, etc.). It is worth noting, however, that all these clusters were formed at a given moment of a language's history and developed for a specific function.

The traditional study of set phrases, of which collocations are a subclass, has introduced an interesting scholarly debate about the terminological character of the general categories and subcategories of phraseology[1]. With regard to the general categories of the phraseological system Mel'čuk (1998: 24-30) uses the terms "set phrases" or "phrasemes" to refer to the total catalogue of word combinations. For Gläser (1998: 126) the whole inventory of idioms and phrases ("phrasicon") of a language is constituted by "phraseological units", whereas Cowie (1998: 5) and Howarth (1996) use the term "word combination". These general categories of the phraseological system may operate either as word-like units, organised at or below the level of the simple sentence, providing a specific semantic role or as sentence-like units endowed with a pragmatic function. Mel'čuk (1988, 1998) considers that word-like units are "semantic phrasemes", Gläser (1988, 1998) includes them under the term of "nomination", whereas (Cowie (1988) calls them "composite", and

---

1 See Cowie 1998: 1-8

Howarth (1996) "composite units". In contrast, the sentence-like units are identified as "pragmatemes" (Mel'čuk 1988, 1998), "propositions" (Gläser 1988, 1998), or "functional expressions" (Cowie 1988, 1998, Howarth 1996).

By focussing on word-like units, where this study is categorised, it is also attested they vary along a continuum which differentiates at least three types of semantic roles: a) an area of opaque and unmotivated meaning composed of formal invariable units where Mel'čuk (1988, 1998) and Gläser (1988, 1998) include "idioms", and Cowie (1988, 1998) and Howarth (1996) "pure idioms"; b) an area of partially motivated meaning, which is a metaphorical extension of an original neutral significance, composed of formal variable units where Mel'čuk (1988, 1998) and Gläser (1988, 1998) include "quasi idioms", whereas Cowie (1988, 1998) and Howarth (1996) include "figurative idioms"; and c) an area of context-motivated meaning in which two or more open-class words operate and in which at least one component of the unit has a literal meaning, whereas the other is figurative and its specific meaning is moulded by its context. In this area I will locate my study which is categorised as "collocations" by Mel'čuk (1988, 1998), "restricted collocations" by Gläser (1988, 1998), Cowie (1988, 1998) and Howarth (1996) and "bound clusters" by Fónagy (2000).

Set phrases should not be simply analysed as arbitrary recurrent items characterised only by a statistical probability of co-occurrence. Certainly, some theories and approaches have been proposed to explain the factors and rationale which determine the use of lexical and grammatical clusters. Thus, a detailed account of lexico-grammatical collocational types has been carried out by Benson (1990), Mel'čuk (1998), Hausmann (2003) who have confirmed both that the meaning of collocations cannot be interpreted on a word-by-word basis ("non-compositionality") and that collocations usually show structural stability. Some other scholars focus on the syntactic and semantic rules which govern the association of words. Thus, Grossmann and Tutin (2003) have examined collocations as pre-constructed syntactic units, Choueka (1988) has studied them as lexically determined elements of grammatical structures, and Gitsaki (1996:17) has emphasized the idea that word associations occur in patterns.

From a different viewpoint pragmatists have stated that structural irregularities and non-compositionality may have an historical and functional source which has been developed in pragmatic regularities (Feilke 1996, 2003, Gledhill 2000). Pragmatists emphasise the rhetorical function of the multi-word expression in discourse. This level of study is particularly interesting because the analyst is involved in the stylistic contrast between marked forms such as "take notice" and the unmarked "notice". The difference is assessed by analysing rhetorical factors, as Moon states: "fixed expressions represent meaningful choices on the part of the speaker/writer" (1994: 117). Nattinger and DeCarrico differentiate unmarked collocations (co-ocurrences of lexical items) from lexical phrases or marked collocations (polywords, institutionalised phrases, phrasal constraints) as different choices of expression. Whereas collocations have a pragmatic function, the unmarked co-occurrence of lexical items are expressions "that have not been assigned particular pragmatic functions by pragmatic competence" (1992:36). However, Gledhill maintains that a "normal text rarely moves in a clear-cut way from unmarked to marked expression...It is more realistic to picture a text as a sequence of different types of discourse signal" (2000:16).

Collocations have also been categorised on statistical bases by reckoning the entire catalogue of tokens and types of co-occurrences of two or more words (Sinclair 1974, Sinclair 1991, Sinclair 2004). This "bottom-up corpus-driven approach"[2], based on lexical/textual analysis, emphasises the statistical probability of some items of co-occurring. Following this method, Clear has studied collocations as a "recurrent co-occurrence of words" (1993: 277); Smadja, as a "recurrent combination of words that co-occur more often than expected" (1993: 143); Benson, as an "arbitrary and recurrent word combination" (1990: 23); Kjellmer, as "a sequence of words that occurs more than once in identical form" (1987: 133). This identification of lexical co-occurrences has been recently reworked in Evert's "distributional approach" (2004), Nesselhauf's frequency-based approach" (2004) or in Siepmann's collocation and colligation typology (2005a, 2005b). This reworking opened the analysis to a wide area of word combination (collocational framework, colligations, etc.).

Some other phraseologists suggest a cultural approach to the study of word associations as these have eventually developed in a given cultural framework. The cultural information that is stored in the phrasicon of a language has been studied, from the perspective of a lingo-cultural approach by Teliya, Bragina, Oparina and Sandomirskaya (1998). Piirainen (2008) describes the connection between figurative phraseological units and culture and maintains that phrasemes reveal cultural relevant concepts. Cross-linguistic and cross-cultural analysis of phrasemes has been carried out by Colson (2008) and Piirainen (2008). According to these scholars phrasemes seem not to be arbitrary recurrent items typified only by a statistical probability of co-occurrence, but by their dependency on cultural domains.

The study of collocations also entails to distinguish the notions of "collocation" and "set" as counterparts of "structure" and "system" in grammatical analysis. Thus, we may emphasize either the collocational structure or the rules that operate within the set. Thus, following Carter (1987: 50), we may select items from lexical sets instead of choosing types of grammatical structures. Collocations, then, may be understood as a "probable co-occurrence of items" (Malmkjaer, 1991: 302), usually linked to a cultural domain (Fónagy 2000), rather than a "set", which

---

2 The traditional approach to phraseology, greatly indebted to Easter Europe scholars, has adopted "a top-down approach which identifies phraseological units on the basis of linguistic criteria" (Granger and Meunier, 2008: 29)

envisages instances of one and the same syntagmatic relation as has been proposed by Halliday (1966: 151-157), who considers that "a strong argument", "he argued strongly", "the strength of his argument" and "his argument was strengthened" as syntagmatically related units. In Halliday's view "strong", "strongly", "strength" and "strengthened" collocate with "argue/argument".

It is also interesting to determine whether the lexeme has its own independent meaning or such a meaning is only shaped by the collocation itself, as Nattinger & DeCarrico (1992: 181-182) have stated. Sinclair (1991: 115-116) also maintains that the "relative frequency of node and collocate determines whether the collocational relation will contribute to the meaning of the node." This seems to be clear in the case of composite predicates in which the support verb has been devoided of lexical meaning as the latter has been displaced to the deverbative noun (e.g. take notice, take care, take advantage, etc.). In broad terms, it is assumed that the greater capacity a lexeme has to develop collocational patterns, the greater restrictions the node has.

The limited data of the HCME, with regard to the collocational framework of the ME *p-Phs*, have restricted my analysis to the notion of collocation provided by Mel'čuk (1998:30) and the notion of "bound utterances" rendered by Fónagy (2000). Rephrasing Mel'čuk's (1998:30) words a collocation is a semantic phraseme formed by two constituent lexemes (**AB**) whose meaning **X** is made up out of both the meaning of one of its two constituents, i.e. of **A**, and the meaning **C** which results from the meaning of **B**, which express **C** only bound to **A**[3] (1998: 30). Besides, social contexts are usually articulated through "bound utterances" (Fónagy 2000), whose constituents are subject to semantic erosion. "As soon as an utterance is globally bound to a recurrent situation, it is subject to semantic loss, since its constituents refer only indirectly and casually to the content they denote in free utterances, even if the utterance still preserves, at least seemingly, its original meaning intact". (Fónagy 2000: 215). Thus, "bound utterances, in contradistinction to *idioms*, do not mean anything *different from* the corresponding free sentences: they simply mean *less*" (Fónagy 2000: 194).

For the sake of clarity, I will tentatively recapitulate the four basic types of word combination with different semantic implications. Thus words may combine:

a) Without restraint and in semantic paratactical occurrence ("free lexematic occurrences"). The meaning of all elements is independent and therefore free to occur elsewhere ("free combination"). The meaning of words which occur in a free combination is known as *compositional*, that is, the meaning of the whole is "composed" from the meaning of its parts. For example in *at the door, on the table,*

---

3 "A COLLOCATION **AB** of language **L** is a semantic phraseme of **L** such that its signified 'X' is constructed out of the signified of one of its two constituent lexemes—say, of **A**—and a signified 'C' ['X' = 'A+C'] such that the lexeme **B** expresses 'C' only contingent on **A**." (Mel'cuk 1998:30).

in the drawer, by the church the significance of this combination of words is the sum of the meaning of the prepositions and their complements.

b) Partially restrainted and in semantic hypotactical occurrence ("conventionalized phrasemes"). The meaning of one of the elements depends on the occurrence of the other, e.g. the combination of base + collocate ("collocations") such as *take care, take a seat,* the "quasi-idiomatic" prepositional phrases such as *at large, at all, at the instance of; in vain, in exchange for, in spite of; on the one hand, on foot; by chance, by heart, by virtue of.* So it is worth noting that the meaning of the words which combine in collocations or in prepositional phrases, such as mentioned above, is *semicompositional*, that is, the collocate (in collocations) or the prepositional complement (in "quasi-idiomatic" prepositional phrases), although they are free to combine in other contexts, have a non free meaning when they occur with the base or with the preposition. Thus, either word can occur in different contexts and combine with other different words, but when *take care, at large, at all, at the instance of,* etc. Combine together, base of the collocation (or the preposition in these "quasi-idiomatic prepositional phrases") does not carry its standard meaning.

c) Partially restrainted and in semantic intertactical occurrence ("conventionalized pragmatemes" = sayings, proverbs, quotations, and speech formulas), semi-compositional.

d) Completely restrainted and in semantic intertactical occurrence ("idioms"). The meanings of all elements are mutually dependent. The meaning of words which combine in idiomatic expressions is *noncompositional*: none of the words has its own semantic connotations as only the whole is provided with meaning. Thus in *kick the bucket* none of the idiom components *kick, the* and *bucket* allude to the idea of death.

1. METHOD AND CRITERIA FOR COLLOCATIONAL PATTERNS SELECTION

Collocational types were typified as follows:

a) I have used the *WordSmith 4* (*WS* hereafter) to compile *word lists* of the HCME. By using *WS Keyword tools* I have also recorded a catalogue of key/salient words contrasting statistically the number of tokens in the corpora.

b) Collocations were retrieved and filtered out following Church and Hanks's Mutual Information (MI) technique (1989) which can be controlled by the *WS*. MI technique compares and assesses the probability of two words occurring mutually bound with the probability of these words occurring separately[4].

---

4 If two items x and y have probabilities of occurrence $p(x)$ and $p(y)$, their mutual information $MI(x,y)$ is formulated as

$$MI(x,y) = log_2 \frac{p(x,y)}{p(x) \cdot p(y)}$$

c) The word lists were previously lemmatized by WS. Thus the spelling variants of a preposition and both the spelling and the morphological variants of the complements of a preposition were joined under the same lemma.

d) The categorization of collocations in this study is based on the following determining factors: a) the degree of probability of a multi-word-item is measured in relation with its degree of *institutionalization* (conventionalized multi-word item); b) the degree of fixedness of the set phrase is also measured in relation to its grammatical restrictions; c) finally, the degree to which the meaning of the set phrase can or cannot be derived from the meaning of its constituent parts is also measured (*non-compositionality* –meaning is not interpreted on a word-by-word basis).

e) Finally, I have restricted my research to the 12 prepositions involved in this study.

2. Corpora

It is worth interesting to note that the HCME shows different texts with external contextual characteristics. Most texts embody extensive linguistic functions (informative, instructional, persuasive, etc.), different styles or prototypical text categories (expository, narrative, imaginative, etc.), different non-technical settings (formal, informal, intimate equal/down/up, distant down/up, interactive, etc.), different types of text (drama, correspondence, fiction, history, romance, etc) and different topics (religion, fiction, etc.). On the contrary, the external contextual features of other texts (legal/academic/scientific texts) are more limiting. Thus legal texts are functionally informative and exhibit both a statutory style and a formal/ professional and distant down setting.

In the following section I will only comment those prepositios which exhibit some collocational framework.

3. Data analysis
Aboue-collocations

The preposition *aboue* tends to be used with open combinatory complements, e.g. *aboue the land, aboue the sea*, etc., however it shows some collocational patterns. *Aboue* occurs frequently associated to the complements *all þinges* (16 occ.), *all other* + N (7 occ.) as in: *The ffirst is: Wurchep God aboue alle thyng. The secunde is: Take not His name in idylnesse* (CMREYNES).

The collocational character of these *aboue*-collocations is shown by means of their constituent lexemes: the preposition *aboue* (**A**), —whose meaning basically

---

When $p(x,y) = p(x) \cdot p(y)$ and the resulting value of $MI(x,y)$ is 0, we may assert that the concurrent appearance of x and y is not significantly recurrent to form a collocation. Whenever $MI(x,y)$ is < 0, then we assume that the two terms (x, y) are mutually complementary and form a collocation.

substantiated a physical position of something/somebody in an area adjacent to the top of another one—, and its complement (**B**). The resulting meaning of both lexemes (**AB**) is fundamentally made up out of both the physical meaning of **A**, and the figurative meaning which results from the meaning of **B**, which express **that figurative meaning** only bound to **A**. Thus the meaning of *aboue*-collocations is framed in an area of context-motivated meaning in which two open-class words operate and in which one component of the unit has a literal meaning (*aboue*), whereas the other (*all þinges, all other*) is figurative and its specific meaning is moulded by its context.

After-collocations

The eME spatial uses of *after* "behind", "moving in the rear of" were gradually replaced in the course of the 13th century and new figurative senses such as "next to in order or importance" and "in imitation of, like" began to appear. From the latter senses some collocational types develop such as *and after þat* (41 occ.) as in *And after that the seid Thomas Stamford beyng atte barre at westminster* (CMDOCU4) and *after al þis* (7 occ.). Scientific cultural domains usually show their collocational framework. For example, CMEQUATO exhibits 13 occ. of *after successioun of signes* as in *& rekne this mene argument fro the white thred after successioun of signes of euery planete* (CMEQUATO). Similarly, in legal documents the collocational pattern *after the fourme and tenour* (5 occ.) is shown as in *be named in dyv~s parties of this your realme, where nede were, after the fourme and tenour of a Co~myssion in the seid Acte specified* (CMLAW).

The collocational character of these *after*-set phrases is revealed in their constituent elements whose meaning is different from the sum of them both. Thus the basic meaning of *after*, "moving in the rear of" or "next to in order or importance" has been slightly altered as has been blended into the whole set phrase shaped by its context. Thus the meaning of *after the fourme and tenour* cannot be controlled by adding the meanings of the preposition and its complement as if they were open-class words.

At-collocations

At is the least specific of the prepositions in its spatial orientation in PDE, however spatial *at-Phs* are numerous in ME (728 occurrences in HCME) and show a wide range of meanings: location in a city or town, at part of/within a building, to be in a given position, location within a region or country, to be at a person, arrival to/in a place, etc. On the contrary the temporal domain of *at-Phs* is more limiting in ME (437 occurrences) and the meanings were restricted to calendar, part of the day and a point in time or within/during a period of time.

As regards collocational patterns, however, no spatial collocations are properly found apart from doubtful collocational framework such as *at London, at*

Westminster. As shown below most *at*-collocations are temporal and some of them figurative. The most frequent are those referring to a point in time: *at that tyme* (24 occ.), *at this tyme* (23 occ.), *at (the, his/my...) comyng* (9 occ.), *at the begyning of* (8 occ.), as in *leped onto him Ser Edmund Stafford, bischop of Chestir, and chaunceler at þat tyme, and þe tresorer, William Scrop, erl of Wiltschere* (CMCAPCHR); *'Youre bounte` may no man prayse halff unto the valew, butt at thys tyme I muste nedis departe* (CMMALORY); *And at þe comyng of þe right high and myghty prynce* (CMOFFICF4); *And notwyttstondyng Waspasion wos not Emparovr at þe begynnyng of þis werke, but he was son aftur* (CMSIEGE).

Temporal collocational framework is also found to indicate that something occurs within a period of time. For example, *at mete* (9 occ.) as in *& on þe next day þat was þe Sonday, whil þei wer at mete at noon with oþer good frendys, he fel in gret sekenes* (CMKEMPE). Some other temporal collocations express the idea that an action occurs during a period of time. For example, *at all tymes* (9 occ.) as in *ye recorde so highly the redinesse of our wille and power at alle tymes to your plesaunce* (CMOFFIC3). At-collocations may also refer to calendar. Some types include: *at the day of* (8 occ.), *at the feste of* (8 occ.), *at this day* (5 occ.) as in *tou wolte þat God haue mercye on þe. And þan ȝiff God assh þe at þe Day of Dome, "Frende, howe entereste þou hidre?"* (CMROYAL); *Provided alwey that this present Acte begyn to take effecte at the fest of Annunciacion of oure Lady next coming* (CMLAW); *in my yong age moche more welthy prosperous & rycher than it is at this day* (CMCAXPRO).

Collocational frames are frequent to indicate part of the day. Our data include: *at middai* (6 occ.), *at þe morne* (6 occ.), *at euen* (5 occ.), *at niht* (5 occ.) as in *Anothir day I wolde knowen the degre of my sonne, and this was at midday in the 13 day of Decembre* (CMASTRO); *with þis sal þu safely hele þam. & gyff þam at drynk þer-of arely at þe morne & late at euen* (CMTHORN).

Figurative collocational framework also occurs to indicate an action subject to the control, will, commandment, request of somebody. For example, *at comaudment of* (5 occ.), *at somebody's will* as in *and Richard of London bischoppis, and Ser Robert Morle at comaundment of þe kyng (þan keper of þe Towre) broute þis knyt* (CMCAPCHR); *At hom withinne his chambre stille, The king he torneth at his wille* (CMGOWER).

There are some verbs that control the preposition *at: Be at* (72 occ.), *holden at* (17 occ.), *sit at* (14 occ.), *do at* (10 occ.), *lay at* (7 occ.), *helpe at* (7 occ.). Some example include: *Yet notwithstanding in a parlement holden at Westm~ the xxxiij yere of the same King Henry the vj* (CMLAW); *Hauelok was war þat Grim swank sore For his mete, and he lay at hom. Þhouthe 'Ich am nou no grom!* (CMHAVELOK); *þan þis kynge com and see þe men sittynge at þe mete and fonde oon þat was not clothed of is weddynge leuere and seid to hym to wordes of my teme, "Frende, how comeste þou in here* (CMROYAL).

Bi-collocations

The role of the preposition *bi*, which is initially related to the spatial and temporal notion of proximity, has evolved, in a specific framework, into a new area of context-motivated meaning in which the preposition *bi* and its complement could be categorised as collocations because, although the complement maintains its literal meaning, the preposition is delexicalised from its initial spatial or temporal role. The most frequent collocational patterns are: *bi cause of* (45 occ), *bi auctorite of* (29 occ), *bi grace of* (16 occ), *by resoun of* (14 occ.), *bi dai* (14 occ.), *bi counseile of* (13 occ), *bi nigt* (12 occ.), *bi dai and nigt* (12 occ.), *bi goddes word* (6 occ), *bi force* 5 (occ), *bi vertue* (5 occ), *bi comaundment* (5 occ), *bi name* (5 occ). Other less frequent collocational patterns include *bi violence, bi assent, bi love, bi ordre, bi wisdom, bi nature, bi cutome, bi strengthe, bi law.*

There are many categories and subcategories of bi-collocational framework. Thus under de category of "by means of" (reasoning, learning) or "motivation" the HCME shows *bi cause of, bi reason of, bi grace of* as in *Also if any man, bi cause of seruyce or other leueful comaundement,* (CMDOCU3); *3e, 3if we be holden bothe to God and man by resoun of dette to don a good dede* (CMWYCSER); *mercy hit shoulde be to your profetes and avayle in tyme comyng by the grace of our Lord* (CMPRIV). Within the category of agency and mediation the corpus exhibits the collocational frames: *bi auctorite of, bi vertue of* as in *yt was also ordeyned enacted and stablisshed by auctorite of the same parliament* (CMLAW); *an helper or sauer of the people by vertues particulare / as that one was by power that other by obedyence / and the thyrde by wysdom* (CMFITZJA). The category "with respect to" includes *bi God* (oaths), *bi godes worde* as in *swa sceal eac þeo sawle libbæn bi Godes worde* (CMBODLEY). Other figurative categories include: in accordance with: *bi assent, bi rede*; in a certain manner: *bi herte*; *bi craft.*

Temporal categories are also displayed. For example, "part of a day" is found in *bi dai, bi nihte, bi þe mourne, bi dai and nigt* as in *is Moni þeof abuten ba bi dei & bi niht. vnseheliche gasttes wið alle unwreaste þeawes* (CMSAWLES).

The preposition *bi* usually pre-collocates heading the passive agent, particularly with verbs such as *made* (21 occ.), *ordained* (15 occ.), *enacted* (7 occ.) and *established* (5 occ.).

Bifore-collocations

The *bifore*-collocational patterns found in the HCME are basically "locative anterior" with the specific meaning of being at a person (usually God, king). Some examples are: *bifore the lord* (5 occ.), *bifore god* (5 occ.), *bifore the king* (5 occ.) as in *for it repentith me that Y made hem. Forsothe Noe foond grace bifore the Lord. These ben the generaciouns of Noe.* (CMOTEST); *(\Misericordia\) nam mid hire (\Pietatem\) and (\Pacem\), and comen before gode, and swiðe eadmodliche him besohten* (CMVICES1); *whan I was byfore the kyng the second day of march* (CMDOCU3).

Bifore-collocations may also express the idea of "earlier than a date or event". For example, *bifore this time* (7 occ.) as in *he wil bryng topi mynde som place þat þou hast wonid in before þis tyme* (CMCLOUD). Although spatial *bifore-Phs* were also predominant in ME, no spatial collocational patterns were detected in the HCME.

In-collocations
The notion of physical enclosed space chiefly connected with the preposition *in* has been extended to other non representational meanings such as *in this manner*. However, a transitional sphere of context-motivated significance (collocations) occurs in *in-Phs*. Thus, phraseological units such as *in accordance*, the post-prepositional element retains its literal meaning, whereas the preposition *in* is devoided of lexical meaning. We may distinguish at least two different categories:

a) Prepositional complements that entail a state of mind: *in herte* (31 occ), *in minde* (14 occ), *in pees* (14 occ), *in spirit* (10 occ),), *in blisse* (10 occ), *in fayth* (8 occ), *in vertu* (7 occ), *in reste* (7 occ), *in loue* (6 occ), *in pride* (6 occ), *in ioy* 6 occ), etc. Examples include: *Mournynge makis me mased and madde, To thynke in herte what helpe Y hadde And nowe has none* (CMYORK); *Þenne myhte vch mon boþ riden & gon in pes wiþ-oute vyhte* (CMPOEMH); *one lyvynge after the pleasur of the worlde, the tother lyvynge here in vertue by grace to come to blysse* (CMINNOCE); *chalt þou triste and hope, þat as þou art felawe with him in peyne and in dissese, litil if it be, so schalt þou be felawe with him in his ioie* (CMHILTON).

b) Subject to, on behalf of or under somebody or something as in *in god* (92 occ), *in soule* 21 occ.), *in body and soule* (17 occ.), *in christ* (15 occ), *in payne* (8 occ.), *in penaunce* (6 occ), *in worship* (6 occ). Some examples include: *We shul do uertu in God, and he shal brynge to nouȝt þe trubland vs* (CMEARLPS); *with-inne schort tyme þei fallen ouþer into werynes and a maner of vnlisty febilnes in body and in soule* (CMCLOUD); *and to spened itt with-oute loue or vaynlikynge of itt, as reson askith, in worship of God, and helpe of thyne evyn cristyn* (CMROLLTR).

Some verbs monitor the in-Phrs in a collocational framework. Consider, for example, *come in* (106 occ.), *made in* (48 occ.) *bilive/ileuve in* (46 occ.), *fall in* (39 occ.), *lay in* (21 occ.), *hope in* (16 occ.).

On-collocations
The whole range of meanings of *on* in ME is not included in the "locative surface" notion ("on the top of" and "at the surface of", Bennett, 1975: 69), nor in the notion of "contact with line/surface" (Dirven, 1993: 78). Although the spatial notion is central, a radial network of meanings expands from it to many other semantic categories and subcategories of time and circumstances (state, means, reason, etc.). Many of these semantic expansions disseminate in a collocational framework.

Thus, the spatial notion of some *on*-phrases ("locative surface", "contact with line/surface") has been partly devoided of their representational meaning and have developed to a sphere of a context-motivated significance (collocations). Thus, in a phraseological unit such as *on life*, the post-prepositional constituent preserves its factual meaning, however the preposition *on* has lost its lexical meaning. Let's consider some categories:

a) Spatial collocations categories

Somebody or something is located in an open place (sea, river, field, road, hill) or within the boundaries of earth, heaven, hell, kingdom, country, region, city, town, etc.) as in *on erthe* (28 occ.), *on londe* (12 occ.), *on world* (10 occ.), *on heuene* (10 occ.). Some examples include: *and alle werk beestis in her kynde, and ech beeste which is moued on erthe in his kynde, and ech volatil bi his kynde* (CMOTEST); *al þat heo wolden. Þat iseʒen Bruttes; þat balu wes on londe. & hu Sæxisce men; isiʒen weoren to heom* (CMBRUT1); *and blissien him mid þisse wordle and ec wunian a wið crist on heofene.* (CMLAMBET); *- for ðan ðe he is god, for ðan his mildsce is hier on world.*' (CMVICES). Collocational framework is also found to express that something or somebody is clasped in, enclosed in, got into somebody's possession, power or control as in *on honde* (16 occ.), *on fote* (15 occ.). Consider: *For ʒee duden Porus of lyue, Whas douʒtter he haþ to wyue. For on honde Ich wil hym take þat he shal don ʒou no wrake.* (CMALISAU); *And lepe on fote, wiþ swerd of steel And gan hym were swiþe wel* (CMALISAU). Within the subcategory of "with regard to a dimension" (*on brede, on heigh, height, on lengthe, on long, on brod*) some collocations are found as in *on heh* (14 occ.). Witness: *Efter him ich iseh on heh ouer alle heouenliche þe eadi meiden his moder marie* (CMSAWLES).

b) Figurative collocations categories

Under the subcategory of "state or manner" indicating a certain physical arrangement in a group, company, sequence (*on hepe, on lump, on roue*); a certain manner, e.g. *on (no, al, this, ani, mani) wise, manner*, the following collocational types, which include more than 5 tokens, were found: *on wise* (45 occ.) and *on þis manere* (27 occ.). Some examples are: *he spake to hure more famyliarly, callyng hur by hur name, seying on þis wise: " Ne timeas, Maria..* (CMROYAL); *þen schalt þou grece it with an oynement þat is ymade on þis manere. Take sulphur vyue. & whit tartre & blak. & grynde him* (CMHORSES).

The subcategory "expressing a certain state or condition" includes the following collocational framework: *on loue, on live, on slep, on witnesse, on fir, on thirst, on game, on cas, on happes, on fer, on god, on egge, on haste, on hed, on heigh, on loft, on mis, on rest, on rune, on (the) strai, on warantise, on blod*. Collocational patterns with five or more tokens include *on life* (22 occ.) and *on ende* (18 occ.). Consider: *& hwu he stiðlucest her on life for Gode libben mihte* (CMVESHOM); *þt lað is luuie men. ant deaðes dunt on ende* (CMHALI).

The preposition *on* forms consistent clusters such as: *haue mercy on* (12 occ.), *on a day* (11 occ.), *on tis manere* (11 occ.), *on tisse liue* (10 occ.), *mercy on me* (7 occ.), *on a tyme* (7 occ.), *on that day* (7 occ.), *on this day* (7 occ.), *on tis wise* (7 occ.), *on ende of* (6 occ.), *on no wise* (6 occ.), *sette him on* (5 occ.), *haue pyte on* (5 occ.). Consider: *haue mercy on me of my mys-levynge me not be-wray haue mercy on me for charyte.* (CMLUDUS); *all they herde hym that were there / My lorde haue pyte on my complaynt whiche is of grete force and murdre that reynard* (CMREYNAR).

It is also worth noting that the HCME exhibits 459 examples of verb-dependent *on* in a collocational pattern as in *ride on, laghe on, vengaunce on, falle on, spit on, mercy on, complain onswere on,* etc.

Ouer-collocations

The preposition *over* plays many different roles in PDE, the most common being (Bennett (1975: 50ff): a) Locative: a^1) locative superior of: "directly above"; and a^2) locative path locative superior of: "on the other side of"; and b) directional: Path: b^1) [Path locative superior of: "passing directly above" (via)], and b^2) GOAL [Goal locative superior of: "to a position directly above" (to)].

From the basic meaning "locative superior" (passing directly above, position directly above) gradually extends to the figurative connotations and some of them acquired a collocational frame such as *ouer all* (32 occ), *ouer all thing(es)* 12 (occ.). Some examples include: *Bot yit will I cry for mercy and call: Noe, thi seruant, am I, Lord ouer all!* (CMTOWNEL); *Þat is oure souereyn desire, and þat bidde we ouer alle þing, þat þin holy name,* (CMVICES).

Þurgh-collocations

The primary spatial and temporal meaning of *þurgh-Phs* ("from end to end of", "from side to side of", "from one surface (or limit) to the opposite", "from the beginning to the end of") developed into the figurative meaning *by means of, by the agency of.* Besides, contrary to *bi,* the preposition *þurgh* tends to be complemented by abstract referents. Some collocational set phrases include: *þurgh the/his/her/goddes grace* (7 occ.), *þurgh the/his/her/goddes mercy* (6 occ.) as in *And scho þat trowed stedfastly Was helid thurgh his mercy.* (CMNORHOM); *And than Seynt Edmond wyst not whate to doo, but at last thurgh the grace of oure Lorde he remembryd his blessyd passhyon.* (CMEDMUND).

4. FRECH INFLUENCE ON THE COLLOCATIONAL FRAMEWORK OF PREPOSITIONAL PHRASES

What follows is an attempt to provide evidence of French influence, through collocations, on the growing number of some types of *p-Phs* in Middle English. The development of the figurative senses of ME prepositions and, more specifically, the increasing use of prepositional phrasemes in ME3 and ME4, was fostered by analogous French counterparts. It is worth noting that 78% of the prepositional noun complements, covered by this study under the categories of "figurative" senses, are abstract French nouns which made their way into English from the early 13th century onwards.

According to the data extracted from HCME, some prepositions such as *aboue, after, at, by* and *in* became much more frequent in ME3 and ME4 due to the influence of the French equivalent preposition (*par-dessus, après, à, par,* and *en*) in collocational patterns. Thus French collocations headed by *par* such as *par autorité (de), par counseil (de), par force (de), par vertu (de),* etc. were directly transposed to English, preserving entirely the network of French senses and subsenses.

My findings will be substantiated by examples extracted from OED, MED and HCME, and also by analogous OF examples found in the *ATILF*[5] (Analyse et Traitement Informatique de la Langue Française).

4.1. Aboue-Phs

As Table 4 (Chapter III) shows *aboue-Phs* are not very frequent in ME. HCME records only 122 examples for the whole ME period. However, their use increases progressively during the ME period, from 0.03‰ in ME1 to 0.3‰ in ME4. Certainly, the core spatial meanings of *aboue-Phs* such as "directly over, vertically up from", "on or over the upper surface" come from OE. However, figurative meanings such as "higher in a rank or position than", "over in authority"; "higher in degree"; "beyond everything" (*aboue alle*) turn out to be of ordinary use from ME3 due to French pressure. Consider some examples in ME and OF:

MED: a) "Higher in rank than, in authority over, superior to".

> E.g. ?a1325 *Þe grace of godde* (Hrl 913) 228: *Þe heiȝ king aboue vs alle.*

Only 12 instances were found in HCME with the meaning of being "higher in rank or position". These instances include: *Bot hey coround kynge abowne all His angells* (CMGAYTRY); *aboven þe hiest ordere of angels* (CMROYAL).

ATILF: *Par-dessus*. «Plus que».

> E.g....recommande Platon et ses ensuians comme philosophes pardessus touz autres (ORESME, *C.M.*, c.1377, 262).

MED: b) "To a greater degree or extent than, more than, beyond, exceeding; (aboue al (al thing everi thing)".

> E.g. (1340) *Ayenb.*(Arun 57) 234: *Uor maidenhod aboue alle oþre states berþ þet gratteste frut.*

---

5 The old French dictionaries, Godefroy (1880-1895) and Tobler-Lommatzsch (1954-.) are included in *ATILF.*

In this category I have detected 49 examples in HCME which show a sense of "higher in degree or quality", e.g. *Ther nys no thyng in gree superlatyf, As seith Senek, above an humble wyf* (CMCTVERS).
ATILF: *Agé au dessus de.* «Âgé de plus de» :

> E.g ...la Court a ordonné et ordonne que ledit curé aura par maniere de provision (...) pour la funeraille de chascun chief d'ostel de sa parroice XV solz parisis, soit homme ou femme, et de chascune autre personne non faisant chief d'ostel, aagée au dessus de sept ans, XIJ solz parisis, et de chascun enfant de VIJ ans et au dessoubz XXX deniers parisis (BAYE, I, 1400-1410, 166).

4.2. After-Phs

The survey of HCME shows that *after-Phs* are very recurrent in ME. I have counted 1001 instances in HCME. According to the data exhibited in Table 5 (Chapter III) *after-Phs* have a similar frequency in all ME subperiods. In like manner, we note that both *après* and *after* had similar spatial and temporal uses. However, figurative meanings such as "next to in order or importance", "in imitation of, in compliance with the wishes of" were fostered by similar French collocational patterns. Consider some examples:

MED: a) "of motion: coming behind, following, in pursuit of".

> E.g. a1131 *Peterb.Chron.*(LdMisc 636) an.1128: *Þa for mid him & æfter him swa micel folc, swa næfre ær ne dide.*

HCME shows 57 examples of *after-Phs* used as complements which express an action involved "in pursuit of, in search of" somebody or something as in *I woll ryde aftir hym and assay hym* (CMMALORY).
ATILF: *Aller après.* «Suivre».

> E.g. Et un deciple lors avoit [S. Jean Baptiste] Qui Andrieu appelé estoit (...) [lequel] tost ala Apres li [Jésus] et pelerina, Et appela et fist venir Pierre, son frere, et li süir. Et l'endemain Jhesus trouva Phelippe qu'ausi appela. Et furent les premiers ces troiz Ses deciples a celle foiz. (GUILL. DIGULL., *Pèler. J.-C. S.*, 1358, 141).

MED: b) "Following (in time): following (sb.) in a chronological series, in succession to; following (sth.) in order of occurrence or existence".

> E.g. a1121 *Peterb.Chron.*(LdMisc 636) an.686: *Heo wæs se þridde abbot æfter Saxulfe.*

The notion that a state or an event is "subsequent to and in consequence of" is detected on 223 occasions in HCME as in & *com to him efter help his flescliche broðer* (CMANCRE).
ATILF: [Avec indication chronol.] *Après qqc.*

E.g. Et atant se taist l'ystoire a parler d'eulx, et parole de Remondin et de sa femme, comment ilz firent aprez la departie de la feste. (ARRAS, c.1392-1393, 45).

MED: c) "Next (in rank, importance, value, etc.), next to, second to".

E.g. a1225(?OE) Lamb.Hom.(Lamb 487)   131: Seinte paul, heȝes[t] larðewen efter ure helende seolfe, speceð on þe halie pistle.

HCME exhibits 36 instances which indicate that a state or event is "next to in order or importance". Thus CMFITZJA includes examples such as the following: *Prudence after him is a wisdom to lede man; And Sapyence after hym stondeth; after him restyth mannys felycyte.*

ATILF: [En parlant de plusieurs choses] *Succéder un après l'autre.* «Succéder l'un à l'autre».

E.g. Et pour ce, un ange peut estre en un lieu sanz soy mouver nonobstant que en ce lieu pluseurs corps succedent un apres l'autre, aussi comme le ray du soleil qui passe par une fenestre n'est pas meu aveques l'aer que le vent emporte ou chace, mais samble demourer tout un combien que non soit, car ce n'est pas du tout semblable. (ORESME, C.M., c.1377, 290).

MED: d) "After the manner of; in imitation of, according to, in conformity with, so as to correspond to, in keeping with, appropriate to".

E.g. ?c1200 Orm.(Jun 1)   ded.2: Broþerr min Affterr þe flæshess kinde.

HCME includes 52 examples which indicate that an action is performed "in imitation of, like".

E.g. *After Ercules hij weren ymad* (CMALISAU).

ATILF: D'après le modèle».

E.g. En ceste eglise, sans nulle menterie, Est le tableau qui par Saint Luc fut fait, Aprés le vif, sur la Vierge Marie Qui sur tout autre est en beaulté parfaict (LA VIGNE, V.N., p.1495, 233).

4.3. At-Phs

As has been shown in Chapter III, the data extracted from HCME show that there is an increasing use of *at*-phrases with a great variety of roles in the course of ME. The use of *at*-phrases to express spatial and temporal senses was dominant. Thus, out of the 1555 phrases headed by *at* in HCME, 671 occurrences had a spatial prepositional complement and 270 instances had a temporal one. Most of the remaining 614 *at*-phrases in the corpus have a figurative or abstract sense, or constitute an idiomatic construction subject to collocational restrictions. Even more significant is that these uses appear for the first time in ME and show a strong imprint of OF *à*-phrases. What follows is a classification of the new senses of *at*-phrases found in ME and their OF *à*-phrase counterparts.

At-Phs recorded for the first time in ME

1. To be at a person "to be in the presence or company of a person" (OED, categories, 3a and 3b; MED, category 2b). To be at a person is recorded by both OED (1205 *Lay.*: *weoren..at Ardure*) and MED (*c*1200 *Orm.*: *to winnen uss att himm*) in the early 13th century.

HCME records 31 *at*-phrases with the sense of being "at the presence of" or "in company with", either in "personal contact with" or "in sensory or perceptional contact with" or "direction towards a person", e.g. *saat..at Ihesu feet, comyn at þe preste, merci is at our Lord, the word was at God, come at hym*, etc. The "direction towards a person" (OED, category 12a) is recorded for the first time in *Ge ne comon æt me* (*c*1000 *Ags. Gosp.* Matt.xxv, 43), while MED (category 2b(b)) includes *comen at* "go to (sb.)" as the first example, *..comeþ nought at hire*, in (a1398) *Trev. Barth.* 277b/a. The HCME includes 6 examples of "direction towards sb."

Consider some examples:
ME:

1. We weoren.. at Ardure þane kinge (OED/1205 *LAY*, 25290).
2. Forr swa to winnen uss att himm, þurrh himm to wurrþenn heʒhenn (MED/?c1200 *Orm.* 13972).
3. He slowʒ an hundreþ in a rawe, þat at his feet laien yslawe. (HCME/c1400 (?a1300) (CMALISAU).

It should be noted that OF includes a similar *à*-phrase pattern: *vingt seront a Tierri, a Carlemagne irez, furent a Guillaume de Blois, aler a vos*, etc.
OF:

1. Et vingt seront a Tierri et Fouchier, *Aym. Narb.* 1501. (ATILF-Tobler).
2. Vingt et un furent a Guillaume de Blois, *eb.* 1504 (ATILF-Tobler).
3. Seignur barun, a Carlemagne irez. (*Rol.*, 70, Müller.) (ATILF-Godefroy).
4. Il s'est mis ou viage d'aler a vos (*Cart. De Champ.*,Richel. I. 5993 f° 79ᵛᵒ.) (ATILF-Godefroy).

2. Arrival at a place, conveying the notion of "intervening space traversed" or "the goal of a movement" (OED, category, 12c; MED, category 3a). OED records this *at*-phrase in *K. Alis.* for the first time (*aryved at Cysile*), whereas MED records it in *Gen. & Ex.*(*cam At a welle*). HCME includes 11 *at*-phrases such as *arryueth.. at the hauene of the cytee of york, At þat cytee entreth, leden þe king.. at Stanford*, etc.

Consider some examples:
ME:

1. The thridde day..He aryved at Cysile (OED/1300 *K. Alis.*).
2. He ðider cam At a welle wið-uten ðe tun (MED/a1325 (c1250) *Gen. & Ex.* 1367).
3. And after arryueth men in Grece at the hauene of the cytee of york or at the hauene of Valone or at the cytee of Duras, & þere is a Duk at Duras, or at oþere hauenes in þo marches & so men gon to Constantynoble (HCME/?a1425 (c1400) (CMMANDEV).

Old French registers parallel *à*-phrases such as *chevaucha a une autre cité, croisa... a Bruges, venu jusques a la, tourner... a Calais*, etc.
OF:

1. Lors..l'empereres..chevaucha a une autre cité qui estoit a une jornee d'olec (VILLEH., 165, Wailly.) (ATILF-Godefroy).
2. Se croisa li quens Baudoins..a Bruges (Villeh. 8) (ATILF-Tobler).
3. Et fist tourner se navie a Calais. (ID., ib., IV, 356, ms. Amiens, f° 100.) (ATILF-Godefroy).

3. Motion directed "against" sb. or the goal of an activity (OED, category 13a; MED, category 3b) OED registers the first example in *Octauian* a1400 with the at-phrase *At me to fyght*. MED records the first example in Chaucer *CT.Kn.* c1385 with the at-phrase *To hunten at the leoun*. HCME includes 15 phrases such as: *at þe pore man hyf drofe (þe stone)*.
Consider some examples:
ME:

1. Swyche twenty n'ere wortht a slo At me to fyght (OED/a1400 *Octauian* 976).
2. To hunten at the leoun or the deer (MED/(c1385) Chaucer *CT.Kn.* A.2150).
3. For þe stone he toke a lofe, And at þe pore man hyf drofe. (HCME/a1400 (c1303), (CMHANSYN).

Old French also uses a similar *à*-phrase structure for the same semantic role: *a els cumbatre, a lui fuison*, etc.
OF:

1. Je me soloie a els cumbatre, Sovent a treis, sovent a quatre, Et il a moi sunt cumbatu (*Brut*, ms. Munich, 14447, Vollmöller.) (ATILF-Godefroy).
2. Vint chevaliers n'orent a lui fuison (*Ogier*, ms. Durh., Bibl. De Cos., V, ii, 17, f° 113ª.) (ATILF-Godefroy).
3. Il y eut assez de gens qui, n'estans pas encor bien leurrez ou affermis a ces bruits et a ces remuemens, commencerent a craindre (Du Villars, *Mém.*, ii, 1551.) (ATILF-Godefroy).

4. "Bodily gestures", "expressions of attitude" and "emotional reactions" (OED, category 13b; MED, categories 7(a)(b)) OED provides the first example c1400 in *Sir Isumb* with *at him faste loghe*, whereas MED records *drede at ʒou* c1384 in

Wbible (1). HCME includes only 13 records of this type, such as *þynche at his writyng, greve þe nought at it, at mete of deth, had grete despite at hym, gnasted at sir Launcelot, besiech at me*, etc.

Consider some examples:
ME:

1. The qwene..at him faste loghe (OED/ c1400 *Sir Isumb*. 625).
2. Se ȝe that he be withoute drede at ȝou (MED/(c1384) *Wbible (1)* Cor. 16.10).
3. Therto he koude endite and make a thyng, Ther koude no wight þynche at his writyng; (HCME/c1387-95) (CMTVERS).

Old French presents similar *à*-phrases: *penet a cel populum, Apreneiz a mi, humiliteit aprengniens a notre signor,* etc.
OF:

1. Jonas propheta habebat mult laboret e mult penet a cel populum (*Fragm. De Valenc.*, Bartsch) (ATILF-Godefroy).
2. Apreneiz a mi (S. Bern., *Serm.*, p. 123, ap. Ste-Pal.) (ATILF-Godefroy).
3. Ensi ke nos mansuetume et humiliteit aprengniens a notre signor (*ib*. P. 256). (ATILF-Godefroy).

5. The object or action which acts as the instrument or cause of a certain activity (OED, category 15b; MED, category 11(a)). OED records the first example, *see this at eye,* in *c*1375 in WYCLIF *Serm*. MED registers the first example in Chaucer *CT c*1385 with the same phrase *seen at eye*. In HCME, 23 records are found, such as *lighte a candle at his lanterne, melte ham at þe fire, been assayed at diverse stoundes, at a dint he slow hem, at two strokys he strake hem downe, toke any dysplesure at my langage.*

Consider some examples:
ME:

1. We may see this at eye (OED/c1375 WYCLIF *Serm. Xxxvi. Sel. Wks.* 1869 I.97).
2. This maistow vnderstonde and seen at eye (MED/c1385 Chaucer *CT. Kn.* A 3016).
3. A man to lighte a candle at his lanterne; (HCME/c1387-95) (CMTVERS).

Old French uses such a pattern in *à*-phrases like: *a ses ieuz le veeit, pooit veoir a oil, Li mostre a l'uel,* etc.
OF:

1. ensi l'escriveit Come il o (*Var*. a) ses ieuz le veeit *Troie*, 106 (ATILF-Tobler).
2. tant que on pooit veoir a oil, ne pooit on veoir se voiles non *Villeh* 120 (ATILF-Tobler).
3. une fenestre Li mostre a l'uel, non mie au doi, *Rcharr.* 4525 (ATILF-Tobler).

6. *The action in which one participates or is engaged* (OED, category 6; MED, categories 6a(a)(b)). OED gives *Æt þǣre bēor-þeʒe* (*Beowulf* 1239) as the earliest record in which sb. takes part in an event ("assisting or present at"). The *Peterborough Chronicle* in its account for the year 1128 includes *at an gefiht*; the only *at*-phrase found in the Chronicle with figurative or abstract use (Lundskær-Nielsel, 1993: 96-7). MED under the category 6a ("Of activities: (a) participating or engaged in (sth.); *present at; at, in; at drinke, ~ ale; at mete, ~ table; at an fighte..; (b) pleien at, play at (a game)..*") records the first occurrence in the *Peterborough Chronicle* An. 1131: *at an gefiht* in *Se eorl wearð gewunded at an gefiht*, in a1131 in *Peterb. Chron.* HCME includes 46 at-phrases such as *at the mete the kyng sate, was at the spoylynge and robbynge of the Fryer Prechourys, seruen the Emperour at the mete, she whos at brekefaste, He miʒte þo at is diner, at drynke & he sall passe owt*, etc. Prins (1952) includes *played at þe bal, At þe echese...pleye, pleyen atte dys, play atte bokeler, at bukler to play*, etc.

Consider some examples:
ME:

1. *Æt þǣre bēor-þeʒe* (OED/1000 *Beowulf* 1239).
2. Se eorl wearð gewunded at an gefiht (MED/a1131 *Peterb. Chron.* An. 1128).
3. Or gif it hym at drynke & he sall passe owt[{e{] of þe euyll faire & wele. (HCME/ c1300 (?c1225) (CMHORN).

OF registers parallel patterns in *à*-phrases like: *jue à la pelote, a billete juer, As eschas jvent*, etc.
OF:

1. As tables juent pur els esbaneier Et as eschas li plus saive e li vieill, *Ch. De R.*, 111 (ATILF-Tobler).
2. Et li plusor vulent jöer As dés, as tables, as eschès (*Durm.* 372) (ATILF-Tobler).
3. Li un jüent a l'escremir, A l'entredeus, por mieux ferir, As tables li conte palès, Li viel et li sage as escès (*CPoit. M.*, 1360) (ATILF-Tobler).

7. *The time at which an event happens* (with the time named or with the time indicated by the event) (OED, categories 29a, 29b; MED, category 4c)). OED records *Att te come off Sannt Johan* (c1200 *ORMIN* 707), whereas MED registers the first record in *Bod. Hom.* 116/4 (c1175): *Æt þisre weorlde endunge, on domes dæʒ*. HCME incorporates 51 at-phrases of this type such as *at þe comyng of þe right high and myghty prynce, At þe fest of Ascencion, at þe set dey, at þe seyd festis of Our Lord, Riʒt at prime tide, evyn at the prechyng tyme, att the comyng of the goode Duke Umfray, at a day assined, at þe oure of mydnyt þe thorusday in estarne Weke*, etc.

Consider some examples:
ME:

1. Att te come off Sannt Johan.. (OED/c1200 *ORMIN* 707).
2. Att te come off Sannt Johan Bigann all ure blisse (MED/c1200, *ibid.*).
3. Riȝt at prime tide, Hi gunnen ut ride, (HCME/c1300 (?c1225) (CMHORN).

Old French uses similar *à*-phrases such as *Al setme meis de l'an, au primier crieur du soir, a l'issue dou mois de mars,* etc.
OF:

1. Al quart an qu'ot suffert li martyrs passiun, Al setme meis de l'an..Vint li reis, *S.Thom.* B¹ 79 a Z.6 (ATILF-Tobler).
2. Lesier oevre en charnage au primier crieur du soir, *Lmest.* 186 (ATILF-Tobler).
3. Onze jors a l'issue dou mois de mars, *Brun. Lat.* 141 (ATILF-Tobler).

8. Distance in time (OED, category 31; MED, category 4c). OED records *att twentiȝ daȝhess end* (1200 *ORMIN* 1893) and MED includes *Æt þisre weorlde endunge, on domes dæȝ* (*Bod. Hom.* 116/4 (c1175)). HCME includes 24 records such as *at the .vc. ȝeres ende, at the ende of .iij. wokes, at the yeeris ende,* etc.
Consider some examples:
ME:

1. Att twentiȝ daȝhess ende (OED/1200 *ORMIN* 1893).
2. He ..swo dide atten ende (MED/a1225 (?a1200) *Vices & B.(1)* 25/3.
3. And at the .vc. ȝeres ende the prestes arrayen here awtere honestly and putten þere vpon spices & sulphur vif & oþer thinges (HCME/?a1425 (c1400) (CMMANDEV).

Old French uses a similar pattern in *a huit jorz, a icel jour, a l'endemain, a un matin,* etc.
OF:

1. Nos vos responurons d'ui a huit jorz, *Villeh.* 19 (ATILF-Tobler).
2. Treinte bastars mena o lui a icel jour, *Bast.* 168 (ATILF-Tobler).
3. onze jors a l'issue dou mois de mars, *Brun. Lat.* 141 (ATILF-Tobler).

9. Price or value (OED, category 27; MED, category 10 (c)). OED records for the first time *at nought* (1325 *Coeur de L.* 362). MED includes *at a certeyn prys* (c1387-95, Chaucer *CT. Prol.* A. 815). In HCME I have found 23 examples, including *at noght, at wages, at land wages, at See Wages, at excessive price, at suche an outrageous price, at such a price, at xx d, at vi d, at a pyn,* etc.
Consider some examples:
ME:

1. He set his stroke at nought (OED/1325 *Coeur de L.* 362).
2. And sette a soper at a certeyn prys (MED/(c1387-95) Chaucer *CT. Prol.* A. 815).
3. and setteth at noght his goode name or loos (HCME/c1390) (CMTVERS).

Old French includes *à*-phrases such as *a droite value de terre, a la value de la dicte rente, a la value de ii s.*, etc.
OF:

1. Li rois de France donra au rei d'Engleterre la value de la terre de Agenois..selonc ce que ele sera prisee a droite value de terre (28 mai 1258, *Tr. d'Abbev.*, Arch. J. 629, piece 1). (ATILF-Godefroy).
2. ...telle comme cilz qui quent la costume de par le roy la voudra prendre, de ci a la value de ii. s. (Est. Boileau, *Liv. des mest.*, 2ᵉ p., xvii, 1).(ATILF-Godefroy).
3. Il facent faire la dicte assiete a value de la dicte rente (1328, *Ass. de terre en Costent,* Arch. kk. 292, f° 1 r°) (ATILF-Godefroy).

The analysis of the data of HCME shows that the spatial and temporal senses of *at*-phrases of OE expand to new uses in ME with more figurative and abstract senses. The first *at*-phrases with a figurative meaning refer to actions in which one participates or is engaged. Thus *at an gefiht* already appears in 1128 (*Peterb. Chron.* An. 1128), although OED dates a similar *at*-phrase in *Beowulf*. The 47 tokens found in HCME show the increase of such a sense, most of them from 1300 onwards. Similarly, the *at*-phrase used to indicate "the time at which an event happens, with the time named" or "with the time indicated by an event; at the time of, on the occasion of" also appears in eME and the first record sems to be found in the *Ormulum*: *Att te come off Sannt Johan* (OED). The 52 tokens registered in the corpus prove the acceptability of this phrase. *At*-phrases with the sense of being "at a person" (31 tokens) also made their way into English by 1200. Thus, the Layamon's *Brut* includes *We weoren.. at Ardure þane kinge* (OED). The other referential-iconic senses are recorded in the course of the 14ᵗʰ century for the first time and their presence in the corpus varies from the 24 tokens found to indicate "distance in time" to the 11 tokens recorded in the corpus to express "arrival at a place (intervening space traversed)." It is worth noting, however, that I have only found 3 types of figurative *At*-phrases in HCME texts prior to 1300. One of these types was used to indicate an action in which one participates or is engaged: *at þan fehte* (Layamon's *Brut*, 1 occ.), the type *at nede* is also found in Layamon's *Brut* (2 occ.), whereas *at will* appears also with a single occurrence in *The Ormulum*.

Most examples of *at*-phrases prior to 1300 occur with a town name or other place name as complement of the preposition (15 instances). The other dominant use is temporal (6 tokens) and most of them refer to the time of the day, e.g. *at middai, at prime* or to the calendar, e.g. *at messe, at circumcisiun, at shrifte*. However, there is only one example with a figurative meaning (*at þan fehte*) and two *At*-phrases which have acquired an idiomatic association (*at ne(o)de* and *at wille*), but with 3 appearances, 2 tokens with *ne(o)de* as complement and 1 whose complement is *will(e)*. This suggests that iconic referential senses (spatial and temporal) of *at*-phrases are used prior to 1300.

However, in the following two centuries there is a significant increase of "symbolic" senses (figurative/abstract and idiomatic). According to the data of HCME before 1300, the extracts from *Vespasian Homilies* (a1150), *Peri Didaxeon* (c1150), *History of the Holy Rood-Tree* (1175), *Hali Meidhad (*The *Catherine* Group) (?c1200), *Juliane (*The *Catherine* Group) (?c1200), *Margarete (*The *Catherine* Group) (?c1200), *Katherine Juliane (*The *Catherine* Group) (?c1200), *Sawles Warde* (?c1200), *Ancrene Wisse* (c1230), The *Proclamation of Henry* III (1258) and *The Thrush and the Nightingale* (?a1300) do not include a single instance of *at*-phrases. The other texts written before 1300 and extracted in HCME show 21 *at*-phrases with spatial (15) and temporal (6) relationships. It is noteworthy that I have found 7 *at*-phrases (7 tokens) with the new ME sense: "to be at a person, at the presence of sb., or to depart from sb".). From the early 14th century on, there is an expansion of *at*-phrases with a varied range of uses. In fact, I have counted one *at*-phrase for every four hundred words (0.255%) from 1300 on with 303 differentiated prepositional complements. Futhermore, by the end of the ME period, abstract, figurative and idiomatic senses matched together with the traditional spatial and temporal roles. Thus, to provide an example, the extracted text in HCME of *York Plays* shows the following *At*-phrases: *at my will, at hys makyng, at his endyng, at thy wylle, at heuyne, an Mane, at your owen wyll, at wyll, at your wyll, at it* (*greue*), *at thy techyng, at thi lare, at my speche, at my biddyng, at thi lare, at asent*, and *at hir boke*.

The transition from the original spatial and temporal senses of OE *At*-phrases, as in *æt Hrofesceastre* (spatial) and *æt sumum cirre* (temporal), to figurative and idiomatic senses such as *at large, at ese*, etc. in ME is still under conjecture. Thus, OF *à*-phrases which were used earlier and with similar senses and which were known by English writers either in bilingual contexts or in the natural process of translation and composition may have contributed to such a transition. Certainly, the symbolic usage of phrasal structures headed by *æt* is rooted in the OE period, but its extensive usage in the course of the fourteenth century seems to be fostered by French.

4.4. Bi-Phs

As has been shown in Chapter III, the use of *bi-Phs* increases notably in ME2 and more significantly in the course of ME3. The data shown in Table 7 (Figure 4, Chapter III) indicate that the 1.2 instances of *bi-Phs* which are found in HCME for every thousand words in ME1 raises to 5.3 in ME3. It is generally assumed[6] that such an increase was largely due to the weight of the OF counterpart *par*. In what follows I intend to prove that French influence was considerably more noticeable in collocational clusters which were taken directly from French, such as *bi auctorite*

---

6 Cf. A.M. Hornero Corisco (1997)

(of), bi grace (of), bi assent (of), bi reson (of), bi counseil (of), etc. In line with this assertion, the data exihibited in Table 21 (Chapter IV) illustrate that there are significant differences in the use of *bi* according to the dialectal area. Thus, the use of *bi-Phs* is very rare in the North in the two subperiods (ME3 and ME4) for which HCME shows data. West Midlands shows a great increase, starting with a rate of 1.4‰ in ME1, but rising to 7.8‰ in ME3. East Midlands starts with a rate of 0.1‰ in ME1 and increases to 0.3‰ in ME3, whereas the Southern area, with no records in ME1 moves to 0.1‰ in ME3. According to HCME data, the collocational *bi*-types have also contributed to raising these rates as they are much more frequent in EMO, EML, and WML, as will be shown in Table 77. In like manner, the data shown in Table 31 (Chapter IV) show that prose doubles the number of *bi-Phs* with regard to poetry throughout the Middle English period. Collocational *bi*-types also occur predominantly in prose (See Table 77).

Bi auctorite (of).
This *bi-Ph* is included in our study (See Chapter VI, Table 68) under the general category F-2 (Figurative meaning -> agency and mediation). This general sense is highly recurrent in ME, as HCME exibits 667 examples which correspond to a ratio of 39.09% within the figurative sense and 29.12 with respect to all *bi-Phs*. Within this semantic category, *bi auctorite (of)* is highly represented in the corpus, with 63 tokens with the meaning "with the approval of", "by power delegated from". This *bi-Ph* began to appear in ME3, coinciding with the massive French borrowing. However, its use was restricted to four texts in HCME: CMDOCU3 (ME3), CMPURVEY (ME3), CMOFFIC4 (ME4) and CMLAW (ME4). Thus, *bi auctorite of* occurs only in two domains: in legal texts (DOCUMENTS) and in religious treatises (henceforward, REL TREAT) as in *Purvey's General Prologue to the Bible* (CMPURVEY) within the expression *bi auctorite of God* ("by the power delegated by God"). This *bi-Ph* was also restricted to EMO, EML and SL dialects.

Auctorite made its way into English c.1230 from O.F. *auctorité*, and *bi auctorite (of) Ph* was directly taken from the OF *par auctorité (de)* whose use was highly extended in all domains in OF with the meaning "faire qqc. *de/par l'autorité de qqn.* "(faire qqc.) sur l'instigation, sous l'impulsion de qqn" (ATILF). However, the French meaning "power to enforce obedience" appears for the first time in English c.1390. Consider some examples:

> MED: a) *bi auctorite (of)*: ("with the approval of", "by power delegated from"). (a1387) Trev. *Higd.*(StJ-C H.1) 1.283: He was i-made kyng..by auctorite [L auctoritate] of pope Steuene. (c1443) Pecock Rule (Mrg M 519) 328: Þey ben ordeyned wijsely.. and bi þe hool autorite of alle hem whiche han riȝt and interes to helpe make þilke ordinauncis.
> MED: b) *bi auctorite (of)*: ("power to enforce obedience"). (1472-3) *RParl.* 6.21a: Please it your Highnes..by the advis and assent of the Lordes..and the Comens in this present Parlement assembled, and by auctorite of the same, to ordeyn [etc.].

HCME: ...of his Rial prerogatif that he grauntede to me by the auctorite of his parlement (CMDOCU3).

Consider similar collocational patterns in OF:

ATILF: *Faire qqc. par l'autorité de qqn.* ("Faire qqc. sur l'instigation, sous l'impulsion de qqn"). Par le conduit et par l'*auctorité* du dict Appius li Poticien, qui estoient une gent qui tousjours avoient acoustumé a estre prestre au grant autel d'Ercule, avoient pris certainz cerfs publiques les drois et les sollempnitez de celui sacrifice (BERS., I, 9, c.1354-1359, 29.9, 53).

Bi cause (of)

This *bi-Ph* is categorised under the general type F-1 (Figurative meaning - > agency, mediation, means, motivation. See Chapter VI, Table 68). This category is the second most frequent *bi-Ph* sense in ME. HCME shows 620 instances, which correspond to a ratio of 36.34% within the figurative sense and 27.07 with regard to all *bi-Phs*. *Bi cause (of)* is found on 22 occasions in the corpus with the meaning "by reason (of), on account (of), because (of)". The senses "for the sake (of)", "in order to prevent" recorded in MED are not attested in HCME.

This *bi cause (of)* is found for the first time in ME3, coinciding with the highest peak of French borrowing. It is important to remark that this *bi-Ph* was confined to 9 texts out of the 91 included in HCME. Eight of these texts were scientific or technical ones (ASTRONOMY, PHILOSOPHY, DOCUMENTS and [Paston] LETTERS). It is also worth noting that the all *bi cause (of) Phs* were only found in EMO and EML dialects.

Cause made its way into English in the early 13th century from French with a variety of meanings "cause, reason; judicial process; lawsuit". *Bi cause (of) Ph* was formed from the OF *par cause (de)*, whose use is recorded in technical and non-technical domains in French with the meaning "sous l'effet, par l'action, en raison de qqc." (ATILF). Consider some examples:

MED: bi cause of: ("By reason (of), on account (of), because (of)"). (a1387) Trev. *Higd.*(StJ-C H.1) 1.321: By cause of [L propter] goodnesse of þe lond. ?a1425(c1400) *Mandev.(1)* (Tit C.16) 109/8: The Ademand..draweth the Iren to him, And so wolde it drawe to him the schipp be cause of the Iren.
HCME: For ther is a versifiour seith that 'the ydel man excuseth hym in wynter by cause of the grete coold, and in somer by enchesoun of the greete heete.' For thise causes.. (CMECTPROS).

OF counterparts are:

ATILF: *Par (la) cause de qqc:* («Sous l'effet, par l'action, en raison de qqc.») ...car nul ne doit improperer ou reprouchier a un homme ce que il est aveugle se il est tel de nature et de nativité ou par *cause* de maladie ou par une plaie. (ORESME, E.A., c.1370, 200).

Bi grace (of god)/bi (godes) grace

This *bi-Ph* is classified in the category F-1 (Figurative meaning -> agency, mediation, means, motivation. See Chapter VI, Table 68). *Bi grace (of god)/bi godes grace* is found 54 times in the corpus with the meaning "by means of (God), through the agency of (God); through or by (God's) faculties; with or through (God's) help, providence, grace", etc.). As the word *grace* made its way into English in eME, *bi grace (of)* is already found in ME2, although a single text of this sub-period from HCME (CMBEVIS) attests it with only two instances.

Its use was widely extended to all domains (ROMANCE, REL TREAT, PHILOSOPHY, DOCUMENTS, LAW, and LETTERS) except technical scientific texts, although it was confined to 13 texts of HCME. It was also found in most of the dialects (EMO, EML, WML, SO), although 50 instances out of 54 occur in EMO.

Grace made its way into English c.1175 from OF with the meaning "God's favour or help". *Bi grace (of god)/bi godes grace* was taken from the OF *par grace (de Dieu)* whose usage was highly extended in colloquial and formal domains in OF with the meaning "par la grace de Dieu", "par la faveur divine" (ATILF). Consider some examples:

> *MED*: a1225 (c1200) *Vices & V.(1)* (Stw 34) 35/13: Of hire we willeð sumdæl keðen be godes grace.
> *HCME*: Somtyme we profite only by grace, and þan we ben licnid vnto Moises, þat for alle þe clymbyng & þe trauaile þat he had into þe mounte, miȝt not com to se it bot seeldom; (CMCLOUD).

OF collocational patterns include:

> *ATILF: Par la grace de Dieu*: En la confiance de l'aide de Nostre Seigneur Jhesu Crist, du commandement de tres noble et tres excellent prince Charles, par la *grace* de Dieu roy de France, je propose translater de latin en françois aucuns livres lesquelx fist Aristote le souverain philosophe (ORESME, E.A., c.1370, 97).
> *ATILF*: («Par la faveur divine»): ...comme par la *grace* de Dieu, du Roy et de sa Court, eusse servi ceans et exercé l'office de graphier par l'espace de seze ans tous entiers et continuez (BAYE, II, 1411-1417, 273).

Bi resoun (of)

This *bi-Ph* is assigned to the general type F-1 (Figurative meaning - > agency, mediation, means, motivation. See Chapter VI, Table 68). *Bi resoun (of)* includes 35 occurrences in HCME. It was first used in the late 13th century with the general meaning of "manner and accord", more specifically, "with reason, for good reason, justifiably, properly" (MED). In the course of the 14th century this *bi-Ph* extended to other senses such as "because of, on account of"; "showing by means of reasoning"; "for this reason" (*bi resoun whi*). All these senses are attested in HCME.

Bi resoun (of) is already detected in ME2 (CMALISAU), although its increase coincides with the massive French borrowing in the course of the second half of the 14th century. This *bi-Ph* is found in 13 texts of HCME and is recorded in most of the domains (ROMANCE, LAW, HISTORY, PHILOSOPHY, DRAMA, REL TREAT, FICTION, SERMON) and in many dialects (EMO, SL, NL, WML). This *bi-Ph* reaches its peak in ME3.

The noun *resoun* made its way into English from French c.1225 with the basic meaning of "statement in an argument," also "intellectual faculty that adopts actions to ends". However, the OF *par raison* was used with a great variety of senses: *Par droit et par raison*. "à juste titre"; "légitimement, à juste titre, à bon droit"; "avec raison, en toute justice"; "logiquement"; "selon le bon sens"; "après réflexion, raisonnnablement"; "comme il convient"; "avec discernement, sagesse, jugement", etc. (ATILF). Many of these senses are also attested en ME such as *bi right and resoun* "by rights, rightly" (MED). Consider some examples:

> MED: a) "Of manner and accord", more specifically, "with reason, for good reason, justifiably, properly": c1330(?a1300) *Tristrem* (Auch) 2023: Bi resoun þou schalt se þat loue is hem bitvene.
> MED: b) "Of learning, knowing, teaching, showing by means of observation, examination, reasoning, judgment, a science": a1425(c1385) Chaucer *TC* (Benson-Robinson) 4.1048: By which resoun men may wel yse That thilke thynges that in erthe falle, That by necessite they comen alle.
> MED: c) "Because of, on account of": (c1325) *Recipe Painting(1)* in *Archaeol.J.1* (Hrl 2253) 65: Mac the sise to goldfoyl, save tac a lutel radel ant grynt to thin asise, vorte loosen is colour, bi resun of the goldfoyl.
> MED: d) "For this reason" (*bi resoun whi*): a1400(a1325) *Cursor* (Vsp A.3) 25165: Bot þar es resun qui vr bon Es noght granted us quilum sun.
> HCME: ("Of manner and accord") "with reason, for good reason, justifiably, properly": "Certes," quod sche, "nothing nys fairere than is the thing that by resoun schulde ben addide to thise forseide thinges." (CMBOETH)

OF shows similar patterns such as:
> ATILF: a) «À juste titre»: Lors un petit pion par droit et par *raison* en presence du roy assauldra un grant [roch] ou un offin. Et s'il saura bien trayre par droyt et par justice ou milieu de l'eschequier et pres du roy et de la royne, il ara sa querelle et la mectra a fin. (MÉZIÈRES, *Songe vieil pèl. C., t.2, c.1386-1389, 182*).
> ATILF: b) «Légitimement, à juste titre, à bon droit» : Bien m'en peusse deporter Se je voulsisse, et par raison, Car de gens de plus hault renom Qu'il n'y a nulz en son parage Sui nez (Mir. ev. arced., c.1341, 108).
> ATILF: c) «Selon le bon sens» : Et ce appert par *raison*, car le mouvement du soleil et des estoilles est tres merveilleusement isnel (ORESME, *C.M., c.1377, 474*).
> ATILF: d) «Avec discernement, sagesse, jugement» : Bien peut le jeune mal fuyr, Si se veult regir par *raison*, Et qu'il s'en vayse recuillir Avec gens de bonne maison. (Pass. Auv., 1477, 119).

Bi counseil (of).
This *bi-Ph* belongs to the general category F-2 (Figurative meaning -> agency and mediation. See Chapter VI, Table 68). Within this semantic category *bi counseil (of)* is highly represented in the corpus with 34 tokens with the meaning "to follow advice; act after due consideration or consultation". This *bi-Ph* began to appear in ME2. Two texts, CMALISAU and CMBEVIS, of this subperiod include 3 and 1 intances, respectively. The highest frequency of tokens occurs in ME3. It has been used in prose and verse in many different domains (ROMANCE, HISTORY, REL TREAT, FICTION, HOMELY and DRAMA). 14 texts out of 91 of HCME include this *bi-Ph* distributed in various dialects: EMO, WML, EML, SL, and NL.

Counseil made its way into English from French in the early 13th century. *Bi counseil (of)* was taken from the OF *par counseil (de) qqn.* that was generally used in all domains in OF with the meaning "suivre l'avis qui est donné" (ATILF). Consider some examples:

> *MED*: (c1390) Chaucer *CT.Mil.*(Manly-Rickert) A.3530: Werk al by conseil, and thow shalt noght rewe. (c1395) Chaucer *CT.Mch.*(Manly-Rickert) E.1485: Werk alle thyng by conseil.
> *HCME*: Belyn þo, by counseil of his folc, grantede him his axing; and so Gutlagh bicome his man; (CMBRUT3).

OF exhibits equivalent patterns such as:

> *ATILF*: a) «Suivre l'avis qui est donné»: Sire, il est bien verité que Hervy de Leon fu ysneaulx chevaliers, courtois et saiges, bien moriginez, et l'ama moult le roy et son nepveu, et usoit le roy moult par son conseil, et estoit Hervy cellui en qui il se fioit le plus. (ARRAS, c.1392-1393, 57).
> *ATILF*: b) «À l'instigation de qqn»: Par le conseil de celeste asistence En excersant mon naturel office, J'ay propheré contre (la) Vie sentence Qui aura lieu, congneu leur malefice. (Cene dieux, c.1492, 140).

Bi assent of
This *bi-Ph* is included in the category F-1 (Figurative meaning - > agency, mediation, means, motivation. See Chapter VI, Table 68). *Bi assent (of)* is found on 22 occasions in the corpus with the meaning "by agreement, unanimously" and "with (one's) consent or approval" (MED).

Bi assent (of) appears for the first time in ME3, coinciding with the highest frequency of French borrowing. This *bi-Ph* is restricted to 9 texts of HCME. All of them were written in prose and in formal domains (HISTORY, LAW, DOCUMENTS, LETTERS and BIOGRAPHY). This *bi-Ph*, however, has an extensive dialectal distribution as it appears in EMO, WML, EML, SL, and SO.

Assent made its way into English c.1300 with the meaning "by agreement, unanimously" and "with (one's) consent or approval." This *bi assent (of) Ph* was formed from the OF *par assent (de)* whose use was mainly recorded in formal domains in French with the meaning "par les conseils, sous la direction de qqn; "par l'approbation, le vote de...." (ATILF). Consider some examples:

> *MED*: a) "By agreement, unanimously": (c1387-95) Chaucer *CT.Prol.*(Manly-Rickert) A.777: If yow liketh alle by oon assent For to stonden at my iuggement.
> *MED*: b) "With (one's) consent or approval": (1439) *RParl.* 5.6a: We, youre seide Communes, graunt to yow, oure Soverain Lord, bi the auctorite and assent aforeseide [etc.].

OF counterparts are:

> *ATILF*: a) *Par l'assens de qqn.* «Par les conseils, sous la direction de qqn» : ... consentez Que me donnez graces et sens De si ouvrer, par vostre assens, Que puisse vivre en chaasté (*Mir. enf. diable*, c.1339, 3).
> *ATILF*: b) *De/par l'assentiment de qqn.* «Avec l'accord, le consentement de qqn» : En celle année, le roy de France morut a Aucerre, et fut enterré en l'eglise Saint Colombe de Sens. Et de l'assentement des François, l'archevesque de Sens fut envoyé en Angleterre pour ramener Loÿs, le filz du roy, pour le mettre ou royalme son pere (*Renart contref.* R.L., t.1, 1328-1342, 271).
> *ATILF*: c) *De/par l'assentiment du peuple/de tous.* «Par l'approbation, le vote de...» : Et einsi de l'assentement de tous Numitor regna des lors an avant. (BERS., I, 1, c.1354-1359, 6.2, 10).
> *ATILF*: d) *Par l'assentiment commun.* «Avec l'approbation générale» : Or ça, Jouvencel, vous voyez que par le commun assentement de tous voz amiz et compaignons (...) estes esleu, par le bon sens et conduitte de nostre guerre qui est en vous, à estre nostre chief (BUEIL, I, 1461-1466, 117).

Bi avis (of)

This *bi-Ph* is categorised under the semantic type F-1 (Figurative meaning -> agency, mediation, means, motivation. See Chapter VI, Table 68). *Bi avis (of)* occurs 19 times in the corpus with the meaning "in accordance with his/her advice, in compliance with his/her orders, under his/her direction". As the word *avis* made its way into English c.1300, the first instances of *bi avis (of)* began to appear in ME3.

Its use was restricted to technical domains (DOCUMENTS, LAW, HANDBOOK/ MEDICINE AND [Paston] LETTERS) and confined to the dialectal areas of EMO (most of the instances) and SO. It is worth mentioning that only 5 texts out of the 91 of HCME include examples of *bi avis (of)* and 3 of them appear in CMLAW.

Bi avis (of) was taken from the OF *par avis (de)* whose usage was highly extended in colloquial and formal domains in OF with the meaning "selon le jugement, la recommandation"; "en vertu de l'opinion"; "avec prudence, avec sagesse" (ATILF). Consider some examples:

> *MED*: "In accordance with his/her advice, in compliance with his/her orders, under his/her direction". (a1393) Gower *CA* (Frf 3) 3.1804: Anon be his avis Ther was a

prive conseil nome. (1418) Grocer Lond.in Bk.Lond.E. 195/6: The same Ordynaunce turnyd in-to englysche be the Avyces of the Fraternite.
HCME: vppon this consideracion that it please you souerain lord by the aduyce and assent of your lordes spirituelx and temporelx assembled in your said parlement and by auctorite (of the same par)lement it was ordeyned that…(CMDOCU4).

OF includes similar patterns:

ATILF: a) *Par l'avis (d'une instance compétente).* «Selon le jugement, la recommandation» : Et par l'aviz et la doctrine D'aucun expert en Médicine, Et mesmement en ceste part Conseillent les Maistres de l'art Que les groz laboreurs des champs Facent saignie en cellui temps D'icelle vaine plainement (LA HAYE, *P. peste,* 1426, 116).
ATILF: b) *Par (bon) avis.* «Avec prudence, avec sagesse» : Sus, compaignons, il fault sortir : Chascun se mecte en ordonnance, Afin que sur luy on ce lance Et vous maintenez par advis. (*Myst. Pass. Troyes* B., a.1482, 698).

Bi comaundement (of)

This *bi-Ph* is classified as F-1 (Figurative meaning - > agency, mediation, means, motivation. See Chapter VI, Table 68). *Bi comaundement (of)* is found 18 times in the corpus. It was first used in ME3 with the general meaning of "on request, in response to an order or instructions" coinciding with the massive French borrowing in the course of the second half of the 14th century. It is worth noting, however, that this *bi-Ph* is only found in 7 texts of HCME, although it is recorded in different domains (DOCUMENTS, HISTORY, ROMANCE, LETTERS and REL TREAT) and in 4 dialects (EMO, SL, EML, WML).

The noun *comaundement* made its way into English c.1250 with the basic meaning of "an order from an authority" [OED]. *Bi comaundement (of)* is taken directly from OF *par commandement (de)* which was used with the meaning "sur l'ordre de" (ATILF). This sense is predominantly attested in HCME. Consider some examples:

MED: "An order from an authority".(1448)*Shillingford* 137: By the commowndment of the seide maier.
HCME: sum tyme Duke of Glouceter, uppon the Satyrday anon as he was a lyght of hys hors he was a-restyde of dyvers lordys for treson by commaundement of the kyng, and men sayde at that tyme. (CMGREGOR).

This collocational pattern is also found in OF:

ATILF: "Sur l'ordre de". Et fu ce jour generalement à Paris faicte abstinence de cher par le commandement de l'evesque de Paris ou ses vicaires. (FAUQ., I, 1417-1420, 180).

Bi vertu (of)

This *bi-Ph* is allocated to the category F-1 (Figurative meaning - > agency, mediation, means, motivation. See Chapter VI, Table 68). *Bi virtu (of)* is found on 17 occasions in the corpus with the meaning "by virtue or authority (of)" (MED). *Bi virtu (of)* is found for the first time in ME3 and was restricted to 9 texts out of the 91 texts included in HCME. All of them were written in prose and for formal domains (DOCUMENTS, PHILOSOPHY, REL TREAT, SERMON, ROMANCE and BIOGRAPHY). This *bi-Ph* appears in the dialectal areas of EMO, WML, SL and SO.

Vertu made its way into English c.1225 with the meaning "moral life and conduct, moral excellence". The phrase *by virtue (of)* was formed from the OF *par vertu (de)* whose use was recorded in OF with the meaning "par le pouvoir, par l'effet de"; "avec force, vigueur, vigoureusement"; "du fait de qqn, sous l'influence de qqn"; "efficacement" (ATILF). ME includes some of these senses, particularly "by the power of (sth.), as a consequence of, through"; "by the power or authority invested in (sb. or sth.)"; "efficacy". *Bi vertu (of)* is also used in in oaths and abjurations. Consider some examples:

> MED: a) "By the power of (sth.), as a consequence of, through": <u>a1425(?a1400) *Cloud* (Hrl 674)</u> 9/19: Bi vertewe of þis werk a man is gouernid ful wisely & maad ful seemly, as wel in body as in soule.
> MED: b) "By the [legal] power or authority invested in (sb. or sth.)": <u>(1331) *Statutes Realm*</u> 1.158: We ... by virtue of the said Commission, do ordain, [etc.].
> MED: c) "In oaths and abjurations": <u>c1330 *SMChron.*(Roy 12.C.12)</u> 569: He suor ... Bi the vertu of Marie sone Nevermore he nolde come ... In the bed ther hire lord lay.

OF includes equivalent frames:

> *ATILF*: a) «Par le pouvoir, par l'effet de»: Par vertu des quelles lettres, parce que nous sommez acertenez que le dit Jehan Bellon a esté jugié, condempné et miz à execucion de mort pour la traison qu'il avoit faicte à nostre dit seigneur du dit chastel (<u>*Doc. Poitou* G., t.4, 1370, 55</u>).
> *ATILF*: b) «Avec force, vigueur, vigoureusement» : Un de sez enfans prinst, plu n'i a atendu, Tout outre la riviere le porta par vertu. (<u>Vie st Eust. 1 P., c.1350-1400, 145</u>).
> *ATILF*: c) «Du fait de qqn, sous l'influence de qqn» : Einsi cil qui furent livré A la mort furent delivré Par la vertu nostre seigneur. (<u>MACH., *C. ami*, 1357, 24</u>).
> *ATILF*: d) «Efficacement» : ...ung legat par vertu Regarda en ses livres, car molt grant clerc il fu, Et dist que... (<u>*Flor. Octav.* L., t.2, c.1400, 493</u>).
> *ATILF*: e) "Par l'autorité de" : Par la vertu et auctorité Des princes, gualant, te commande, Et sur paine de grant esmende, Que vieignhes ceste croix porter. (<u>*Pass. Auv.*, 1477, 192</u>).

Bi lawe

This *bi-Ph* is assigned to the general category F-2 (Figurative meaning -> agency and mediation. See Chapter VI, Table 68). Within this semantic category *bi lawe* includes 14 tokens with the meaning "according to custom or law, lawfully" (MED). This *bi-Ph* appears for the first time in ME2 in HCME. Its use was used in a varied range of texts (REL TREAT, PREFACE, PHILOSOPHY, DOCUMENTS, LAW, SERMON, BIBLE) and in most dialectal areas (EMO, EML, KL, SL, NO).

Lawe, though of Scandinavian provenance, was increasingly used headed by *bi* from 1300 onwards, fostered by the OF counterpart, *par loi* with the meaning "conformément au droit, à la justice" (ATILF). Consider some examples:

> MED: "Of manner and accord" (general sense), more distinctively, "according to custom or law, lawfully". (c1390) Chaucer *CT.Pri.*(Manly-Rickert) B.1824: Wilde hors he dide hem drawe, And after that he heng hem by the lawe. a1400(a1325) Cursor (Vsp A.3) 13052: Þi broþer wijf, þat þou agh not to haf be lau.
> HCME: þat es, when we will noghte do to Godd Almyghten ne till Haly Kyrke, ne till oure euencristyn, þat vs awe for to do by dett and by lawe, bot anely haldes þat we hafe for ese of oure selfen (CMGAYTRY).

OF shows similar counterparts such as:

> ATILF: a) *Par loi.* «Conformément au droit, à la justice» : ...afin que l'en peust savoir quant par loy et par droit l'en povet faire aucune chose (BERS., I, 9, c.1354-1359, 46.5, 87).
> ATILF: b) *Par loi de.* «Selon les usages de» : ...moult grief sembloit aux communes qui acoustumé avoient à vivre par loi de ville, et estre subjects à leur seigneur par raison (CABARET D'ORV., *Chron. Loys de Bourb. C.,* 1429, 166).
> ATILF: c) *Par la loi de.* «En manière de» : Mais je sers a la char par la loy de pechié, quant je obeis plus a ma sensualité que a raison. (*Internele consol. P.,* 1447, 245).

Bi ensample of

This *bi-Ph* is classified as F-2 (Figurative meaning -> agency and mediation. See Chapter VI, Table 68). Within this semantic subclass *bi ensaumple* is found on 11 occasions with the meaning "to learn from, be warned by; to set a precedent, furnish a pattern of behavior or action" (MED). This *bi-Ph* is found for the first time in ME3 in HCME. It was used in a varied range of texts (REL TREAT, PREFACE, PHILOSOPHY, SERMON, FICTION AND HANDB/ASTR) and in 4 dialectal areas (EMO, EML, KL, SL).

Ensample appears in the late 14th century, and *bi ensample* is recorded in (a1382) *WBible(1)* (Dc 369(1) (MED) with the meaning "furnish a pattern of behavior or action", which comes directly from French *par essample* "fait que l'on cite à l'appui d'une assertion"; *faire qqc.* (une punition) *en exemple*; "personne ou comportement qui peut être proposé comme modèle à imiter" (ATILF). Consider some examples:

> MED: a) "To learn from, be warned by": (a1398) * Trev. *Barth.*(Add 27944) 17a/a: Þe liknes of god..Hy fongiþ by ʒifte and ʒeueþ forþ by example.
> MED: b) "To set a precedent, furnish a pattern of behavior or action": (a1382) *WBible(1)* (Dc 369(1)) *Esth.1.18:* Bi this exsaumple alle the wiues..shuln dispise the hestis of ther husbondis.

OF counterparts are:

> *ATILF*: a) "Fait que l'on cite à l'appui d'une assertion" : Par ceste usurpacion, laquelle le Pape fait en la temporalité, nous veons cités destruire, et païs perir, et le povre pueple a gleve mourir, conme nous en avons prest exemple en la cité de Cesaine, en Ytalie, en laquelle tout le pueple, par la guerre de Nostre Saint Pere, a esté destruit et mis a mort. *(Songe verg. S., t.1, 1378, 212).*
> *ATILF*: b) «Ce qui peut servir de leçon ou d'avertissement» : Exemple de Moyse qui fut repris par Jetro. (GERS., P. Paul, a.1394, 490).
> *ATILF*: c) "Modèle, type": faire tailler et mectre en forme de patrons et monstres de monnoie, les exemples de florins d'or et de monnoie d'argent (*Comptes Lille* L., t.1, 1439-1440, 370).
> *ATILF*: d) *Faire qqc.* (une punition) *en exemple.* «Le faire pour l'exemple» : ...fut ataché nud à ung pal et fut sagité en son visage et, après qu'il fut mort, fut mis sur une roe en exemple (SIMON DE PHARES, *Astrol.*, c.1494-1498, f° 115 r°).
> *ATILF*: e) "Personne ou comportement qui peut être proposé comme modèle à imiter»:
> Et que ire soit plus naturele il appert par example d'un homme qui fu repris de ce que il avoit feru son pere, et il respondi que aussi son pere avoit feru le sien pere et icelui aussi le sien en retournant dessus. (ORESME, *E.A.*, c.1370, 384).

Bi force (of)

This *bi-Ph* is allocated to the general category F-2 (Figurative meaning -> agency and mediation. See Chapter VI, Table 68). Within this semantic category *bi force (of)* is represented in the corpus with 10 tokens with the general meaning of "agency, mediation, means, motivation" and more precisely "by virtue or authority (of)". This *bi-Ph* began to appear in ME3. It has only been used in prose, although in many different domains (ROMANCE, DOCUMENTS, LAW, LETTERS and PHILOSOPHY). This *bi-Ph* does not have an extensive dialectal distribution, as it appears only in EMO, WML, and EML and is restricted to 6 texts.

Force is found in English c1300, from O.F. *force*, with the meaning "body of armed men, army". The *bi force (of) Ph* meaning "by virtue or authority (of)" was taken from the OF *par force (de)* (ATILF). Consider some examples:

> *MED*: a) "By sheer force, in a violent manner, violently": c1330 *7 Sages(1)* (Auch) 474: Par force [vr. strengthe] he dhadde [read: hadde] me forht inome. (c1375) Chaucer *CT.Mk.* (Manly-Rickert) B.3561: She that helmed was in starke stoures And wan by force townes strong and toures.
> *MED*: b) "By the efficacy, effect, power, or virtue (of a thing)": (c1390) Chaucer *CT.Mcp.*(Manly-Rickert) H.228: The tiraunt is of gretter myght, By force of meynee for to sleen doun right.
> *MED*: c) "Of necessity": (c1390) Chaucer *CT.Ph.*(Manly-Rickert) C.205: This worthy knyght..Moste by force his deere doghter yeuen Vnto the iuge.
> *MED*: d) "By virtue or authority (of)": (1439) *RParl.* 5.5b: By force of the seid Graunte. (1442) *RParl.* 5.37b: And that the seid Collectours, by force of the same Certeficate, sursease of eny levy to make of eny suche Towne.

HCME: And thys good knyght, her brothir, mette with the knyght that helde hir to paramoure, and slew hym by force of hys hondis. (CMMALORY).

OF shows similar phrasemes, such as:

ATILF: a) *Par force* : ...Et se du contraire s'efforce, Oste li le cierge par force Hors de ses mains. (<u>Mir. femme, 1368, 228</u>).
ATILF: b) *Avoir* (une femme) *par force* : ...car sachiez de certain, pour en mourir ne pour en estre desheritee, je n'auray ja le roy d'Aussay a mary, non pas que il ne vaille mieulx que a moy n'appertiengne, mais pour tant qu'il me veult avoir par force. (<u>ARRAS, c.1392-1393, 148</u>).
ATILF: c) *Par force d'armes*. «Au moyen, par la puissance des armes» : ... Si se mist a pays conquerre, Par force d'armes (<u>CHR. PIZ., M.F., II, 1400-1403, 211</u>).
ATILF: d) *Par force*. «Par nécessité, forcément, nécessairement» : Vueillez jusques au pape aler Dire li qu'il me fault parler Par force a li. (<u>Mir. prev., 1352, 267</u>).
ATILF: e) *Par force de*. «Par l'effet de ; par le moyen de» : ..ceuls qui se acoustument a ces estudes ou desirs sont demy sauvages et (...) se conforment.et acoustument a monstres et choses estranges par force de leur meurs. (<u>FOUL., Policrat. B., I, 1372, 104</u>).

Bi order

This *bi-Ph* is categorised as F-2 (Figurative meaning -> agency and mediation. See Chapter VI, Table 68). Within this semantic category *bi order* is represented in the corpus with 10 tokens with the general meaning "in order, in sequence, in an orderly arrangement or manner". This *bi-Ph* began to appear in ME3. It has been mostly used in prose and in many different domains (HANDB/ASTR, PHILOSOPHY, SCIENCE/MED, LAW, FICTION and SERMON). The 9 instances found in HCME appear in 6 different texts and are confined to the dialectal areas of EMO and EML.

Order made its way into English c.1225, with the meaning "body of persons living under a religious discipline." The meaning "command, directive" is first recorded in 1548, from the sense "to keep in order". The meaning of this *bi-Ph*, "of manner and accord"; "one after another, in a row", "in order, in sequence, in an orderly arrangement or manner"; according to rank", was taken from the OF *par order*: "une chose après l'autre, en détail; "position, rang (qu'occupe une personne) dans une succession régulière" (ATILF). Consider some examples:

MED: a) "In order, in sequence, in an orderly arrangement or manner": <u>(a1382) WBible(1) (Bod 959)</u> 1 Esd.3.4: Þei maden þe solempnete of tabernaclis, as it is writen, & brent sacrifise alle daiys bi ordre [L per ordinem] after þe comaunded werk of þe dai. <u>(a1382) WBible(1) (Bod 959)</u> Gen.43.7: The man askide vs by ordre [L per ordinem] our progenye, ȝif þe fader lyuyde, ȝif we hadden a broþer.
MED: b) "According to rank": <u>c1425(a1420) Lydg. TB (Aug A.4)</u> 2.1004: Sessions wer made on euery syde Only þe statis by ordre to deuyde.

OF uses analogous collocations:

ATILF: a) *Par ordre*. «Une chose après l'autre, en détail» : ...Je cheï en moult grant pensée Et par ordre a recorder pris Tout ce qu'elle m'avoit apris De point en point, car bien pensoie Qu'encor grant mestier en aroie. (MACH., R. Fort., c.1341, 108).

ATILF: b) "Position, rang (qu'occupe une personne) dans une succession régulière» : Au jour d'ui, maistre Guillaume de Celsoy, conseiller du Roy nostre Sire en la Chambre des Enquestes, a protesté que la reception de maistre Pierre Buffiere en la Grant Chambre par vertu de certein mandement royal ne lui prejudicie point, attendu que par l'ordre il precedoit et devoit avant venir en la dicte Grant Chambre que ledit Buffiere. (BAYE, I, 1400-1410, 92).

We may conclude that the increase of *bi-Phs* in ME3 and ME4 was largely due to the influence of the OF counterpart *par*. Some of them were particularly recurrent, such as *bi auctorite, bi grace, bi reson, bi counseil*. The senses of all these *bi-Phs*, with the exception of *bi-christ*, are categorised as figurative with the meaning "agency, mediation, means, motivation" (F1 and F2). Only 4 out of the 14 *bi-Phs* included in Table 77 appear in ME2. The other ones occur in ME3 or ME4, coinciding with the massive French borrowing. The data exihibited in Table 77 show that there are significant differences in the use of these *bi-Phs* according to the dialectal area. Thus, the use of *bi-Phs* is very rare in the North in the two subperiods (ME3 and ME4) for which HCME shows data. It is also significant that the 14 *bi-Phs* shown in Table 77 appear in EMO, 10 out of the 14 occurring in EML, 8 in SL, 6 in WML, and 3 in SO. It is also important to show that these *bi-Phs* were mostly restricted to a few texts. Thus *bi-counseil*, which is the most extensively used, appears only in 14 texts out of the 91 of HCME. This confirms that these phrases were a matter of idiolect. With regard to text types, we may assert that there is no preference for a specific domain, as all text types are represented. It is worth noting, however, that these *bi-Phs* of French provenance were mostly confined to prose.

Table 77: Bi-collocational patterns

Bi-Noun complement	Occ	sense	ME Sub-period	Dialects	N° of HCME texs	Text types	Comp. type (+70%)
auctorite	63	F2	ME3, ME4 SL	EMO EML	4	LAW, LETTERS, REL TREAT, DOCUMENTS	Prose
grace	54	F1	ME2 ME3, ME4	EMO EML WML SO	13	LAW, LETTERS, REL TREAT, DOCUMENTS	Prose
reson	35	F1	ME2 ME3, ME4	EMO SL NL WML	13	ROMANCE, LAW, HISTORY, PHILOSOPHY, DRAMA, REL TREAT, FICTION	Prose
counseil	34	F2	ME2 ME3, ME4	EMO EML SL NL WML	14	ROMANCE, HISTORY, REL TREAT, FICTION, HOMILY, DRAMA	Prose
cause	22	F1	ME3, ME4	EMO, EML	9	SCIENCE ASTRONOMY, PHILOSOPHY, DOCUMENTS [Paston] LETTERS	Prose
assent	22	F1	ME3 ME4	EMO WML EML SL SO	9	HISTORY, LAW, DOCUMENTS, LETTERS and BIOGRAPHY	Only prose
advice	19	F1	ME3 ME4	EMO SO	5	DOCUMENTS HANDBOOK/MEDIC. LAW [Paston] LETTERS	Only prose
comandment	18	F1	ME3 ME4	EMO WML EML SL	7	DOCUMENTS HISTORY ROMANCE, LETTERS REL TREAT	Only prose
virtue	17	F1	ME3 ME4	EMO WML SL	9	PHILOSOPHY DOCUMENTS BIOGRAPHY, ROMANCE REL TREAT	Only prose

Table 77: Bi-collocational patterns (continuation)

Bi-Noun complement	Occ	sense	ME Sub-period	Dialects	N° of HCME texs	Text types	Comp. type (+70%)
law	14	F2	ME2 ME3, ME4	EMO EML SL KL NO	12	PHILOSOPHY DOCUMENTS, SERMON LAW REL TREAT PREFACE BIBLE	Only prose
christ	11	F5					
example	11	F2	ME3 ME4	EMO EML SL NL	9	REL TREAT, PREFACE, PHILOSOPHY HANDB/ASTR SERMON, FICTION	Prose HOMILY
force	10	F2	ME3 ME4	EMO EML WML	6	PHILOSOPHY DOCUMENTS LAW ROMANCE LETTERS	Only prose
order	10	F2	ME3 ME4	EMO EML	6	HANDB/ASTR PHILOSOPHY SCIENCE/MED LAW FICTION SERMON	prose

4.5. In-Phs

In-Phs were related to a spatial or temporal sense in OE and many of them still preserved these domains in ME. Thus, 3113 occurrences out of 9437 have a spatial connotation, and 456 a temporal one. However, throughout the ME period many *in-Phs* lost much of their referential meaning and by way of metaphorical extension developed into a figurative sense. From this latter sense, some *in-Phs* turned into *in*-collocations. Thus, some *in-Phs* maintain a spatial or temporal reference i.e. *in (þe) midde(l) of* as in *in the middel of this plate* (CMQUATO), *in mydde of the day* (CMASTRO). However, some other *in-Phs* acquired a quasi-idiomatic meaning, i. e. *in þe mene tyme* (CMBRUT3), *in the mene whyle* (CMGREGOR), *in þe ende* (CMGREGOR), *in the begynnyng* (CMINNOCE), *in sumer tide* (CMHANSYN), etc.

I intend to show that the transition from abstract domains to quasi-idiomatic roles of *in-Phs* was fostered by French phrasal influence. Phraseological units such as *in doubt, in vayn, in speciall, in generall, in despite*, were adopted from French counterparts. Consider: (i) *The whiche fourthe partie in speciall shal shewen a table of the verrey moeving of the mone* (CMASTRO); (ii) *in general his falsenesse were ayeinsaide* (CMDOCU3*)*; (iii) *þe wicked tempted my soule in vayn* (CMEARLPS).

What follows is a detailed account of French *en-Phs* which made their way into Middle English as *in-Phs*. I will confine to collocational patterns which include at least two instances in HCME:

In maner(e)

In maner(e) is allocated to the category F-2[7] (Figurative meaning -> manner: "in a form, shape or manner"). *In (the) maner(e)(of)* occurs 156 times in HCME with different meanings such as "in the nature, guise, or capacity of"; "in likeness of, after the fashion of"; "after the custom of; according to custom" (*MED*). *In no(ne)/ani manere* "in any way, by any means, at all" is highly recurrent in HCME. This *in-Ph* is found for the first time in ME2, although two texts (CMALISAU and CMEROBLO) of this subperiod include just a single instance each of them. *In (the) maner(e)(of)* was extensively used in ME3 and ME4, as 44 out of the 91 texts of HCME include this *in-Ph*. Its use appears in many dialectal areas (EMO, SO, EML, KL, WML and SL) and covers all domains (REL TREAT, HOMILY, DRAMA, HISTORY, LETTERS, HANDBOOK, etc.).

Maner(e) is found in English c.1175. *In (the) maner(e) (of)* was taken from OF *en la manere de* with similar sense as in English. Consider these examples:

> MED: a) *in (the) manere of* "in the nature, guise, or capacity of; in likeness of, after the fashion of". E.g. a1375 *WPal.*(KC 13) 821: Boþe þe þrusch & þe þrustele..Meleden ful merye in maner of here kinde.
> ATILF: *En la maniere de.* "De la même façon que" : Avecques ce fit tant qu'a l'ayde de maistre de l'artillerie Jehan de la Grange, le capitayne des Allemans et les dictz Allemans que l'artillerie fut tiree et menee par les dites Arpes et montaignes par le col des hommes en la maniere de chevaulx en montant icelle (LA VIGNE, *V.N.*, p.1495, 278).
> MED: b) *in no(ne)/ani manere* "in any way, by any means, at all". E.g. c1330(?c1300) *Spec.Guy* (Auch) 628: He þat wole him heinen here, þat nele be make in none manere, In litel while he shal..falle..swiþe lowe. a1375 *WPal.*(KC 13) 892: ȝif ich miȝt in ani maner þe amende, y wold.

---

[7] I have identified 1811 occurrences which denote a certain form, shape or manner. The instances for this section represent the high rate of 33.71% in relation to all figurative instances and 19.19% when compared with all *in-Phs* found in the corpus.

ATILF: En aucune maniere (avec nég.)/*nulle maniere*. "Aucunement, d'aucune façon" : Ce n'est pas chose droituriere ne raisonnable en nulle maniere de ensuivir les fortunes en jugeant de la felicité ou de la misere d'un homme. (ORESME, E.A., c.1370, 133).
MED: c) *in manere* "After the custom of; according to custom". E.g.(a1382) *WBible(1)* (Bod 959) 4 Kings 17.11: Þei brenden þere encense vp on þe auteris in maner of heþene.
ATILF: En/selon la maniere accoutumee. "Selon l'usage, comme d'habitude" : Si fu mis hors d'icelle question, mené choffer en la cuisine en la maniere acoustumée, et en après ramené en jugement sur les quarreaux. (*Reg. crim. Chât.*, I, 1389-1392, 233).

In part

In part is allocated to the category F-2 (Figurative meaning -> manner: "in a form, shape or manner; in the presence, sight, or hearing of somebody"). *In part* occurs 55 times in HCME with the basic meaning of "in part, partially" (*MED*). This *in-Ph* is found for the first time in ME2. It is highly representative, as 16 out of the 91 texts of th HCME include this *in-Ph*. Its use appears in many dialectal areas (EMO, SO, EML, KL, WML and SL) and covers all domains (REL TREAT, HOMILY, DRAMA, HISTORY, DOCUMENTS, LETTERS, HANDBOOK, etc.).
Part is found in English c.1000. *In part* was taken from OF *en parte* with similar sense as in English. Consider these examples:

MED:a)*inpart*"inpart,partially".E.g. c1300*SLeg.Lucy*(LdMisc108) 68: Woldestþou gon þare-Inne, In part, riche man þou were i-nouȝ.
MED: b) *in ani part* "in any part or respect, at all". E.g. (1463-4) *RParl.* 5.505a: Noo woman Wydowe but such as have possessions of the seid yerely value of xl li..were.. eny Girdell harneysed with gold or with silver in eny part therof overgilt.
ATILF: Aucune part. «À un endroit indéterminé» : Se aucune part en cest escript et libelle j'ay erré ou failli, il me soit pardonné, car ce a esté par ignorance. (*Somme abr.*, c.1477-1481, 99).
MED: c) *in everi part* "in every part or piece; in every respect, completely". E.g. a1425(?a1400) *RRose* (Htrn 409) 2245: For pride is founde in every part Contrarie [F tout le contraire] unto loves art.
ATILF: Toute part. «Partout» : Et qui veulent long chemin faire Par air puant, trouble et contraire, Doivent garder soigneusement De l'inspirer abondamment, Et porter o soy toute part Des pommes, confites par art, De bonne oudeur et sentement. (*LA HAYE, P. peste*, 1426, 140).
MED: d) *in gret part* "to a great extent". E.g. (1426) *Paston* 1.6: Þe processe, in gret part ther-of, is fal[se].
MED: e) *in som part* "to some extent, somewhat". E.g.(a1393) *Gower CA* (Frf 3) prol.64: Yit woll I fonde To wryte and do my bisinesse, That in som part..The wyse man mai ben avised.
ATILF: En quelque part : ...puis qu'il se trouvoit en quelque part a descouvert avecques quelque belle fille, il luy monstroit qu'il estoit homme. (*C.N.N.*, c.1456-1467, 303). Prenés loysir Pour y aler, - et le varrons en quelque part. (*Pass. Auv.*, 1477, 188).
MED: f) *in no part* "in no way, not at all". E.g. c1425(a1420) Lydg. *TB* (Aug A.4) 5.2051: Fro þens forþe to seile I gan, Dreven with wynde, & no part socoured.

ATILF: *Ne ...en aucune part.* «En aucun lieu» : SAINCT MARTIN. Je ne puis maintenant courir Në aller en aulcune part. Pour ce d'y vouloir recourir, Vous voyez qu'il est ja trop tart. (LA VIGNE, *S.M.*, 1496, 411).

In (e)special

In (e)special is also categorised in this study as F-2 (Figurative meaning -> manner: "in a form, shape or manner"). *In (e)special* is attested in HCME with 30 tokens, with a varied range of meanings such as "with reference to a particular instance, purpose, or act"; "with particularity or detail; in detail"; "to an unusual or exceptional degree; more than others, most of all; chiefly, especially" (*MED*). This *in-Ph* first appeared in ME2 and was used in 18 texts out of the 91 of HCME. This phraseme is represented in all dialects and is used in all text types.

(E)Special is detected in English from the early 13th century with the meaning of "better than ordinary," *In (e)special* was taken from OF *en especial* with identical senses. Consider these examples:

> *MED*: a) "With reference to a particular instance, purpose, or act". E.g. (c1390) Chaucer *CT.Mel.*(Manly-Rickert) B.2423: Ye han..taught me as in general how I shal gouerne me..But now wolde I fayn that ye wolde condescenden in especial, and telle me [etc.].
> *ATILF:* ...par ledit mons. le prevost, fu dist qu'il deist verité des larrecins et murdres par lui fais, et en especial d'un certain murdre commis et perpetré le mercredi IIIJe jour de novembre (*Reg. crim. Chât.*, I, 1389-1392, 154).
> *MED*: b) "With particularity or detail; in detail". E.g. a1500(a1450) *Gener.(2)* (Trin-C O.5.2) 1081: Right as the writeng seyth in especiall.
> *ATILF:* ...si comme en une cité ou l'en sacrifice a Braside en especial. (ORESME, *E.A.*, c.1370, 304).
> *MED:* c) "To an unusual or exceptional degree; more than others, most of all; chiefly, especially". E.g. a1475(?1445) ?Lydg. *Cal.*(Rwl B.408) 30: Kepe us dayly from al maner of synne..in especyal from pryde.
> *ATILF*: .li fu demandé par ledit mons. le prevost et enjoint que elle deist verité des autres biens par elle prins ou coffre d'iceux mariez, et en especial d'une verge d'or petite, dont elle n'avoit rien confessé (*Reg. crim. Chât.*, I, 1389-1392, 197).

In pein

In pein is categorised under the type F-3[8] (Figurative meaning -> "expression of a certain state or condition"). *In pein* is found on 29 occasions in HCME with the meanings "subject to a punishment or fine" and "under the condition that one feels when hurt, opposite of pleasure" (*MED*). This *in-Ph* is already attested for the first time in ME2, and it is represented in 19 texts of HCME. It was widely used throughout England, as it appears in the following dialectal areas: SL, EMO, EML,

---

8 This sense is recurring in ME as HCME exibits 2776 instances. This number represents half of all figurative examples (51.67%) and 29.41% within the whole number of *in-Phs*. They regularly occur with a noun implying a state: faith, truth, haste, pain, doute, peace, will, hope.

NL and WMO. This *in-Ph* is also attested in most domains (REL TREAT, DRAMA, BIOGRAPHY, FICTION, DOCUMENTS, HISTORY, SERMON, ROMANCE, PHILOSOPHY).

Pein is found in English c.1300 with the meaning "punishment," "condition one feels when hurt, opposite of pleasure". *In pein* was taken from OF *en peine* with similar sense as in English. Consider these examples:

> *MED*: "subject to a punishment or fine". E.g. c1450(1410) Walton *Boeth*.(Lin-C 103) p.242: Than han þe wicked certanly..Somwhat of good, when þat þey ben in peyne [Chaucer *Bo*.: punyschid; L puniuntur].
> *ATILF*: *En peine de*. "Sous une astreinte de" : Mais il n'en diroit mot si les dictes parties ne se soubzmettoient, en peine de dix nobles, que de tenir ce qu'il en diroit [Un arbitre a trouvé une solution à un conflit] (*C.N.N.*, c.1456-1467, 393).

In grace

In grace is also categorised as F-3 (Figurative meaning -> "expression of a certain state or condition"). There are 28 instances of this *in-Ph* in HCME, with different meanings such as "in the good graces of (sb.)"; "mercy, pardon"; "to grant (sb.) pardon"; "cast (oneself) on (someone's) mercy". (*MED*). This *in-Ph* is already attested in ME1 and was used in 13 texts of HCME. Its use is extended to most dialectal areas (EMO, EML, KL, WML, WMO, SL, NL). It was recurrently used in religious domains (REL TREAT, SERMON and BIBLE), although it also occurs in DRAMA, HISTORY and LETTERS.

Grace is found in English in the late 12th century with the meaning "God's favor or help". *In grace* was taken from OF *en grace* with similar senses as in English. Consider these examples:

> *MED*: a) "In the good graces of (sb.)". E.g. (a1393) Gower *CA* (Frf 3) 7.878: He schal..stonde in mochel grace Toward the lordes..And gret profit and thonk deserve.
> *ATILF*: *Avoir qqn en grace*. "Favoriser" : ...il sembloit, tant les hot en grace Fortune, que (...) Fussent droiz signeurs du paÿs (CHR. PIZ., *M.F.*, IV, 1400-1403, 73).
> *MED*: b) "Mercy, pardon; to grant (sb.) pardon; cast (oneself) on (someone's) mercy". E.g. a1375 *WPal*.(KC 13) 531: I giue me holly in his grace, as gilty for þat ilk.
> *ATILF*: *Recevoir qqn en grace*. "Accorder son pardon à qqn" : Lequel, par le conseil des cardinaulx, prelas et aultres princes rommains, qui prisonniers estoient, ledit pappe Anaclet iie le recepust en grace et a mercy. (LA SALE, *Salade*, c.1442-1444, 169).

In form (of)

In form (of) is also categorised as F-2 (Figurative meaning -> manner: "in a form, shape or manner"). *In form (of)* is found 28 times in HCME with a varied range of meanings such as "the physical shape of something"; "the figure or shape (of a person), body"; "the correct or appropriate way of doing something: established process or procedure"; "customary or traditional usage"; "prescribed ritual or formal etiquette"; "in accordance with prescribed usage, properly, correctly; according to legal procedure" (*MED*). This *in-Ph* appeared in ME3 for the first time and was used in 10 out of the 91 texts of HCME. All occurrences appear only in EMO and EML areas. This phraseme is found in a varied range of text types (RULE, FICTION, LETTERS, PHILOSOPHY, REL TREAT, DOCUMENTS and HANDBOOK) but its use is particularly recurrent in official letters and documents with the meaning "in accordance with prescribed usage, properly, correctly; according to legal procedure".

Form is found in English from the early 13th century with the meaning of "form, mold, shape". *In form (of)* was copied from OF *en (la) forme (de)* with the same senses as in English. Consider these examples:

> *MED*: a) "The physical shape of something, contour, outline; the figure or shape (of a person), body" E.g. (c1410) York *MGame* (Vsp B.12) 18: Eiþer in plat fourmes, eyþer engleymed or pressed.
>
> *ATILF: En (la) forme de* + subst. "Sous l'apparence de" : Aussi li dieu les gens muoient En quelque forme qu'il voloient Et les deesses ensement, Car on vëoit appertement Les uns mués en forme d'arbre, Les autres en pierre de marbre. (MACH., *Voir*, 1364, 494).
>
> *MED*: b) "The correct or appropriate way of doing something: established process or procedure; customary or traditional usage; prescribed ritual; formal etiquette". E.g. c1400(?c1390) *Gawain* (Nero A.10) 1295: Gawan..Ferde lest he hade fayled in fourme of his castes.
>
> *ATILF: En forme*. «De façon explicite, formellement» : Car humilité les recors De ton cuer a Dieu si enforme Que j'essauce et soustien en forme Les priéres de ta parole. (*Mir. parr.*, 1356, 38).
>
> *MED*: c) "In accordance with prescribed usage, properly, correctly; according to legal procedure". E.g. c1325(c1300) *Glo.Chron.A* (Clg A.11) 9174: ȝif bissop oþer abbod in þis lond ded were..Þat me ne chose in riȝte fourme an oþer anon.
>
> *ATILF: En forme*. "Selon les règles" : Et ainsi, se nous concedons Qu'il soit Crist, mal y procedons Se nous ne venons par arroy Le prendre et faire nostre roy En fourme et vraye obeïssance. (GRÉBAN, *Pass. J.*, c.1450, 208).

In hast(e)

In hast(e) is also categorised under the type F-3 (Figurative meaning -> "expression of a certain state or condition"). *In hast(e)* is found 24 times in HCME with different meanings such as "speedily, quickly, in a hurry"; "in a short time, soon"; "presently"; "suddenly". (*MED*). This *in-Ph* is found for the first time in ME3 and was used in 10 texts of HCME. Its use is extended to most dialectal areas (SO, EML, KL, WML, WMO, SL, NL). It was used in a varied range of domains (REL TREAT, HOMILY, DRAMA, HISTORY and LETTERS).

Hast(e) is found in English c.1300 with the meaning "quickly, in a hurry". *In hast(e)* was taken from OF *en hast(e)* with a similar sense as in English. Consider these examples:

MED: a) *in haste* "speedily, quickly, in a hurry; in a short time, soon; presently; suddenly". E.g. c1350(a1333) Shoreham *Poems* (Add 17376) 60/1691: And 3yf hys make mone craueþ, Ine leyser oþer in haste, Lykynde, He mo3t hy3t do wyþ sorye mod.
ATILF: «Rapidement» ...c'est force que j'escheve en haste l'escript que j'ai encommancé (*C.N.N., c.1456-1467, 151*).
MED: b) *in al haste* "with all speed, at once; as soon as possible". E.g. (a1393) Gower *CA* (Frf 3) 2.1542: He cam forth in alle haste.
ATILF: *En (grande) haste.* «Rapidement» : Un jour advint qu'en son palais (...), Un message vint en grant haste, Qui disoit a tous : «On me haste, Parler m'estuet a la roÿne.» (MACH., *Voir*, 1364, 438).

In pes

In pes is categorised as F-3 (Figurative meaning -> "expression of a certain state or condition"). *In pes* is found on 24 occasions in HCME with the meaning "reconcile"; "be/dwell in peaceful relationship"(*MED*). This *in-Ph* is already attested for the first time in ME2, and it is represented in 15 texts of HCME. It was widely used throughout England, as it appears in the following dialectal areas: SL, EMO, KL, NL, EML and WMO. This *in-Ph* was also attested in most domains (REL TREAT, SERMON, HISTORY, FICTION, LETTERS, DOCUMENTS, ROMANCE, RULE and BIBLE).

Pes is found in English c.1140 with the meaning of "peace, tranquility, absence of war". *In pes* was taken from OF *en pais* with a similar sense as in English. Consider these examples:

MED: a) *setten in pes* "reconcile (two parties)". E.g. a1450(?c1421) Lydg. *ST* (Arun 119) 1083: The noble Citezeyns..Shope a way to mak hem of accord And to set hem in quyete and in pees.
ATILF: *Mettre paix entre des personnes* : Et il les .II. bestes partoit, Entr' eulx loyale paix metoit, Puis leur donnoit a mariages ..II.. filles, qu'il avoit moult sages. (CHR. PIZ., *M.F.*, II, 1400-1403, 299).
MED: b) *be/duellen in pes* "be/dwell in peaceful relationship". E.g. c1330(?a1300) *Tristrem* (Auch) 61: He preyd hem as his frende To duelle wiþ him in pes.
ATILF: Estre/vivre en paix : ...tant demoura Remondin en la terre de Guerrande qu'il mist accord entre aucuns des Bretons qui estoient en discencion, et fist tant que ly pays fu tous en paix. (ARRAS, c.1392-1393, 76). Vivons en paix, exterminons discordá; Ieunes et vieulx, soyons tous d'ung accordá: La loy le veult, l'apostre le ramaine Licitement en l'espitre rommaine. (VILLON, *Poèmes variés* R.H., c.1456-1463, 63).

In cas

In cas is also categorised in this study as F-2 (Figurative meaning -> manner: "in a form, shape or manner"). *In cas* is attested in HCME with 18 tokens, with a varied range of meanings such as "it may be, perhaps" (*in cas*), "if it chance that, in the event that, if" (*in cas that/if*). (*MED*). This *in-Ph* appeared in ME2 and was used in 12 texts of HCME. These texts belong to all dialects except NO and

WML. Most text types include this phraseme: ROMANCE, FICTION, LETTERS, PHILOSOPHY, DOCUMENTS and HANDBOOK.

Cas is detected in English from the early 13th century with the meaning of "an event," or "a chance. *In cas* was copied from OF *en cas* with identical sense. Consider some examples:

> *MED*: a) "During the event (*in the cas*)" E.g. ?a1425 *Chauliac(1)* (NY 12) 44b/ b: Of þe cure [of þe pestilence], it was labored in preseruacioun byfore þe case or fallyng [L ante casum] & in cure in þe case [L in casu].
> *MED*: b) Die through misfortune or an accident, die miserably "(*die in cas*)". ?c1450 *St.Cuth.*(Eg 3309) 3212: It is teld in þis space How a man dyed in a case; he fell oute of a hy tre.
> *MED*: c) "It may be, perhaps (*in cas*)". E.g. (a1398) * Trev. *Barth.*(Add 27944) 38a/ a: Þe vertu of worchinge in case [L forte] worchiþ no þing perfitliche or at þe fulle.
> *MED*: d) "If it chance that, in the event that, if". (*in cas that, if*). E.g. (a1393) *Gower CA* (Frf 3) 4.1917: He schal noght the deth ascape In cas that he arryve at Troie.
> *MED*: e) "With the purpose of, in order to (*in cas to*)". E.g. c1540(?a1400) *Destr.Troy* (Htrn 388) 532: Hit sittes..to a sure knyghte Þat ayres into vnkoth lond auntres to seche, To be counseld in case to comfford hym-seluyn.
> *MED*: f) "For example (*in a cas*)". E.g.c1475(c1445) Pecock *Donet* (Bod 916) 170/9: Riȝt as, in a caas, a white stoon and a white stok ben euen lijk white bodies.
> *MED*: g) "To be subject to (a law) (*ben in the cas of*)". E.g. (1414) *RParl.* 4.58a: To the which Statut we fre tenauntz of the Coroune owe not to obeye, for we be not in the cas of the Statut, and ne oughte not to answere lyk as bondemen of byrthe shulde, for the whiche the forseide Statut was made.
> *MED*: h) "To be in a legal position to (demand sth.) (*ben in the cas to*)". E.g. (1461) *Paston* 4.20: Sche is in the cas to have the lyf in stede of damages.
> *MED*: i) "To be brought into court (*comen in cas*)". E.g. a1450 *Castle Persev.*(Folg V.a.354) 3324: Ne had mans synne neuere cum in cas, I, Mercy, schuld neuere in erthe had plas.
> *MED*: j) "In this (that) situation, under these (those) circumstances, in this (that) instance (*as in this (that) cas, in this (that) cas*)". E.g.(1340) *Ayenb.*(Arun 57) 46/12: Ine þet cas, he ssolde hit yelde to him þet hit heþ ylore.
> *MED*: k) "Under no circumstances, not at all (*in no cas, in no maner cas*)". E.g. c1390(?c1350) *SVrn.Leg.*(Vrn) 88/1561: He nolde not in no cas Biholde a wommon in þe fas.
> *MED*: l) "In any way, at all (*in ani cas*)". E.g.c1450(?a1400) *Wars Alex.*(Ashm 44) 1362: Þis kyng..castis in his mynd How he miȝt couir in any cas to come to þe cite.

Consider similar uses in OF:

> *ATILF*: *En cas de* «Si la situation l'exige»..mais tant nettement l'avoit alors despendu [le trésor] en cas de toute necessité qu'il ne lui estoit demouré que la bourse platte et esvuydee (*Percef. IV*, R., c.1450 [c.1340], 821).
> *ATILF*: *En cas de qqc.* «En fait de qqc., en ce qui concerne qqc.»: ...lesquelles joustes, en cas de pompes et de riche arroiement en armes, estoient outrepasses (CHASTELL., *Chron.* K., t.3, c.1456-1471, 309).

ATILF: En cas de qqc. "Dans telle situation ou état existant ou pouvant exister, dans la réalité ou dans l'éventualité de telle chose" : Mais briefment, je di que nulle ignorance de ce que l'en est tenu a savoir ne excuse et chascun doit savoir que il doit traire et que il doit faire et que il doit eschiver et en cas de doubte il s'en doit enformer. (ORESME, E.A.C., c.1370, 180).
ATILF: En ce cas/en tel(s) cas. «Dans de telles circonstances» : ...les corps les pevent soustenir ; il fault aucune foiz faire evacuacion jusques a deffeccion, en ce cas on doit tousjours regarder se la vertu est forte pour soustenir. (SAINT-GILLE, A.Y., 1362-1365, 57).
ATILF: «Cause qui doit être jugée» : ...il avoient esté à monsr le Chancellier, auquel ont requiz qu'il leur seellast l'adjornement en cas d'appel fait des gens de la Chambre des Comptes (BAYE, I, 1400-1410, 20).
ATILF: [Dans une propos. affirm.] *En aucun cas.* «En certaines circonstances» : Et semblablement appartiennent a magnificence toutes grans choses qui sont faites pour la chose publique et pour le bien commun, si comme il convient en aucun lieu et en aucun cas largement despendre et donner, comme seroit au prince des galees ou du navire pour son ost, ou faire un convit et donner a disner a toute la cité. (ORESME, E.A., c.1370, 244).

In batail(l)e

In batail(l)e is included under the category F-1[9] (Figurative meaning -> in the course of an action: "in an action or in a course of action, engaged in something, during an action or process"). *In batail(l)e* is attested in HCME with 15 tokens with the meaning "in combat; in fighting". (*MED*). This *in-Ph* appeared in ME2 and is represented in 11 texts of HCME. The use of this phraseme was extended to all dialects and text types.

Batail(l)e is found in English from the late 13th century with the meaning of "battle, single combat," also "inner turmoil, harsh circumstances; army, body of soldiers." *In batail(l)e* with the sense of "in combat; in fighting" was taken literally from OF *en bataille* with the meaning of "en ordre de bataille". Consider some examples:

MED: "In combat; in fighting". E.g. c1300 *SLeg.Cross* (LdMisc 108) 336: In weorre and batoylle he was so muche þat þare-of nas no fin.
ATILF: Se mettre en bataille. "Se ranger en ordre de bataille" : Ils abillierent leurs chevaus, Et issirent de leurs vaissiaus Bien et bel et arreement, Sans avoir nul empeechement ; Puis se meïrent en bataille ; Chascuns l'espée qui bien taille Tenoit en sa main toute nue. (MACH., P. Alex., p.1369, 77).

In presence (of)

In presence (of) is assigned to the F-2 category (Figurative meaning -> manner: "in a form, shape or manner; in the presence, sight, or hearing of somebody"). *In presence (of)* appears 13 times in HCME with the meaning "in the presence of (sb.

---

9 In the survey of HCME I have found 609 examples of *in-Phs* under this category indicating that sb. or sth. is engaged in an action. They are basically used with prepositional complements

or sth.), before (sb. or sth.)"; "in attendance, present" (*MED*). This *in-Ph* is attested for the first time in ME3, and it is represented in only 6 texts of HCME. It is attested in 3 dialectal areas: EMO, EML and WMO. This *in-Ph* covers 5 domains (REL TREAT, PHILOSOPHY, DRAMA, LETTERS, DOCUMENTS and ROMANCE).

Presence is found in English in the early 14th century, meaning "the fact of being present." *In presence (of)* was taken from OF *en presence (de)* with a similar sense as in English. Consider these examples:

> *MED*: a) *in presence* "in attendance, present". E.g. (a1393) Gower *CA* (Frf 3) 7.2065: Ther was a worthi povere kniht, Which cam..forto sein His cause..Wher Julius was in presence.
> *ATILF*: *En presence.* "publiquement" : ...en presence et en destour, Soit loing soit prés amis sera Qui parfaitement amera. (MACH., *Voir*, 1364, 652).
> *MED*: b) *in presence of* "in the presence of (sb. or sth.), before (sb. or sth.)"
> c1425(a1420) Lydg. *TB* (Aug A.4) 1.3369: No venym may lasten nor endure In þe presence of þis rich stoon.
> *ATILF*: *En (la) presence de qqn.* «Qqn étant présent, devant qqn» : Car einsi com la fueille en tramble Contre le vent fremist et tramble, Leur trambloit li corps et les james En la presence de leurs dames, Voire, dès li piet jusqu'en chief, Tant avoient il de meschief (MACH., *D. Lyon*, 1342, 196).

In substaunce

In substaunce is included in this study under the type F-3 (Figurative meaning -> "expression of a certain state or condition"). *In substaunce* appears on 12 occasions in HCME in 6 texts with the meaning "in the main, generally". The first instance is found in CMBBOETH in ME3. HCME texts in which this *in-Ph* appears belong to EMO, EML and SL dialectal areas, and cover the following domains: REL TREAT, PHILOSOPHY, DOCUMENTS, HISTORY and DRAMA.

Substaunce is found in English c.1300 with the meaning "essential nature." *In substaunce* was taken from OF *en substance* meaning "en résumé, pour donner l'idée essentielle, pour s'en tenir à l'essentiel". Consider these examples:

> *MED*: "in the main, generally". E.g. c1425(a1420) Lydg. *TB* (Aug A.4) 1.976: Of þe charge þat he on hym leyde..Þis was þe somme pleinly, in substaunce.
> *ATILF*: *En substance.* «En résumé, pour donner l'idée essentielle, pour s'en tenir à l'essentiel» : Parler briefment, en substance et en bien... (DESCH., *Oeuvres* R., t.7, c.1370-1407, 208).

In honour

In honour is also included in the category F-5[10] (Figurative meaning -> "benefit: on behalf of"). *In honour* appears on 9 occasions in HCME with the meaning of

---

implying an action: battle, war, quarrel, fight, works. The examples found under the category F-1 represent a rate of 11.33% in relation to all figurative instances and 6.45% when compared with all *in-Phs* found in HCME.

10 I have found 129 *in-Phs* with the sense "for the benefit of sb., on behalf of sb., for the service of sb, etc. These phrases represent a ratio of 2.40% with regard to all figurative *in-Phs* and 1.36% taking into account all *in-Phs* in the corpus.

"revered, worshipped"; "in honor of (sb. or sth.), out of respect for (sb. or sth.)" (*MED*). This *in-Ph* is already attested for the first time in ME2, although it was restricted to 6 texts of HCME. The dialectal areas in which it appears are: SO, EML, EMO and NL). FICTION, LETTERS, DOCUMENTS and BIBLE are the domains in which this *inPh* is recorded.

Honour is found in English c.1200 with the meaning "glory, honor, dignity, reputation," *In honour* was taken from OF *en honour* with a similar sense as in English. Consider these examples:

> *MED*: *in honour (of)* "revered, worshipped; in honor of (sb. or sth.), out of respect for (sb. or sth.)". E.g. c1300 *SLeg.*(LdMisc 108) 419/40: Þat ech man..In þe honour of alle haluwene made þane day feste.
> *ATILF: En l'honneur de.* «À la gloire de» : Je vous ay voué, fleur de lis, Que jamais de ma char delis Ne sera en vostre honneur fais [«À votre gloire, jamais je ne m'abandonnerai aux plaisirs de la chair»]. (*Mir. enf. diable*, c.1339, 3).

In doute

This *in-Ph* is included in our study in the general category F-3 (Figurative meaning -> "expression of a certain state or condition"). Within this semantic category *in doute* is represented in the corpus with only 8 tokens with the meaning "a feeling of uncertainty, doubt, or perplexity" or "a cause or reason for fear; something to be feared" (*MED*). This *in-Ph* began to appear in ME3 coinciding with the massive French borrowing. However, its use is restricted to 6 texts in HCME: CMBENRUL (ME3), CMCAXPRO (ME4), CMCURSOR (ME3) and CMGOWER (ME3), CMLUDUS (ME4) and CMPRICK (ME3). *In doute* occurs in a varied range of domains: RULE, HISTORY, PREFACE, FICTION, DRAMA and REL TREAT. However, it was restricted to the dialectal areas of EMO, EML and NL.

Doute appears in English early 13th Century. The original Latin sense of "hesitation" developed to the new sense of "fear" in OF and from this language made its way into English. *In doute* was directly taken from the OF *en doute* whose usage was highly extended in all domains in OF with the meaning "être agité par l'inquiétude à cause de" and "craindre de" (ATILF). Consider some examples:

> *MED*: a) "A feeling of uncertainty, doubt, or perplexity". E.g. c1300 *SLeg.*(LdMisc 108) 376/9: For þis Mis-bileue men him cleopeden 'Thomas longue in doute'.
> *ATILF: Estre en (grant) doubte de.* "Être agité par l'inquiétude à cause de" : Et je te promet et te jur Que je te feray asseür De ce dont yes en si grant doubte. (MACH., *R. Fort.*, c.1341, 75).
> *MED*: b) "A cause or reason for fear; something to be feared". E.g. (c1395) Chaucer *CT.Mch.*(Manly-Rickert) E.1721: Neuere tromped..Theodamus yet half so cleere At Thebes, whan the citee was in doute.
> *ATILF: Estre en doubte de* + inf. "Craindre de" : Si deving merancolieus, Tristes, pensis et plain d'anoi, S'au pis assez c'onques mais n'oi ; Quar vraiement j'estoie en doubte De perdre m'esperance toute. (MACH., *Voir*, 1364, 86).

HCME: What we schal haue aftir þis lif it is in doute, saue we hope veryly (CMCAPSER).

In merci

In merci is categorised as F-3 (Figurative meaning -> "expression of a certain state or condition"). *In merci* appears on 8 occasions in HCME with the meaning "in the (your, his, her..) power (mercy)" (*MED*). This *in-Ph* is already attested for the first time in ME2, although it is confined to 5 texts of HCME. The dialectal areas in which it appears are only SL, EMO and EML. This *in-Ph* is mostly attested in religious domains (REL TREAT, SERMON, HISTORY and and BIBLE), and usually in the context of "in God's reward, gift, kindness; power/mercy".

Merci is found in English in the late 12th century with the meaning of "reward, gift, kindness; power". *In merci* was a copy from OF *en la merci de* with a similar sense as in English. Consider these examples:

> *MED*: a) *in the/thi/his merci* "in the (your, his, her..) reward, kindness, power (mercy)". E.g. a1375 *WPal.*(KC 13) 665: I am Meliors, neiȝh marred, man for þi sake; I meke me in þi merci, for þow me miȝt saue.
> *ATILF*: *(Estre) en la merci de qqn.* «Être au pouvoir de qqn, voir son sort dépendre de qqn» : Se vous n'avés pité de ces honmes qui sont en vostre merchi, toutes aultres gens diront que ce sera grans cruaultés, se vous faites morir ces honestes bourgois qui de lor propre volenté se sont mis en vostre ordenance pour les aultres sauver. (FROISS., *Chron.* D., p.1400, 847).
> *MED*: b) *don (putten, stonden) in merci* "put/be (oneself) at (someone's) mercy". E.g. c1400(?a1300) *KAlex.*(LdMisc 622) 1834: He sent a lettre..To Alisaunder and gretyng, Þat he shulde come as amy, And don hym in his mercy, And amende his trespas.
> *ATILF: Se mettre en la merci de qqn.* "Se livrer à qqn (parfois pour éviter le pire)" : Car vos gens tellement menez Par combatre ont voz annemis Qu'en vostre merci se sont mis Com prisonnier. (*Mir. Amis,* c.1365, 12).

In vein

In vein is assigned to the type F-2 (Figurative meaning -> manner: "in a form, shape or manner"). *In vein* appears on 7 occasions in HCME in 5 texts with the meaning "worthless, useless, without value; meaningless, insignificant". The first instance is found in CMEARLPS in ME2. This *in*-Ph has been extensively accepted as it was used in various dialectal areas: EMO, EML, SL and NL covering different domains: REL TREAT, BIBLE, RULE and DRAMA.

Vein is found in English c.1300 with the meaning "devoid of real value, idle, unprofitable". *In vein* was taken from OF *en vein* meaning "sans résultat, sans nécessité, inutilement" (ATILF). Consider these examples:

1) Used adjectivally:

> *MED*: a) "worthless, useless, without value; meaningless, insignificant." E.g. (c1380) Chaucer *CT.SN.*(Manly-Rickert) G.285: Alle ydoles nys but a thyng in veyn, For they been dombe and ... deue.

ATILF: *En vain.* «Sans résultat, inutilement» : DOYEN. Sans le temps en vain dispencer, Selon noz droiz et estatus, Chantre, veillez tost commancer (LA VIGNE, S.M., 1496, 394).
MED: b) "futile, ineffectual; to no purpose, fruitless, pointless; maken in vein, to break (a covenant, commandment)." E.g. (a1382) *WBible(1)* (Bod 959) Judg.2.1: Y haue ... byhoote þat y sholde not make in veyn [*WB(2)*: make void] my couenaunt wiþ Zow.
ATILF: Loc. adv. *En vain.* "Sans effet, inutilement" : ...car Joachim et saincte Anne brehaings estoyent et steriles, et pour neant et en vain ceste(s) chose(s) ilz demandoyent. (GERS., *Concept.*, 1401, 395).

2) Used adverbially:

MED: a) "meaninglessly, pointlessly; frivolously, idly; *oppress in vein*, to force (sb.) to work without reward; *serve in vein*, work (for sb.) without pay; *stonden in vein*, be of no use (to sb.)". E.g. (a1382) *WBible(1)* (Bod 959) Gen.29.15: Wheþer, for þou ert my broþer, in vayn [*WB(2)*: frely; L gratis] þou schall serue to me? Sey what of mede þou schalt take.
ATILF: *En vain.* "Sans nécessité, inutilement" : Amours, je t'ay donné le bail De moy, et encor le te bail. Mais bien voy qu'en vein me travail, Qu'adès te truis Preste pour moy faire travail. (MACH., *Compl.*, 1340-1377, 244).
MED: b) "groundlessly, without cause; falsely, deceptively; also, foolishly; *taken (mistaken) in vein*, to appropriate (a name) improperly". E.g. (a1398) Trev. *Barth.*(Add 27944:Seymour) 745/21: More freliche þey ben þere yclepide Agereni þan Sareceni, þogh þei mystake þe name of Sarra in vayne.
ATILF: Loc. adv. *En vain.* "Sans nécessité, inutilement" : Amours, je t'ay donné le bail De moy, et encor le te bail. Mais bien voy qu'en vein me travail, Qu'adès te truis Preste pour moy faire travail. (MACH., *Compl.*, 1340-1377, 244).
MED: c) "*taken in vein*, to invoke (God's name) falsely, profanely, or frivolously". E.g. (a1382) *WBible(1)* (Bod 959) Ex.20.7: Þou schalt not take þe name of þe lord þi god in vayn [L in vanum].
ATILF: Loc. adv. *En vain.* «Sans nécessité, pour des motifs futiles» : Tu ne jureras point le nom de Dieu en vain. (LA SALE, *J.S.*, 1456, 37).

In armes

In armes is included in this study in the category F-1 (Figurative meaning -> in the course of an action: "in an action or in a course of action, engaged in something, during an action or process"). *In armes* is attested in HCME with only 6 tokens with the meaning "armed" or "in battle". (*MED*). This *in-Ph* appeared in ME2, although it is confined to 3 texts in HCME: CMTRUSH (ME2), CMHORN (ME2) and CMALISAU (ME2). These texts were written in the SL and EMO areas and assigned to the domains of FICTION and ROMANCE.
Armes is found in English from the late 11[h] century with the meaning of "armed" or "in battle". *In armes* was literally taken from OF *en armes* with the meaning "en armes" ("armed; in battle") (ATILF). Consider some examples:

MED: a) "Armed". E.g. (c1385) Chaucer *CT.Kn.*(Manly-Rickert) A.874: Al his hoost in armes hym bisyde.
ATILF: *En armes* : L'EMPEREUR. (...) hastez vous Tant que pourrez. LE CONTE. En armes prest me trouverez Au revenir. (*Mir. fille roy*, c.1379, 70).
MED: b) "In battle". E.g. a1425(c1385) Chaucer *TC* (Benson-Robinson) 5.1718: Myn owen deth in armes wol I seche.
ATILF: *En armes* : Mais tant sont de foible marrien Qu'en armes il ne valent rien, Eins s'en fuient comme chevriaus. (MACH., *P. Alex.*, p.1369, 62).

In charge (of)

In charge (of) is included in the category F-2 (Figurative meaning -> manner: "in a form, shape or manner"). *In charge (of)* is found on 6 occasions in HCME with 3 different meanings: "under orders", "instruct, request" and "in (one's) power". This *in-Ph* appeared in ME3 and is limited to 5 texts of HCME (CMTVERS, CMDOCU3, CMDOCU4, CMMANKIN and CMREYNES). These texts were also restricted to the dialectal areas of EMO and EML. Text types vary from FICTION and DRAMA to DOCUMENTS and HANDBOOK.

Charge is found in English from the early 13th century, although the meaning of "responsibility, burden" is mid-14th century. *In charge (of)* was copied from OF *en charge (de)* with similar senses. Consider some examples:

MED: a) *Haven in charge* "be under orders". E.g. c1425(a1420) Lydg. *TB* (Aug A.4) 2.8033: An hundrid schipes..Gan proudly saille, as þei had in charge.
ATILF: Avoir en charge de + inf. : Or avoit en charge cestui conte de le mener de Louvain à Brusselles, où estoit la ducesse (CHASTELL., *Chron. K.*, t.3, c.1456-1471, 198).
MED: b) *Yeven in charge* "instruct, request". E. g. (c1390) Chaucer *CT.Sh.*(Manly-Rickert) B.1622: Keep bet thy good; this yeue I thee in charge.
ATILF: *Mettre qqc. en charge à qqn*. «Confier (un message à transmettre) à qqn» : Et moult doulcement luy dirons Ce que nous avez mys en charge (LA VIGNE, *S.M.*, 1496, 534).
MED: c) *Ben in charge* "be in (one's) power". E.g. (c1387-95) Chaucer *CT.Prol.*(Manly-Rickert) A.733: Who so shal telle a tale after a man, He moot reherce..Euerich a word, if it be in his charge.
ATILF: Avoir (une troupe) *en sa charge*:...ledit seigneur de Sempy à l'heure que devoit venir à guet, avoit en sa charge, hommes d'armes et archers tant du pays de Picardie comme de Hainau (CHASTELL., *Chron. K.*, t.3, c.1456-1471, 153).

In comparison

In comparison (of) is classified under the category F-2 (Figurative meaning -> manner: "in a form, shape or manner"). *In comparison (of)* is found on 6 occasions in HCME. This *in-Ph* appeared in ME3 and was restricted to 4 texts of HCME (CMMANDEV, CMROYAL, CMCLOUD, CMINNOCE). These texts were only found in the dialectal areas of EMO, SL and EML. Text types vary from TRAVELOG to SERMON and REL TREAT.

Comparison is found in English from mid-13th century with various meanings: "in comparison (with sth.)"; "as distinct (from sth.)"; "in like manner, similarly, likewise"; "in relation to (sth.)". *In comparison (of)* was copied from OF *en comparison (de)* with a similar sense. Consider some examples:

> *MED*: a) "as compared (with sth.), in comparison (with sth.), comparatively; in reference or respect (to sth.). E.g. (a1382) *WBible(1)* (Dc 369(1)) Wisd.7.8: And richesses I seide no thing to ben in comparisoun of it [wisdom].
> *MED*: b) "as distinct (from sth.); on the other hand". E.g. (a1398) * Trev. *Barth.*(Add 27944) 236b/a: A vellana is a feld note..in comparisoun to þe frensshe note.
> *MED*: c) "in like manner, similarly, likewise". E.g. (a1393) Gower *CA* (Frf 3) prol.916: For as the man hath passioun Of seknesse, in comparisoun So soffren othre creatures.
> *MED*: d) "in relation to (sth.)". E.g. (a1398) * Trev. *Barth.*(Add 27944) 68a/a: As..a pece of gold..is in comparisoun to þe money wiþ perfite coyne, so is al disposiciouns of oþir beestes in comparisoun to man.
> *ATILF*: *en comparaison*. «Comparer» : Et se nous voulons entrer en compareison, quelle chose peult estre plus divine en contemplation, plus juste a bien vivre, plus honneste en humanité, plus riglee en meurs, plus proufitable a chacun, plus paisible pour tous, plus garnie de bonne esperance et tendant a souverain guerdon, que sainte crestienté ? (CHART., *L. Esp.*, c.1429-1430, 127).

In absence

This *in-Ph* is incorporated in the F-3 category (Figurative meaning -> "expression of a certain state or condition"). Within this semantic category *in absence* is recorded in HCME only 5 times with the meaning "the state of being away from a place, absence" or the state of being "absent" (*MED*). This *in-Ph* appeared in ME3, although its few occurrences were restricted to 2 texts in HCME: CMOFFIC3 (ME3) and CMCLOUD (ME3). The dialect of both texts is EMO and the domains were LETTERS and REL TREAT, respectively.

Absence appears in English in the late 14th century with the meaning of "be away". *In absence* was a copy from the OF *en absence* with the meaning "en l'absence de qqn; sans la présence de, à défaut de" (ATILF). Consider some examples:

> *MED*: a) "The state of being away from a place, absence". E.g. (c1384) *WBible(1)* (Dc 369(2)) Phil.2.12: ʒe han obeischid not in my presence oonly, but moche more now in myn absence.
> *ATILF*: *En l'absence de qqn* : Ve les cy devant ta presence, Je n'ay riens dit en leur absence, Ils scevent bien ce que j'ay dit. (MARCADÉ, *Myst. Pass. Arras* R., a.1440, 143).
> *MED*: b) "Absent". E.g. a1425(c1385) Chaucer *TC* (Benson-Robinson) 3.1300: And if I do, present or in absence..lat sle me with the dede.
> *ATILF*: En l'absence de. «Sans la présence de, à défaut de» : Par formes abstraictes et separees de matere en l'absence du corps et par raison, c'est a dire par la vertu de l'ame raisonnable congnoist [l'âme] la nature des corps et des choses corporeles. (*Somme abr.*, c.1477-1481, 136).

In accord(aunce)

This *in-Ph* is categorised in the type F-3 (Figurative meaning -> "expression of a certain state or condition"). Within this semantic category *in accord(aunce)* is witnessed in HCME on only 5 occasions with the meaning "have the same attitude" or "be at peace" (*MED*). This *in-Ph* is already shown in ME3, although it was found only in 3 texts in HCME: CMEARLPS (ME2), CMGOWER (ME3) and CMCLOUD (ME3). These texts are located in the EMO and EML areas, being assigned to the domains of BIBLE, FICTION and REL TREAT, respectively.

Accord appears in English in the early 12th century, whereas *accordance* "agreeing" is found from 1300 onwards. *In accord(aunce)* was a borrowing from the OF *en acord(ance)* with the meaning "estre/mettre en accord" (ATILF). Consider some examples:

> *MED*: a) "Have the same attitude". E.g. (a1393) Gower *CA* (Frf 3) 1.2250: For al schal deie..Als wel a beggere as a lord, Towardes deth in on acord Thei schullen stonde.
> *ATILF*: *Estre en accord* : Grant merci, dame ; or sommes en acort. (MACH., *J. R. Beh.*, c.1340, 108).
> *MED*: b) "Be at peace". E.g. (a1393) Gower *CA* (Frf 3) 1.115: And tolden how thei weren glade Of that thei stoden in acord.
> *ATILF*: *Mettre en accord.* «Réconcilier» : Li roys leur [Pollinicés et Thideüs] prie que paix facent Pour s'amour, et de ce qu'ilz chacent, S'il peut, les metra en accort (CHR. PIZ., *M.F.*, II, 1400-1403, 300).

In aventure

In aventure is also categorised in this study as F-1 (Figurative meaning -> in the course of an action: "in an action or in a course of action, engaged in something, during an action or process"). *In aventure* is attested in HCME with only 5 tokens with the meaning "at adventure". (*MED*). This *in-Ph* appeared in ME2, although it was restricted to 3 texts in HCME: CMALISAU (ME2), CMMALORY (ME3) and CMTHORN (ME4). These texts were written in the NO, WML and EMO areas and their domains were ROMANCE and HANDBOOK.

Aventure is detected in English from the early 13th century with the meaning of "chance, fortune, luck". *In aventure* was plainly copied from OF *en aventure* with a similar sense. Consider some examples:

> *MED*: a) "At adventure". E.g. (a1393) Gower *CA* (Frf 3) 8.1118: And for he wolde unto hire winne Upon som cooste a Sepulture, Under hire heved, in aventure, Of gold he leide Sommes grete.
> *ATILF*: *Estre en aventure de* + inf. : Se tu t'armes, en aventure Seras d'estre a desconfiture (MACH., *C. ami*, 1357, 118). Lasse ! je sui en aventure De morir de mort einsi dure Com li biaus Narcisus mori (MACH., *Motés*, 1377, 496).
> *MED*: b) "To put (sth.) in jeopardy, to risk (oneself, one's life, one's goods)". E.g. c1380 *Firumb.(1)* (Ashm 33) 89: His body wold he putte in auntre.

ATILF: Estre en (grant) aventure. "Être en (grand) danger" : Mais mieus me vaut en aventure Estre en vos mains de pechié pure Que par pechié mon Dieu offendre (MACH., C. ami, 1357, 7).

In general

In general is also categorised as F-1 (Figurative meaning -> manner: "in a form, shape or manner"). *In general* is attested 5 times in HCME with different meanings such as "without exception, universally; in one body"; "as a rule, generally"; "not specifically, in general terms, in general" (*MED*). This *in-Ph* appeared in ME3 for the first time and was only used in 3 texts of HCME (CMECTROS, CMDOCU3 and CMMETHAM) which belong to the EMO and EML dialectal areas. This phraseme is found in the following text types: PHILOSOPHY, DOCUMENTS and HANDBOOK.

General is found in English c.1300 with the meaning of "relating to all, of a whole class". *In general* was taken from OF *en general* with senses matching the English ones. Consider these examples:

MED: a) "Without exception, universally; in one body." E.g. (c1390) Chaucer CT.ML.(Manly-Rickert) B.417: To the feste cristen folk hem dresse In general, ye bothe yonge and olde.

ATILF: En general. "D'une manière qui intéresse l'ensemble des cas ou des individus" : ...renommée estoit que tant en general, es faiz d'estude comme autrement, et es particuliers et singuliers suppostz ladicte Université se gouvernoit mal (BAYE, I, 1400-1410, 122).

MED: b) "As a rule, generally." E.g. ?c1425(c1390) Chaucer *Fort.*(Benson-Robinson) 56: Wikke appetyt comth ay before syknesse: In general, this reule may nat fayle.

ATILF: En general : Mais ne vueil pas mettre m'entente A rimer en especial Tout ce qu'il fist en general, Eins m'en passeray plus briefment. (MACH., C. ami, 1357, 49).

MED: c) "Not specifically, in general terms, in general." E.g. (c1385) Chaucer CT.Kn.(Manly-Rickert) A.2285: How she dide hir ryte I dar nat telle, But it be anythyng in general.

ATILF: En general. «En ne considérant que des cas, des caractères généraux ; en général» : Mais regardons en general Quans grans princes en fait rural Ont par leur sens leurs anemis Subjuguez et au dessoubz mis (CHR. PIZ., Chem. estude P., 1402-1403, 212).

In ordre

In ordre is allocated to the type F-3 (Figurative meaning -> "expression of a certain state or condition"). *In ordre* is found on 5 occasions and in 5 texts of HCME (CMBOETH, CMCLOUD, CMTVERS, CMROLLTR, CMWYCSER) with the meaning "in order, in sequence, in an orderly arrangement or manner". This *in-Ph* is attested for the first time in texts of ME3 which belong to the EMO and EML dialectal areas. PHILOSOPHY, SERMON, REL TREAT and FICTION are the domains in which it is found.

Ordre is found in English in the early 13th century with the meaning "body of persons living under a religious discipline." *In ordre* was taken from OF *en ordre* meaning "dans la succession convenable". Consider these examples:

> *MED*: "in order, in sequence, in an orderly arrangement or manner". E.g. (a1398) * Trev. *Barth.*(Add 27944) 141a/b: And suche foules..makeþ a kyng amongis hem and beþ obedient to hym and fleþ in ordre [L ordinate] & in aray.
> *ATILF: En ordre*. "Dans la succession convenable" : Icy prent Jhesus le pain et benist, et leur baille tout en ordre (GRÉBAN, *Pass. J.*, c.1450, 240). Item, aprés marcha l'artillerie en ordre requise (LA VIGNE, *V.N.*, p.1495, 282).

In comfort

In comfort is included under the category of F-3 (Figurative meaning -> "expression of a certain state or condition"). *In comfort* is only attested in two texts of HCME: CMJULNOR (3 occ.) and CMOFFIC4 (1 occ.) with the meaning of "For the benefit of"(*MED*). This *in-Ph* appeared in ME4 in EML and within the domains of REL TREAT and LETTERS.

Comfort appears in English in the early 13th century, replacing the OE *frofor* "comfort, strength." *In comfort* was taken from OF *en comfort* with a similar sense. Consider these examples:

> *MED*: "For the benefit of". E.g. c1400(?a1387) PPl.C (Hnt HM 137) 6.75: Lordene sones..For þe ryght of þis reame ryden a-ʒens oure enemys, In confort of þe comune and þe kynges worshep.
> *ATILF: En confort de qqc.* "Au renfort, au profit de qqc." : ...une somme de deniers (...) en confort de son dit voiage. (CHASTELL., *Chron. K.*, t.3, c.1456-1471, 13).

In pece(s)

In pece(s) is allocated in this study to the semantic type F-2 (Figurative meaning -> manner: "in a form, shape or manner"). *In pece(s)* only appears on 4 occasions in HCME, in three texts (CMECTPROS, CMREYNES ANS CMVICES4) with the meaning "into pieces". The first instance is found in ME3 (CMECTPROS). The three texts in which this *in-Ph* is found belong to the EML dialectal area and cover three different domains: REL TREAT, HANDBOOK, and PHILOSOPHY.

Pece(s) is found in English early in the 13th century with the meaning of "fixed amount, measure, portion". *In pece(s)* was taken from OF *en piece(s)* meaning "(*Rompre*) *en pieces* ". Consider these examples:

> *MED*: in pece "into pieces". E.g. (a1398) * Trev. *Barth.*(Add 27944) 220b/b: Þe flour..is best þat is..nought y-broke in gobettes and peces [L fragmenta].
> *ATILF: Rompre en pieces* : ...et rompi son glaive en pechies [var. piechies, pieces]. (HENRI FERR., *Modus et Ratio, Songe pest. T.*, c.1354-1377, 180).

In figure

This *in-Ph* is included under the category F-2 (Figurative meaning -> manner: "in a form, shape or manner; in the presence or sight of somebody"). Within this category *in figure* is recorded 3 times in a single text of HCME (CMFITZIA) with the meaning "in visible or tangible shape or form" (*MED*). This *in-Ph* appeared for the first time in ME4 in EMO.

Figure is found in English in the early 13th century with the meaning of "a shape, form, figure". *In figure* was taken from the OF *en figure* with the meaning "En forme de" (ATILF). Consider these examples:

> *MED*: "Visible or tangible shape or form; general appearance"
> (a1393) Gower *CA* (Frf 3) 4.2563: Bothe in substance and in figure, Of gold and selver the nature.
> *ATILF: En figure de*. "en forme de" : ...et voit Melusigne en la cuve, qui estoit jusques au nombril en figure de femme (ARRAS, c.1392-1393, 242).

In pacience

In pacience is included in this study under the type F-3 (Figurative meaning -> "expression of a certain state or condition"). *In pacience* only appears on 3 occasions in HCME in three other texts (CMBENRUL, CMHILTON and CMROLLTR) with the meaning "the calm endurance of misfortune, suffering". The first instance is found in CMBENRUL in ME3. The texts above mentioned belong to the NL and EMO dialectal areas and cover the religious domains of RULE and REL TREAT.

Pacience is found in English in the early 13th century with the meaning of "quality of being patient in suffering". *In pacience* was taken from OF *en pacience* meaning "avec patience, résignation". Consider these examples:

> MED: a) *in pacience* "The calm endurance of misfortune, suffering, etc.; steadfastness against temptation". E.g. a1325(c1280) *SLeg.Pass.*(Pep 2344) 426: In ʒoure pacience [vr. suffrance] ʒe shulleþ ʒoure soules wytie.
> *ATILF*: courtois et discrez, Et qu'il endure en pacience Tout ce qui iert a la plaisance De sa dame pour qui il vuet Auques valoir, se valoir puet. (MACH., D. verg., a.1340, 39).
> MED: b) *taken in pacience* "accept (sth.) with resignation"; E.g. (c1385) Chaucer *CT.Kn.*(Manly-Rickert) A.1084: For Goddes loue take al in pacience Oure prisoun, for it may noon oother be.
> *ATILF*: Loc. adv. *En pacience*. «Avec patience, résignation» : ...moult doucement li enorte Qu'il soit pleins de bon reconfort, Car il ara joie et confort, Mais qu'il soit loiaus et secrez, Dous, humbles.

In certain

In certain is incorporated under the general type of F-3 (Figurative meaning -> "expression of a certain state or condition"). *In certain* is attested in HCME in ME3 with only 3 occurrences with the meaning "be in certain" (*MED*). They are found in three different texts (CMBRUT3, CMDIGBY and CMGOWER) in the dialectal areas of EMO and WML. They also cover three domains: HISTORY, DRAMA and FICTION.

Certain made its way into English c.1300 with the meaning of "determined, fixed". The collocational phraseme, *in certain*, was a reproduction from the OF *en certain* whose meaning was also "C'est une certitude, assurément" (ATILF). Consider some examples:

> *MED*: "Be in certain". E.g. a1450 *Gener.(1)* (Mrg M 876) 7437: And as for hir, I am in certeyn That she wil not be therageyn.
> *ATILF: En certain*. "C'est une certitude, assurément" : Je saip bien qu'il est tempz paisséz certennement Que deusse estre allér querre en certain maintenant Cely qui fist jaidis de moy l'angenrement (*Lion Bourges* K.P.F., c.1350, 415).

In avauntage

In avauntage is incorporated in this study in the category F-1 (Figurative meaning -> in the course of an action: "in an action or in a course of action, engaged in something, during an action or process"). *In avauntage* is exhibited in HCME with only 2 tokens in CMROYAL with the meaning "dominant, privileged, or advantageous position". So it was restricted to the domain of SERMON in the dialectal area of SL.

Avauntage is found in English in the early 14th century with the meaning of "position of being in advance of another". *In avauntage* was literally taken from OF *en avantage* with the meaning "état de supériorité" (ATILF). Consider some examples:

> *MED*: "Dominant, privileged, or advantageous position; supremacy, superiority" or "Pecuniary profit, monetary gain." E. g. a1450 *Forest Laws* (Dc 335) 242: Also if the wardeyn..of the forest rewseth ony maisterfull bowes of the kinges okes or ony other tree in a vauntage for the sale rather than the sustenaunce of the kinges deere, ye shul do vs to wite.
> *ATILF: Estre en avantage*. "Être en état de supériorité" : Et quant le dit Mery vit qu'il fut en son avantaige, il tira une espée qu'il avoit et en donna au dit Jehan Girault ung cop sur la teste (*Doc. Poitou* G., t.8, 1446, 237).

In chef

In chef is also categorised in this study as F-4 (Figurative meaning -> "as something or in the form of something"). In this category I have included 47 instances of *in-Phs* which indicate that something appears as something or in the form of something, e.g. *in conclusioun, in ensaumple, in signe, in cause, in token, in witnesse*.

In chef is attested in HCME with only 2 tokens in CMDIGBY with the meaning "primarily, principally, chiefly, especially" (*MED*). This *in-Ph* appeared in ME4 in EMO and within the domain of DRAMA.

Chef is detected in English c.1300 with the meaning of "leader, ruler, head" (of something). *In chef* was literally copied from OF *en chef* with similar senses. Consider some examples:

> *MED*: a) *Holden in chef* (law) "to have a fief immediately from the Crown in return for specified services, be a vassal of the king". E.g. c1300 *SLeg.Becket* (LdMisc 108) 588: No man þat of þe kinge heolde ouȝt In chief oþur In seruise.
> *ATILF: En chef et en membre.* «Dans le fief pris en totalité et dans ses parties»: avec touz leurs biens, tant en chief comme en membres (PHIL. VI VALOIS, *Doc. paris.* V., t.2, 1342, 174).
> *MED*: b) "Primarily, principally, chiefly, especially". E.g. a1450(?c1421) Lydg. *ST* (Arun 119) 3715: He wol han the domynacioun First in chief to hym-silf reserued, As hym thouht he hadde wel disserued.
> *ATILF*: "En premier lieu, tout d'abord" : Qui sera cellui qui me puist mectre avant ung hault honneur rendu pour vertueux service ne une seule correction pour deliz infiniz commiz en chief contre toute ordonnance d'armes et au revers des loys et coustumes des preux et des vaillans ? (CHART., *Q. inv.*, 1422, 59).

In conclusioun

In conclusioun is included under the type F-4 (Figurative meaning -> "as something or in the form of something"). *In conclusioun* is shown in HCME with only 2 tokens in CMASTRO and in CMOFFIC3 with the meaning "in the end, finally"(*MED*). This *in-Ph* appeared in ME3 in EMO and within the domains of LETTERS and HANDBOOK/ASTR.

Conclusioun appears in English in the mid-14th century with the meaning of "deduction or conclusion reached by reasoning." *In conclusioun* was literally taken from OF *en conclusion* with equal sense, "à la fin, finalement", (ATILF). Consider some examples:

> *MED*: "In the end, finally". E.g. (c1390) Chaucer *CT.ML.*(Manly-Rickert) B.683: For this miracle, in conclusioun, And by Custances mediacioun, The kyng..Conuerted was.
> *ATILF*: «À la fin, finalement»: D'unnes choses et d'autres asséz on devisa, Mais en conclzion li conssaus s'acorda Qu'au gentil Esmeret la tiere demoura (*Flor. Rome W.*, c.1330-1400, 225).

In nature

In nature is included in this study as type F-3 (Figurative meaning -> "expression of a certain state or condition"). *In nature* only appears twice in a single text (CMBOETH) of HCME with the meaning "in itself". CMBOETH belongs to ME3 and is found in the EMO dialectal area and to the domain of PHILOSOPHY.

Nature is found in English c.1300 with the meaning "essential qualities, innate disposition." *In nature* was taken from OF *en nature* meaning "dans son état d'origine". Consider these examples:

MED: "in itself". E.g. c1400(?a1300) *KAlex.*(LdMisc 622)   293: Þe mone in propre nature Of adamaunt bare þe coloure.
ATILF: En nature. "Dans son état d'origine, avec les qualités de fonctionnement qui lui sont propres, en bon état" : ...et que ou cas que elle ne cognoistroit autre chose que dit est dessus, attendu que lesdiz deux aneaux et verge d'or sont en nature et restituez à iceulx mariez, que, au jeudi absolu, elle feust eslargie de prison (*Reg. crim. Chât., I, 1389-1392, 196*).

In trouble

In trouble is incorporated under the general type of F-2 (Figurative meaning -> manner: "in a form, shape or manner"). Only CMMANKIN and CMMETHAM texts include this *in-Ph,* with a single occurrrence each, and with the meaning "in confusion, in disorder" (*MED*). Both texts are assigned to ME4 and are found in the EML dialectal area and cover the domains of DRAMA and HANDBOOK, respectively.

Trouble made its way into English in the early 13th century with the meaning of "confusion, disorder, political unrest"; "to trouble, make turbid" (MED). The collocational phraseme, *in trouble*, was a reproduction from the OF *en trouble* with a sense similar to English. Consider some examples:

MED: "in confusion, disorder, political unrest". E.g. (1458) *Visit Hen.VI* (Vsp B.16) 55: God preserue hem..And london, for thei..Kepten the peas in trowbel & aduersite.
ATILF: Mettre en trouble : N'est expedient que pour le confort d'une seule personne on mette en tourble ung royame entier (CHASTELL., *Temple Boc.* B., 1463-1464, 163).

We may conclude that *in-Phs* were predominant in ME3 and ME4, fostered by their French counterpart, *en-Phs*. They were highly prolific, particularly because many of them were recurrently used. They represented all figurative senses, although F2 (manner: "in a form, shape or manner") is the most frequent one. *In-grace* is already found in ME1, and 12 out of the 134 *in-Phs* included in Table 78 appear in ME2, the other ones occurring in ME3 or ME4 coinciding with the peak of French borrowing. The data shown in Table 78 indicate that there are no significant differences in the use of these *in-Phs* according to the dialectal area, with the exception of the Northern dialect. It is also significant that 31 out of the 34 *in-Phs* shown in Table 78 appear in EMO, 24 out of the 34 occur in EML, 14 in SL, 7 in WML and 7 in SO. Other dialects were hardly represented. It is also worth mentioning that these *in-Phs* were author-dependent. With the exception of *in manner,* which is found in 44 texts out of the 91 of HCME. Regarding text types, we may affirm that there is no preference for a specific domain, as all text types are represented. It is worth noting, however, that these *in-Phs* were mostly restricted to prose.

Table 78: *In-collocational patterns*

In-Noun complement	Occ.	sense	ME Sub-period	Dialects	N° of texts	Text types	Comp. type (+70%)
manere	156	F2	ME2 ME3, ME4	EMO,EML, WML,SO, KL, SL	44	HISTORY, DRAMA, REL TREAT, HOMILY, LETTERS, HANDBOOK	Prose
part	55	F2	ME2 ME3, ME4	EMO, EML, WML,SO, KL, SL	16	RULE, HISTORY, DRAMA, REL TREAT, HOMILY, LETTERS, HANDBOOK, ETC.	Prose
(e)special	30	F2	ME2 ME3, ME4	ALL DIALECTS	18	HISTORY, DRAMA, REL TREAT, FICTION, HOMILY, LETTERS, ETC.	Prose
pein	29	F3	ME2 ME3, ME4	EMO EML WMO,KL SL	19	REL TREAT, DRAMA, BIOGRAPHY, FICTION, DOCUMENTS, HISTORY, SERMON, ROMANCE, PHILOSOPHY	Prose
grace	28	F3	ME1 ME2 ME3, ME4	EMO, EML, KL, WML, WMO, SL, NL	13	REL TREAT, SERMON, BIBLE, DRAMA, HISTORY, LETTERS.	Prose
form	28	F2	ME3, ME4	EMO, EML	10	RULE, FICTION, LETTERS, PHILOSOPHY, REL TREAT, DOCUMENTS, HANDBOOK	Prose
haste	24	F3	ME3, ME4	SO, EML, KL, WML, WMO, SL, NL	10	REL TREAT, HOMILY, DRAMA, HISTORY, LETTERS	Prose
pes	24	F3	ME2 ME3, ME4	SL, EMO, KL, NL, EML, WMO	15	REL TREAT, SERMON, HISTORY, FICTION, LETTERS, DOCUMENTS, ROMANCE, RULE, BIBLE	Prose
cas	18	F2	ME2 ME3, ME4	ALL DIALECTS EXCEPT NO and WML.	12	ROMANCE, FICTION, LETTERS, PHILOSOPHY, DOCUMENTS, HANDBOOK	Prose

Table 78: *In-collocational patterns*

In-Noun complement	Occ.	sense	ME Sub-period	Dialects	N° of texts	Text types	Comp. type (+70%)
bataille	15	F1	ME2 ME3, ME4	ALL DIALECTS	11	ALL TEXT TYPES	Prose
presence	13	F2	ME3 ME4	EMO, EML, WMO	6	REL TREAT, PHILOSOPHY, DRAMA, LETTERS, DOCUMENTS, ROMANCE	Prose
substance	12	F3	ME3, ME4	EMO, EML, SL	6	REL TREAT, PHILOSOPHY, DOCUMENTS, HISTORY, DRAMA	Prose
honour	9	F5	ME2 ME3, ME4	SO, EML, EMO, NL	6	FICTION, LETTERS, DOCUMENTS and BIBLE	Prose
doute	8	F3	ME3, ME4	EMO, EML, NL	6	RULE, HISTORY, PREFACE, FICTION, DRAMA, REL TREAT	Prose
merci	8	F3	ME2 ME3 ME4	SL, EMO, EML	5	REL TREAT, SERMON, HISTORY, BIBLE, REL TREAT	Prose Prose
vein	7	F2	ME2 ME3, ME4	EMO, EML, SL, NL	5	REL TREAT, BIBLE, RULE, DRAMA	
armes	6	F1	ME2 ME3, ME4	SL, EMO	3	FICTION, ROMANCE	Prose
charge	6	F3	ME3, ME4	EMO, EML	4	FICTION, DRAMA, DOCUMENTS, HANDBOOK	Prose
comparison	6	F2	ME3 ME4	EMO, SL, EML	4	TRAVELOG, SERMON, REL TREAT	Prose
absence	5	F3	ME3, ME4	EMO	2	LETTERS, REL TREAT	Prose
Accord(ance)	5	F3	ME2 ME3, ME4	EMO, EML	3	BIBLE, FICTION, REL TREAT	Prose

Table 78: *In-collocational patterns*

In-Noun complement	Occ.	sense	ME Sub-period	Dialects	N° of texts	Text types	Comp. type (+70%)
aventure	5	F2	ME2 ME3, ME4	NO, WML, EMO	3	ROMANCE, HANDBOOK	Prose
general	5	F2	ME3 ME4	EMO, EML	3	PHILOSOPHY, DOCUMENTS, HANDBOOK	Prose
order	5	F2	ME3, ME4	EMO, EML	5	PHILOSOPHY, SERMON, REL TREAT, FICTION	Prose
comfort	4	F3	ME4	EML	2	REL TREAT, LETTERS	Prose
pece	4	F2	ME3, ME4	EML	3	REL TREAT, HANDBOOK, PHILOSOPHY	Prose
figure	3	F2	ME4	EMO	1	SERMON	Prose
pacience	3	F3	ME3, ME4	NL, EMO	3	RULE, REL TREAT	Prose
certain	2	F3	ME3, ME4	EMO, WML	3	HISTORY, DRAMA, FICTION	Prose
avauntage	2	F1	ME4	SL	1	SERMON	Prose
chef	2	F4	ME4	EMO	1	DRAMA	Prose
conclusion	2	F4	ME3, ME4	EMO	2	LETTERS, HANDBOOK/ASTR.	Prose
nature	2	F3	ME3 ME4	EMO	1	PHILOSOPHY	Prose
trouble	2	F2	ME4	EML	2	DRAMA, HANDBOOK	Prose

CHAPTER EIGHT

IDIOMATIZATION

1. Theoretical framework

1. 1. Definition

There has been much debate about phrasemes and idioms in the last decades, and there is no agreement about their formal definition and typology. Thus there is not an accepted term to name these structures properly. The term "idiom" seems to be the most widely accepted one to refer to a large set of expressions which include non-free words. These set (fixed, frozen) phrases are then usually called idiomatic expressions or idioms, although other more restrictive terms such as "phraseological units", "speech formulas", "lexical solidarities" (Coseriu 1967) and "fixed syntagms" (Rothkegel 1973) have also been used in studies of phraseology and idiomaticity.

The study of set phrases, of which idioms are a subclass, has brought in an interesting academic dispute about the terminological character of the general categories and subcategories of phraseology[1]. Regarding the general categories of the phraseological cataloguing Mel'čuk (1998: 24-30) employs the terms "set phrases" or "phrasemes" for the whole directory of word combinations. Gläser (1998: 126) uses the term "phraseological units" for the total catalogue of idioms and phrases ("phrasicon") of a language. Cowie (1998: 5) and Howarth (1996) use the term "word combination".

Word combination vary along a continuum which distinguishes at least three types of meanings depending on the degree of semantic transparency: a) an area of opaque and unmotivated meaning composed of ritual invariable units where Mel'čuk (1988, 1998) and Gläser (1988, 1998) include "idioms", and Cowie (1988, 1998) and Howarth (1996) "pure idioms"; b) an area of greater semantic transparency (semantic transparency is perceived via a metaphorical extension of an original unbiased meaning of at least one component of the unit) and partially

---

1 See Granger and Paquot (2008: 27-50)

motivated connotations composed of formal variable units where Mel'čuk (1988, 1998) and Gläser (1988, 1998) locate "quasi idioms", whereas Cowie (1988, 1998) and Howarth (1996) categorised them as "figurative idioms".; and c) an area of semantic transparency and context-motivated meaning in which two or more open-class words co-occur and in which at least one component of the unit has a literal meaning, whereas the other is figurative or metaphorically extended by its context. As has been shown in the previous chapter, in this area Mel'c#uk (1988, 1998) categorises "collocations", whereas Gläser (1988, 1998), Cowie (1988, 1998) and Howarth (1996) call them "restricted collocations".

Handl (2008: 50-55) puts forward the notion of "continua" to differentiate idioms, collocations and free ad-hoc combinations. The first continuum is semantic transparency (semantic dimension) which is chiefly responsible for the distinction of free ad-hoc combinations, collocations and idioms". Maximum semantic transparency implies that words associate in a free co-occurrence, whereas idioms and compounds locate in the other extreme point on the scale (minimum opaque semantic transparency). Collocations are located in the central "core area" of this scale. Another continuum is the collocational range (lexical dimension), "which is simply the number of potential collocates a node...can take" (2008: 52). "The endpoints of the scale are again reserved for idioms and compounds in the case of very small ranges, and for free combinations if there is a large range" (2008: 55). The third continuum is frequency (statistical dimension) which exhibits an analogous allocation of collocation, idiom/compound and free co-occurrence. The highest statistical scores is assigned to free co-occurrence of words, the lowest to idioms and compounds, whereas the central area of the scale is assigned to collocations (2008: 55).

In oder to outline a conceptual framework of idioms I will start with that definition heard by Mel'čuk from one of his tutors: "An idiom is what we beat Chomsky with". The interpretation of this "idiom" seems to be clear in Mel'čuk's words:

> A syntax-geared linguistic theory is not a very appropriate framework to deal with idioms. Idioms have an internal syntactic structure, so that they do undergo syntactic processing, but not *qua* idioms: on the surface, they are treated by syntactic rules the same way all free phrases are (1995: 168 footnote).

Evidence for this claim could be put forward with this common example of idiom: *kick the bucket*. Certainly, the internal syntactic structure of this idiom cannot be subject to syntactic variations such as *kick a (/his/her/any) bucket, kick a black(/small..) bucket, kick the pail*, etc. without altering the semantic connotations of the idiomatic expression. For the sake of putting the point within limits I will depart from Mel'čuk's interpretation of idioms. Mel'čuk (1995: 179) classifies idioms into two categories: pragmatic phrasemes ("pragmatemes" = sayings, proverbs, quotations, and speech formulas) and semantic phrasemes (idioms, collocations and quasi-idioms). For the present purposes I will concentrate only on one subset of semantic phrasemes: quasi-idioms.

Idiomatic set phrases are traditionally defined as "conventionalized complex expressions" (Everaert, van der Linden, Schenk and Schreuder 1995: 3) which are semantically noncompositional and unanalysable and syntactically fixed or frozen. There are still contending theories with regard to the meaning of idiomatic expressions. Some scholars argue that only the idiom as a whole is provided with meaning, and none of its constituents has a semantic role (Nicolas 1995, Schenk 1995), while some other idiomaticity researchers consider that the constituents of an idiomatic expression have semantic connotations and so the meaning of the whole depends on the meaning of the parts (Gazdar, Klein, Pullum and Sag 1985; Gibbs 1995). Finally, a third theory holds that the meaning of an idiomatic expression is localized in a subset of its constituent elements, whereas other elements of the whole are meaningless (Bresnan 1982).

It is traditionally assumed that idiomatic expressions were originally metaphorical and innovative but in the course of time they have become semantically conventionalized and syntactically frozen as lexical items that exist in the speaker's word list. This means that idiomatic expressions have to be learnt as a unit which has lexical co-occurrence restrictions. Thus, on the one hand, idiomatic expressions are traditionally viewed as noncompositional, that is, their conventional, non-literal meaning is not determined through the meanings of their individual words, but from the meaning of the whole. On the other hand, this traditional approach also highlights the idea that idioms have a very restricted potential to undergo syntactic and morphological operations such as passivization, the presence or absence of articles, modification, etc. (Weinreich 1969; Chafe 1968; Fraser 1970; Katz 1973; Nicolas 1995). This extended interpretation of idiomaticity has been challenged by some other authors such as Nunberg (1978), Wasaw, Sag and Nunberg (1983), Gibbs and Nayak (1989), Cacciari and Glucksberg (1990), Cacciari (1993), Glucksberg (1993) and Gibbs (1995) who have experimentally shown that the components of many idioms still have a figurative meaning and therefore the whole is analysable. They also emphasize that idioms do not emerge arbitrarily but as a problem-solving, that is, motivated by a specific context. In line with this view of compositionality and motivation of idioms, Cacciari and Glucksberg (1990; cf. also Cacciari 1993: 45-48; Glucksberg 1993: 16ff; Flores D'Arcais 1993: 80-81) prefer a compositional classification of idioms in the following terms: a) *compositional-opaque*, e.g. *kick the bucket*. This idiomaticity type includes those idioms whose parts and the idiom itself have no apparent semantic relation; b) *compositional-transparent*, e.g. *break the ice*. In this type of idioms the meaning of the parts is relevant for understanding the meaning of the whole; c) *quasi-metaphorical*, e.g. *giving up the ship*. In this case, idioms are interpreted as a "prototypical or stereotyped instance of an entire category of people, events, situations, or actions" (Glucksberg 1993: 18). Thus

giving up the ship is interpreted both as a prototypical act of surrendering and as an instance of complete surrender.
Regarding this compositional and analysable view, Gibbs states:

> A great deal of evidence in linguistics and psychology shows that many idioms are, at least to some extent, compositional and analyzable. People do not simply assume that the meanings of idioms are arbitrary or fixed by convention. Instead, people make sense of idiomatic expressions precisely because their ordinary metaphorical and, to a lesser extent, metonymic knowledge that provides part of the link between these phrases and their figurative interpretations (1995: 98-99).

The basic claims suggested by this new approach (Cacciari and Glucksberg 1990; Gibbs 1995: 98 ff) are substantiated in the following premises: idiomatic expressions certainly have a metaphorical origin and certainly they have lost some of their metaphoricity over time but not to such an extent that they have turned into "stock formulas or "dead metaphors". Furthermore, if the meaning of the idiomatic expression is not predictable from the meaning of its parts, then the meanings of idioms are "arbitrary" and "unmotivated". In Gibbs' opinion (1995:99), although in a very common example of idiom, *kick the bucket* ("die"), apparently none of the elements provide a definite or vague clue to determining the meaning of the whole, we must assume that a historical event, the knowledge of which is still uncertain for contemporary speakers, has to be the origin of this idiom, otherwise it would emerge as an abstract, unmotivated and arbitrary linguistic form. Gibbs (*ibid.*) also argues that idioms do not constitute a homogeneous class, as there are many "syntactic, lexical, semantic and pragmatic differences" among them. Thus *kick the bucket* seems to be much more noncompositional and unanalysable than *pop the question* or *blow your stack* which are "almost completely compositional and analyzable" (1995:100).

1. 2. Acquisition and processing of idioms

A twin theoretical issue which is still unresolved is how idioms are processed, and how they are represented and stored in our mind. The following questions are still under conjecture: Are there different mechanisms to process figurative and literal language? If both the literal and the figurative meanings are available, which comes first to the listener? There are then many questions regarding the factors that may activate idiomatic meanings, and also practical problems, for example, if idioms are fossilized items, we may assume that they are stored as unitary lexical entities and therefore retrieved as frozen and conventionalized chunks, unable to undergo syntactical variations and transformations e.g. passivization, presence and absence of articles and auxiliary verbs. This means that idioms have to be learnt and remembered before retrieval (cf. Swinney and Cutler 1979, Estill and Kemper 1982; Cacciari and Tabossi 1988). However, if idioms are considered to be processed like any other word sequence, we may presume that they are stored and retrieved like any other item in our word list. Another important problem we face is how to elucidate the mechanisms of access that a speaker has when s/he uses an idiom and how s/he chooses an idiomatic expression instead of a literal version or interpretation, particularly when both are available. Various experimental psychological studies have been carried out to elucidate the mechanisms of access to idiomatic expressions (Ortony, Schallert, Reynolds and Antos 1978; Van Lancker and Canter 1981; Gibbs 1986, 1995; Botelho da Silva and Cutler 1993) and some hypotheses have also been proposed. Thus, by assuming that idioms are stored as single lexical items, Swinney and Cutler (1979) have developed a "Lexical Representation Hypothesis" based on the premise that we access the lexicalized meaning of an idiomatic expression at the same time that we access the literal meaning of its individual words. Consequently they predict that the process of recognition of an idiomatic (figurative) expression comes first because the literal meaning has to be computed, whereas the figurative one, which has already been stored in our mind, only needs to be retrieved (cf. Tabossi and Zardon 1993: 146).

Gibbs (1980, 1986), Gibbs and Nayak (1989), Gibbs, Nayak and Cutting (1989) have put forward a "Decomposition Hypothesis" based on the principle that idioms are not a homogeneous class and consequently they vary in compositionality. According to this approach, the meaning of the individual words of an idiom actually provides the key to open the overall meaning of the idiom. Consequently we access the meaning of the idiom depending on the analysis of its compositionality. They also consider that the recognition of the literal and the figurative meanings of an idiom are not parallel processes. The computation of the literal meaning comes after the recognition of the figurative meaning and only starts when idiomatic meaning is de-contextualized.

Cacciari and Tabossi (1988) and Tabossi and Zardon (1995) have developed, from a psychological approach, a "Configuration Hypothesis" based on the psychological activating mechanisms we have to recognize an idiom. They argue that the overall meaning of an idiomatic expression emerges with the recognition of the meaning of its key word. There is, then, a key word that provides the necessary input to recognize the configuration of a word string as an idiom. They have also noted that the processing of literal or idiomatic meanings depends on whether the idiomatic sequences are predictable or not. The more unpredictable an idiomatic string is the faster is the access to the literal meaning, and vice versa: the more predictable an idiomatic string is the faster is the processsing of the idiomatic meaning.

Regarding the processing of idiomatic meaning, Levorato 1993: 119ff) has also tried to propose a model of idiom acquisition based on the analysis of "Figurative Competence". According to her, a speaker can be considered truly competent in figurative language (idioms) when s/he has acquired the following skills:

> "the ability to break down an idiom into its component parts and to make semantic inferences about these; the ability to comprehend idiomatic expressions even when

they have been subjected to lexical substitution or syntactic or lexical variations; the ability to generate new idioms by means of syntactic and lexical variation on existing idioms" (1993: 122).

In like manner, Omazič (2008: 72) says that idiom processing involves a complex functional relationship of three interrelated factors: a) cognitive mechanisms (conceptual metaphor and metonymy, conceptual mapping between and within domains); b) knowledge of the language (semantics, syntax, etymology, discourse analysis); and c) knowledge of the world (cultural and historical background, imagery symbolism).

1. 3. Idiom formation

The idiom formation is the result of a historical development which exhibits various phases:

a) Before initiating an idiomatic status all the constituents were unrestricted and free to be used under the rules of grammar, e.g. *[accordant]* + *[to/with]*. Before being used as part of a complex preposition, *accordant* was an adjective with the meaning of "suitable, fitting, appropriate", e.g. 1413 Lydgate *Pylgr. Sowle* ii. lviii. 56 (1859) *Sothly, this lykenes is accordaunt*. It is to be noted that *accordant* has a lexical qualitative meaning.

b) In a second stage the relation between the lexical units of the set phrase becomes stabilized, "rigidicized" or "routinicized". In the course of this process, grammatical categories "decategorialize" by losing many of their morphological and syntactical properties. Thus a major grammatical category such as nouns loses some of its characteristic features such as case, number and gender, and restricts the use of articles, quantifiers, and the property of being modified or referred to by an anaphoric pronoun. Semantically, in the course of this process the nouns involved in idiomatization evolve from concreteness to abstractness (semantic erosion). Thus, *accordant* came to be reiteratively used followed by *to* and sometimes by *with*. By combining together *accordant* + *to/with*, the adjective loses many of its morphological and syntactical properties and progressively undergoes a process of decategorilization by adopting the grammatical function of relational word (preposition), e.g. c1315 Shoreham 89 *Acordaunt to thy trauayl, Lord, graunte me thy coroune* (OED).

c) In the third stage, there is a reanalysis of the constituent structure (Brinton and Akimoto 1999: 7-8). Thus X + [*be* + *accordant*], X being head (NP) and *accordant* either modifier (within the NP) or predicative complement, undergoes the following process of reanalysis of its constituent structure: *[it]* + *be* + *[accordant to/with]* X, X being also head of a NP, but functioning as prepositional complement. This process involves, then, lexical co-occurrence restrictions and changes in the assignment of morphological boundaries, that is, there is a reassignment of the morphological properties of the phraseological unit.

d) In the fourth stage, all the constituents are idiomatized into a single lexical unit ("lexicalization"), e.g. *setten spel on ende* ("come to the point"; *Dame Sirith*, 61). By turning into an idiomatic "conventionalized" set phrase it also became semantically noncompositional and unanalysable and syntactically fixed or frozen.

In the previous Chapter, I have tentatively reviewed the four basic types of word combination by considering that words may combine:

a) Without restraint and in semantic paratactical occurrence ("free lexematic occurrences"). The meaning of all elements is independent and therefore free to occur elsewhere ("free combination").

b) Partially restrainted and in semantic hypotactical occurrence ("conventionalized phrasemes"). The meaning of one of the elements depends on the occurrence of the other (collocations).

c) Partially restrainted and in semantic intertactical occurrence ("conventionalized pragmatemes" = sayings, proverbs, quotations, and speech formulas).

d) Completely restrainted and in semantic intertactical occurrence. The meanings of all words are mutually dependent ("idioms"). None of the words has its own semantic connotations as only the whole is provided with meaning.

This study, however, is not a corpus-based study of idioms in ME, but a tentative survey of the meaning of idiomatic prepositional phrases in ME.

2. IDIOMATIC SENSES OF MIDDLE ENGLISH PREPOSITIONAL PHRASES

What follows is then an attempt to scrutinize the itinerary of semantic erosion in *p-Phs* in their transition from OE to ME. In the first Chapter of this work I tried to show how adverbs were recruited as prepositions to cover the range of new functional relations which emerged in the language system, due to the loss of the inflectional system. Initially these new grams were used to specify two primary functional relationships: spatial and temporal. In this stage of the language, prepositions and their complements appeared in free lexematic occurrences. Many prepositions were interchangeable. Thus the early ME texts of the HC show, for example, that words such as *weorld, fot, night* could be headed by various prepositions to express the same idea, e.g. *aboue þe weorld, at þe weorld, bi þe weorld, in þe weorld, on þe weorld, ouer þe weorld* and *þurgh þe weorld* tend to be used with the meaning "all over the world". Similarly *in þe niȝt, at þe niȝt, on þe niȝt, bi þe niȝt, ouer þe niȝt* were often interchangeable to express the meaning "during the night". However, in the course of time, prepositions and their complements tended to acquire both a more rigidicized or routinicized occurrence and, via metaphorical extension, they tend to shift from a concrete domain (spatial or temporal) to a more abstract or figurative one. Finally, some prepositional phrases shifted from figurative domains to idiomatic or quasi-idiomatic roles. What follows is a detailed account of the transition of the *p-Phs* dealt with in this study from figurative meanings to quasi-idiomatic meanings or "phrasemes" (henceforth, **Phms**). Four prepositions (*bifore, biside, bihinde* and *under*) do not exhibit any trace of idiomaticity in ME, but the rest will be discussed in detail now.

2. 1. Aboue-Phms

As was mentioned in Chapter V, the primary semantic domain of the preposition *aboue* indicated a physical position of something (rarely somebody) in an area adjacent to the top of another one. From this spatial role it extended to other spatial domains such as "resting upon"; "beyond, further than", etc. Then, in the course of time and from these spatial meanings, *aboue-Phs* developed into a varied range of figurative meanings, namely, "superior to", "higher in rank or position" and "higher in degree or quality". Finally, from this latter figurative subsense ("higher in degree or quality"), which had gained a large presence in ME (the HCME includes 54 instances out of 122 of all *aboue-Phs*) it developed into the phraseme *aboue al(l)*. Then *aboue all þings* developed into "aboue all" which gradually lexicalized into an adverb "before every other consideration, specially". Examples include: *he that cometh from heuene, is aboue alle* (CMNTEST); *as it were semynge aboue al* (CMCHAULI). It is worth noting, however, that the survey of the HCME shows only 3 instances.

2. 2. After- Phms

The basic locative meanings of *after-Phs* indicating either a position at the rear of (spatial) or following (in time) developed to new figurative meanings in ME such as "next to in order or importance" and "in imitation of". Within these figurative fields some *after-Phs* tend to be more phraseological units or speech formulas. Examples which I have found in the HCME with an idiomatic content include phrasemes such as *word after word* "word by word", as in *and ic ou wile seggen word efter word* (CMLAMBET), *on after on* "one after the other", e.g. *& nimeð an efter an* (CMHALI), and *after (one's) word* "reliance on one's trustworthy word", e.g. *Efter þi word qð ha mote me iwurðen* (CMHALI). Phrases such as *after lengthe* "lengthwise" (MED); *after more and (or) lesse* "as to greater and (or) lesser" (MED) do not appear in the corpus. Finally, some other set phrases which recap known information such as *after þat* (with 41 instances), *after (al) þis* (7 occ.) are relatively frequent in the corpus and they were included in the section of collocations.

2. 3. At- Phms

The primitive locative domains of *at-Phs*, expressing basically at a point in place or time, developed into a large variety of figurative roles to indicate an ample range of states, situations, activities and circumstances (*at ese, reste, pes,* etc) as shown in Chapter V. The process towards phraseological units of many *at-Phs* was steady and progressive. Some phrasemes developed directly from temporal roles. Thus many temporal phrasemes such as *at frymþe* "in the beginning", *at frome* "at first", *at the erst* "for the first time", *at þe next* "next", *at þe laste, at ende* "at last, in the end", *at the ferrest* "at the latest", *at ene(s), at one(s)* "at once" (cf. MED) are found in the HCME, e.g. *And at þe laste after þe restynge* (CMCHAULI); *þan at erst, and none er, he renniþ to þe welle to wasche hym* (CMCLOUD); *þerfore at þe laste sche fondede to overcome hym wiþ gile* (CMPOLYCH); *'þou ʒeuest two tymes at ones, and I haue bot o steryng at ones.'* (CMCLOUD). The review of the HCME shows 17 temporal phrasemes.

It is also noteworthy that another 27 *at-phms* recorded in the HCME developed from figurative domains of *at-Phs*, e.g. *at þe best* (wei), "in the best way"; *at þe leste* (wei) "to the least extent, at least"; *at all* "in every way", *at evene* "exactly at"; *at unimete* "infinitely", *at þe fulle* "completely", *at regard of* "as regards", *al al degres* "in every respect" (cf. MED). Examples include: *hir schrewednesse ne were fynissched at the leste weye by the owtreste deth* (CMBOETH); *Of plesaunt prosperyte I lakke non at alle!* (CMDIGBY); *and none bot he, is sufficient at þe fulle, and mochel more, to fulfille þe wille and þe desire of oure soule* (CMCLOUD).

2.4. Bi-Phms

The initial locative role of the preposition *bi*, which is associated with the idea of proximity (space) and the temporal notion that an event occurs during a period of time, developed to new figurative roles and phraseological units via metaphorical extension. As regards phrasemes I have not found in the corpus any spatial instance, but 15 instances were detected as temporal *bi-Phms*, such as *dai bi dai* "on and on"; *bi day and nighte; yer bi yer* "every year", e.g. *day by day to the laste* (CMQUATO); *i sall clens my consciens, passand ilk nyght by nyght* (CMROLLPS). The figurative domains of *bi-Phs*, related to motivation, agency, mediation, manner, etc, (cf. chapter V) developed to new phraseological units such as *pas bi pas* "step by step"; *word bi word* "in detail"; *bi lyttel and lyttle* "little by little, gradually"; *bi no mene(s)* "in no way"; *bi name (of)* (cf. MED). In this category I have found 67 occurrences, e.g. *Wylliam Mydwyntter whent to London, as aull wholl getherars wher sent for be wryt be the mene of Pettyt* (CMPRIV); *we swere noghte by His name* (CMGAYTRY).

2.5. In-Phms

In-Phs were associated with a spatial or temporal sense in OE, but in the course of ME many of them lost much of their original referential meaning and via metaphorical extension developed into a more figurative or abstract domain. From these latter roles, some *in-Phs* turned into *in-Phms*, although most of them continued to be associated with spatial or temporal references such as *in (þe) midde(l) of.* This phraseme is detected on 36 occasions (0.51% in relation to all *in-Phs*) and denotes a position in the midst of persons or things e.g. *in the middel of this plate* (CMQUATO). *In (þe) midde(l) of* is also used to indicate the midpoint of a given period of time, as in *in mydde of the day* (CMASTRO). I have also found other examples which could be categorized as phrasemes, which only indicate a temporal relationship. Within this category I have classified 31 in-*Phms* (that is, a rate of 6.36% of all temporal instances and 0.32% of all examples in the corpus) such as *in þe mene tyme*, e.g. *in þe mene tyme* (CMBRUT3), *in the mene whyle* (CMGREGOR), *in þe ende* (CMGREGOR), *in the begynnyng* (CMINNOCE), *in sumer tide* (CMHANSYN), etc.

The shift from figurative domains to quasi-idioms is detected in 267 instances of the HCME. This transition is displayed in some phraseological units such as *in deed, in doubt, in vayn, in speciall, in generall, in certayn, in despite*, etc. The Phm *in deed* is the most frequent as it is found on 51 occasions, e.g. *and þis was fulfillid in dede* (CMCAPCHR). *In special* appears 23 times, e.g. *The whiche fourthe partie in speciall shal shewen a table of the verrey moeving of the mone* (CMASTRO). *In general* is found on 12 occasions, e.g. *in general his falsenesse were ayeinsaide* (CMDOCU3). *In vain* and *in despite* occur 11 times each, e.g. *þe wicked tempted my soule in vayn* (CMEARLPS); *þou has him and his in despite* (CMCURSOR). The figures in this category represent only a ratio 4.73% as far as the whole number of figurative instances are concerned and 2.82% with regard to all *in-Phs* found in the corpus.

2.6. On-Phms

As was mentioned in Chapter IV, Lundskær-Nielsen has already found 9 occurrences of *on-Phs* which had a figurative or abstract sense in the *Anglo-Saxon Chronicle* (years 892-900) (1993:88). He has also found 25 instances with a figurative sense in the *Peterborough Chronicle* for the years 1122-54, whereas he has not detected any figurative *in-Phs* and only one example of *æt-Ph* may be considered figurative (1993: 96). I have also observed that *on-Phs* were well in the lead in the formation of phraseological units (phrasemes) in ME. Thus, in my analysis I have found that 17.17% of *on-Phs,* within spatial references, had acquired a quasi-idiomatic status. It is worth noting, however, that *on-Phs* decreased steadily and progressively in the course of ME (cf. Chapter II) and therefore their use became more and more restricted and dependant on the complement of the preposition or on the verb which preceded the preposition.

Semantically, it seems reasonable that the notion of "contact" originally conveyed by *on* developed to a radial network expanding to other figurative domains which indicate "circumstance", "state", "means", "reason", etc. As Dirven (1993: 78) states, *on* seems to develop in chains of meaning from physical into mental. Therefore the areas covered by this preposition were so numerous that it had a greater chance of shifting to phrasemes. Thus *on-Phs* which originally expressed a physical situation, e.g. *On oure side were ded Edward* (CMCAPCHR), in the course of time developed into phrasemes denoting a figurative position or direction.

I have detected 151 spatial *on-Phms* in the HCME (17.17% within the spatial sphere and 5.61% when related to all other *on-Phs*). Most of them indicate position: ("in or from a certain direction") *on side* "to the side, aside"; *on eche half (a side)* "into every part"; *on everi half (honde)* "from all sides"; *on high* "high up"; *on height* "up high"; *on eche (either, everi, his, that other, right, this) half; on honde(s)* "close at hand"; *on sides honde* "privately"; *on (either, his, the right) hand; on either (hire) partie; on eche (either, everi, his, that other, right, this, our, thi) side; on both hands, parties, sides.* They were also used in correlated constructions: *on half..on other half; on the on (the right) hand..on the other (the lift) hand); on that parte, on the other parte; on the one side..on the other side* (cf. MED). Examples include *on þe French side were but fraude* (CMCAPCHR). It is worth noting that 80 instances out of the 151 found for this category occur with the complement *side*. The *on-side* phrases denote a position in or from a certain direction, that is, "to the side, aside". The complement *side* tends to include some type of determiner such *on eche half side* "into every part", *on everi half side* "from all sides", *on eiþer, his, that oþer, riȝt, this, our, þi side*.

The second highest number of spatial figurative *on-Phs* occur with *on part(ie)*, of which there are 21 instances, most of them showing a parallel construction with regard to *side*. Thus *part(ie)* also tends to be used with determiners, e.g. *on þe partye of þe seyd William* (CMOFFIC4). Within the figurative spatial heading are other *on-Phs* such as *on high* "high up", of which there are 12 instances, and *on height* "up high", of which there are 5, e.g. *Bot goth toward the deyss on hih* (CMGOWER); *bute steauene on heh in hire heorte* (CMJULIA); *and cryed on hyghe* (CMMALORY), *þis on þe wal steiȝ on heiȝ* (CMALISAU). Some figurative spatial on-Phs are used in correlated constructions such as "on the one side..on the other side" (4 instances), e.g. *sette on that oo syde an ymage of oure Lady and a-nother on that other syde of Seint Iohn* (CMAELR3).

The HCME also shows 19 *in-Phs* which could be classified as phrasemes in ME, denoting a temporal relationship such as *on alre erest* (7 instances), *on firste* (4), *on frume, on frumthe* (4), *on ende* (3), e.g. *were on alre erst ikennen* (CMCATHE), *on ða lange firste* (CMVICES1), *on fruman do þas sealfe* (CMPERIDI), *And I shal setten spel on ende* (CMSIRITH). Idiomatic *on-Phs* show a rate of 6.18% within the examples found in temporal categories, and 0.70% of all *on-Phs* in the corpus.

The shift from figurative usage to a quasi-idiomatic role in the following *on-Phs* is still very difficult to explain. Let us consider some of them: a) arrangement in a group, company, sequence: *on hepe, on lump, on roue*; b) dressed or covered with:

on blod; c) state or condition: *on loue, on live, on slep, on witnesse, on fir, on thirst, on game, on cas, on happes, on fer, on god, on egge, on haste, on hed, on heigh, on loft, on mis, on rest, on rune, on (the) strai, on warantise*.

As was stated in Chpater V, these *on-Phs* have been considered under the label of figurative, but depending on the criteria we use to determine the framework of phrasemes, they could also be classified as phraseological units and therefore quasi-idioms.

CONCLUSIONS

The analysis of the 12 types of *p-Phs* covered in this study allows the following conclusions to be drawn:

1. *Aboue-Phs* are scarcely used in ME, although their use increases progressively in the course of ME. The East Midland dialect seems to favour the use of *aboue-Phs*, whereas the southern and eastern parts of England do not show any examples in early Middle English (ME1). The small number of instances found in other areas in this period indicates that there is not sufficient evidence to conclude that *aboue-Phs* were predominant in the Midlands in ME1.

The analysis of the semantic domains of *aboue-Phs* shows a varied range of figurative meanings, namely, "superior to", "higher in rank or position" and "higher in degree or quality". Finally, we may also conclude that the reiterative use of the phrase *aboue all þinges* developed into the phraseme *aboue al(l)*, which gradually lexicalized into an adverb "before every other consideration, especially".

2. *After-Phs* have a similar frequency in all subperiods of ME, although there is a decline in ME2. The analysis of these *p-Phs* shows some discrepancies with regard to the dialectal area. In broad terms, the East Midland dialect includes more *after-Phs* than the other dialects in the course of ME, whereas the Northern dialect shows the smallest number of examples.

In semantic terms, the locative meanings of *after-Phs* extended to new figurative meanings in ME, such as "next to in order or importance" and "in imitation of". From these semantic areas they evolved into some phraseological units such as *word after word* "word by word"; *on after on* "one after the other"; *after (one's) word* "reliance on one's trustworthy word"; *after more and (or) lesse*, etc.

3. *At-Phs* are restrictively used in ME1 and ME2. From 1350 on, there is an expansion of *at-Phs* with a varied range of uses. In fact, from 1150 to 1350 I have only found 201 *at-Phs*, whereas 1354 were recorded from 1350 to 1500. There are significant variations with regard to the dialectal distribution of *at-Phs*. Thus, on the one hand, the Southern dialect includes more examples than the other dialects in all the subperiods of ME, while on the other hand the Kentish one scarcely contains any *at-Phs*. The rest of the dialects do not present considerable differences among them.

From a semantic point of view, the primitive locative domains of *at-Phs*, expressing basically "at a point in place or time" developed into a large variety of figurative roles to articulate an ample range of states, situations, activities and circumstances (*at ese, reste, pes,* etc). The process towards phraseological units of many *at-Phs* was steady and progressive in the course of time. Some phrasemes developed, on the one hand, from temporal roles such as *at frympe* "in the beginning", *at frome* "at first", *at the erst* "for the first time", *at þe next* "next", *at þe laste, at ende* "at last, in the end", *at the ferrest* "at the latest", *at ene(s), at one(s)* "at once"; and, on the other hand, from figurative domains as in *at þe best* (*wei*), "in the best way"; *at þe leste* (wei) "to the least extent, at least"; *at all* "in every way", *at evene* "exactly at"; *at unimete* "infinitely", *at þe fulle* "completely", *at regard of* "as regards", *al al degres* "in every respect".

4. The use of *bi-Phs* increases progressively in the course of ME1, ME2 and ME3, but the number of 5.3 instances recorded for every thousand words in ME3 drops to 4.2 in ME4. The data provided in this study illustrate that there are noteworthy differences according to the dialectal area. The East and West Midland areas seem to favour the use of *bi-Phs,* whereas the Northern dialect shows the smallest number of examples. In broad terms, the increase of *bi-Phs* in the course of ME is not homogeneous. In fact, there is an important variability within each region, except in the North where the use of *bi-Phs* is very rare in the two subperiods from which we have data (ME3 and ME4). West Midland shows great variation, starting with a rate of 1.4‰ in ME1, then rising to 5.3‰ in ME2 and 7.8‰ in ME3, but then that ratio diminishes to 1.1‰ in ME4. However, the increase of *bi-Phs* seems to be steady in the East Midlands and in the South with a moderate upsurge in ME3.

In semantic terms the initial locative role of the preposition *bi*, which is associated with the idea of proximity (space) and the temporal notion that an event occurs during a period of time, developed to new figurative roles and phraseological units via metaphorical extension. From temporal domains some *at-Phs* evolved into phrasemes such as *dai bi dai* "on and on"; *bi day and nighte; yer bi yer* "every year". Similarly from figurative roles some *at-Phs*, related to motivation, agency, mediation, manner, etc, developed into new phraseological units such as *pas bi pas* "step by step"; *word bi word* "in detail"; *bi lyttel and lyttle* "little by little, gradually"; *bi no mene(s)* "in no way"; *bi name* (*of*).

5. *Bifore-Phs* are scarcely used in ME. Thus only 1 instance is found for every two thousand words. The number of occurrences varies significantly in the four subperiods. Thus the use of *bifore-Phs* in ME1 decreases in ME2, but recovers again in ME3 and falls again in ME4. There is also a great deal of fluctuation within each dialect in the course of ME. Thus, the West Midland dialect shows a similar ratio in the four subperiods of ME, but East Midland displays a great oscillation (the ratio of 1.1‰ in ME1 falls to 0.2‰ in ME2).

The semantic analysis of *bifore-Phs* shows that the primary meaning of the preposition *before*, characterized as "locative anterior" (spatial and temporal) extended into new abstract subsenses such as "in the mental view of; in the knowledge of; in preference to, etc. I have not found any phraseological unit formed by *bifore-Phs*.

6. *Bihinde-Phs* were hardly used in the course of ME. I have only detected 24 instances in the corpus. Their use was similar in all the subperiods of ME. The increase shown in ME3 is not indicative of a greater preference in daily talk in this subperiod because 5 out of the 11 instances belong to a single text (CMMALORY). The number of *bihinde-Phs* found in the corpus are not sufficiently indicative so as to measure their dialectal distribution.

In semantic terms, the preposition *behind* initiates its role as a preposition in the course of the 13th century with the meaning of "locative posterior position". This physical semantic connotation was gradually extended to refer to abstract entities such as events, states and manner and figurative subsenses ("in the absence of"). I have not found any phrasemes formed by *bifore-Phs*.

7. *Biside-Phs* are very unusual in ME. Thus ME1 exhibits only 2 examples (both of them in CMBRUT1) and ME2 includes no more than 9 instances. This figure rises to 22 in ME3 and falls again in ME4 (9 occ.). The number of *biside-Phs* found in the corpus are not sufficiently indicative so as to measure their dialectal distribution.

The study of the semantic domains of *biside-Phs* shows that the initial locative meaning "by the side of" a place, person or thing developed new figurative meanings such as "in the mental view of"; "in the knowledge of"; as well as, in addition to". No phraseological units were detected in the corpus.

8. *In-Phs* are uncommon in the first period of ME. Thus only 5.6 instances are recorded for every thousand words. However, their use increases significantly in ME2 and ME3 as the rate shifts to 15.5‰ and 19.3‰, respectively. It is worth noting, however, that *in-Phs* became less frequent in the last period of ME. There are noteworthy variations depending on the dialectal area. Kentish and Southern areas hardly include any *in-Phs* in ME1, although the Kentish dialect exhibits a great increase in ME2 and ME4.

The semantic analysis indicates that the number of temporal instances is very small, as they only represent a rate of 5.15% with regard to all *in-Phs* found in the corpus. Our analysis also shows that a great number of *in-Phs* have acquired a figurative or abstract sense. In fact, *in-Phs* are subject to a massive transition from a spatial referential meaning to a more abstract one from 1350. I have also found some examples which could be categorized as phrasemes within temporal domains such as *in þe mene tyme, in the mene whyle, in þe ende, in the begynnyng, in sumer tide*, etc. The shift from figurative domains to quasi-idioms is detected in 267 instances of the HCME. This transition is displayed in some phraseological units such as *in deed, in doubt, in vayn, in speciall, in generall, in certayn, in despite*, etc.

9. *On-Phs* were predominant in ME1, but their frequency decreased steadily and progressively throughout the ME period. Thus more than 10 *on-Ph* are found for

every thousand words in ME1, whereas only 2.5 instances are identified in ME4 for the same number of words. There are significant variations with regard to dialect. Kentish and Southern areas include more than 2 *on*-occurrences in ME1 for every hundred words (2.19% and 2.17%, respectively), whereas the East Midland dialect records 1.10% and the West Midland area falls to 0.15%. ME2, ME3 and ME4 show, however, a similar distribution of *on-Phs* in all dialects.

From the semantic perspective, the locative uses of *on-Phs* to indicate a position of sb. or sth. placed on the top of an object or in close contact with a surface shows a very low rate in ME. On the other hand, the location of sth. or sb. in an open place (sea, river, ground, field, road, street, way, hill) is highly represented. The position above (not touching) or around (surrounding), suspended from or fixed to, in proximity to, close to, near, is also very commonly expressed by *on-Phs*. Equally, movement on or onto a position such as *on fot, on hors, on bac* is regularly expressed by *on-Phs*. The number of temporal instances is less than half those found in spatial uses. Figurative or abstract senses became very common in ME and I have also attested that *on-Phs* are well in the lead in the formation of phraseological units (phrasemes) in ME. Thus, in my analysis I have found that 17.17% of *on-Phs*, within spatial references, had acquired a quasi-idiomatic status. Most of them indicate position: ("in or from a certain direction") *on side* "to the side, aside"; *on eche half (a side)* "into every part"; *on everi half (honde)* "from all sides"; *on high* "high up"; etc. The HCME also shows *on-Phs* which could be classified as phrasemes in ME, denoting a temporal relationship such as *on alre erest, on firste, on frume, on frumthe, on ende*, etc. There is also a shift from their figurative usage to a quasi-idiomatic role to indicate either arrangement in a group, company or sequence as in *on hepe, on lump, on roue*, or state/condition as in *on loue, on live, on slep, on witnesse, on fir, on thirst, on game, on cas, on happes, on fer*, etc.

10. The number of *ouer-Phs* declines progressively, although slightly, in the course of the ME period. The rate of 0.8‰ of ME1 falls to 0.5‰ in ME4. The data from the corpus prove that all dialects include *ouer-Phs* in all subperiods of ME. It is also noticeable that there ane no significant variations in the dialectal distribution of these phrases.

The semantic study of these *p-Phs* indicates that the central meaning "locative superior" (passing directly above, position directly above) of the preposition *ouer* gradually extends to other figurative fields such as "to a greater degree or extent". I have not found any phraseological unit formed with *ouer-Phs*.

11. *Þurgh-Phs* were predominant in ME1, exhibiting a rate of 4 instances for every thousand words. This ratio diminishes to 1.1‰ in ME2 and only 0.6‰ were found in ME3 and a similar rate (0.7‰) has been recorded in ME4. The dialectal distribution is not homogeneous. Thus, except for the Southern dialect, which shows a progressive tendency to reduce *Þurgh-Phs* in the course of ME, the other dialects show a great deal of oscillation in their figures.

In semantic terms, the central meaning of "going across/along" of *þurgh-Phs* developed into other figurative semantic fields such as "through the mediation of a holy being or person"; "by means of virtue, grace, violence", etc. I have not detected any phraseological unit formed with *þurgh-Phs*.

12. I have only found 261 *under-Phs* in the HCME, that is, less than one instance for every two thousand words. It is also noteworthy that its use decreases in late ME. The figures exhibited in the corpus show that *under-Phs* are used in all dialects. There are, however, significant variations in the dialectal distribution of *under-Phs*. Thus, the Kentish dialect hardly includes the preposition *under*. In fact, we have to check about six thousand words to find a single instance of *under-Phs* in the subperiods (ME1 and ME2) recorded in the HCME. However, it seems to be clear that East Midland areas use more *under-Phs* than other dialectal areas.

The semantic analysis of *under-Phs* indicates that the primary role of *under-Phs*, indicating a position beneath or below, developed into a varied range of figurative meanings such as "subordination or subjection to a person"; "beneath the rule of, during the reign of"; "under the protection of", etc. No phraseological units were detected in the corpus.

As general conclusion, it is a noteworthy fact that *on-Phs* were predominant in ME1 with respect to all other prepositions, particularly with regard to *at, in* and *bi* which contended to cover a similar range of semantic connotations, but from ME2 *on-Phs* decreased steadily and progressively, whereas *at, in* and *bi* increase their usage in the course of ME.

APPENDIX

The main prepositions in the HCME

Preposition/Text	about	above	after	ageins	among	at	bi	bifore	bihinde	biside	bitwine	for	from	in	into	of	on	out of	ouer	to	purgh	under	up-on	wiþ	wiþut
CMAELR3	6	0	5	2	1	5	7	0	0	0	0	19	2	60	0	99	2	4	0	69	3	0	0	0	0
CMAELR4	0	0	1	0	0	1	6	0	0	0	0	13	1	29	5	81	2	4	0	33	0	0	0	14	2
CMALISAU	0	0	21	6	6	31	40	1	1	3	9	31	7	156	12	206	96	4	11	121	15	15	0	101	0
CMANCRE	1	0	16	6	0	1	17	0	2	0	2	73	16	32	0	160	31	6	11	117	36	8	11	108	2
CMASTRO	0	3	19	6	6	7	50	3	0	0	5	24	45	140	4	362	23	4	10	55	3	18	45	35	3
CMAYENBI	2	5	2	3	1	3	69	2	0	0	1	2	0	234	2	370	7	6	4	125	0	1	0	4	9
CMBENRUL	0	0	0	0	0	3	0	0	0	0	0	5	1	40	0	50	3	1	0	30	0	5	0	5	2
CMBESTIA	0	0	3	0	2	3	11	0	0	0	0	5	10	60	0	42	34	0	4	54	11	2	4	4	0
CMBEVIS	0	1	10	0	0	4	24	0	0	0	0	25	6	81	15	87	20	9	6	0	10	4	0	0	4
CMBODLEY	3	0	20	0	0	9	19	1	1	0	1	12	6	0	0	15	1	0	0	71	35	0	2	54	0
CMBOETH	3	2	3	0	6	7	110	3	0	2	0	34	20	81	19	357	135	6	3	132	0	0	1	13	19
CMBRUT1	0	0	9	0	0	5	23	0	0	1	0	11	0	27	4	115	8	5	13	158	19	2	8	0	3
CMBRUT3	2	0	23	14	7	12	19	2	1	0	13	16	13	73	48	256	55	7	4	65	0	3	6	24	0
CMCAPCHR	3	0	24	13	2	37	25	10	0	0	8	30	18	120	19	294	11	7	0	91	3	0	5	75	3
CMCAPSER	0	0	2	0	0	40	8	0	0	0	0	8	7	4	0	66	37	2	0	21	1	0	0	9	0
CMCAXPRO	0	0	16	0	4	8	49	0	1	0	4	40	6	35	7	240	1	6	2	77	1	3	3	12	1
CMCHAULI	9	5	36	0	0	12	43	1	0	0	15	19	15	20	4	257	5	5	9	68	1	1	5	37	1
CMCLOUD	3	14	23	4	3	6	88	7	1	0	2	64	28	486	15	528	6	3	2	105	11	5	3	98	41
CMCTPROS	0	0	9	3	0	19	100	7	0	0	1	41	12	187	11	298	48	4	6	66	8	10	5	16	11
CMCTVERS	5	1	6	0	0	5	38	5	0	0	2	34	8	109	4	152	5	9	6	43	15	3	15	48	5
CMCURSOR	5	0	0	4	0	25	9	0	0	1	3	29	0	140	0	69	26	1	6	61	11	9	1	135	22
CMDIGBY	3	2	4	8	5	24	13	1	0	0	1	22	11	63	10	58	44	3	6	26	11	2	8	57	9
CMDOCU2	0	0	0	1	1	4	1	0	0	0	0	2	0	4	1	17	12	0	0	1	6	0	0	1	0
CMDOCU3	4	0	33	8	11	40	102	13	0	0	5	86	18	289	15	676	19	7	1	236	3	7	28	42	12
CMDOCU4	2	1	17	1	5	46	93	13	0	0	6	60	21	190	13	546	51	6	3	146	8	10	38	72	8
CMEARLPS	1	0	1	0	4	10	4	0	0	1	0	33	15	442	20	559	16	10	5	297	6	2	71	8	3
CMEDMUND	0	0	9	0	1	18	15	4	0	0	1	25	16	92	9	80	32	1	0	67	6	1	10	19	0
CMEQUATO	3	0	16	3	0	8	34	0	0	0	0	18	58	201	3	400	14	37	4	33	4	5	11	1	0

The main prepositions in the HCME

Preposition/Text	aboute	aboue	after	ageins	among	at	bi	bifore	bihinde	biside	bitwine	for	from	in	into	of	on	out of	ouer	to	burgh	under	up-on	wiþ	wiþut
CMFITZJA	5	1	18	0	5	9	72	1	1	0	11	31	28	141	6	258	6	0	0	77	1	2	0	9	0
CMFOXWO	0	0	—	3	0	2	5	0	0	0	0	9	0	17	0	20	3	1	1	19	0	3	0	1	4
CMGAYTRY	0	0	1	8	2	7	5	0	0	0	0	11	8	90	0	150	24	2	6	61	18	2	0	24	13
CMGOWER	1	1	11	0	5	9	12	0	1	0	3	31	5	57	4	117	19	0	3	18	12	3	0	43	6
CMGREGOR	0	0	27	0	2	59	25	3	0	0	0	27	13	109	3	290	23	10	0	55	12	0	27	13	0
CMHALI	2	0	15	7	2	2	11	0	0	0	0	33	13	60	7	186	41	4	16	68	22	13	1	93	15
CMHANSYN	2	1	8	9	0	31	11	8	2	2	3	47	17	127	1	136	31	6	6	84	12	0	5	59	4
CMHILTON	0	2	8	6	3	1	13	2	0	2	6	18	9	67	1	202	82	4	3	61	12	6	3	25	7
CMHORN	6	0	11	6	0	23	40	8	0	2	2	11	12	56	21	92	53	2	2	76	18	0	15	37	7
CMHORSES	7	1	16	2	6	11	18	2	0	3	0	14	6	117	0	225	29	5	11	20	1	12	14	66	4
CMINNOCE	1	1	13	1	2	3	27	4	0	0	0	15	8	137	1	129	3	0	0	61	7	0	0	17	5
CMJULIA	3	3	11	3	0	0	7	1	2	3	0	26	14	81	6	117	24	8	6	87	2	1	7	70	16
CMJULNOR	0	0	10	0	0	3	5	4	0	0	0	23	5	120	0	97	4	0	6	72	1	1	2	25	6
CMCATHE	2	0	2	2	0	0	3	0	2	3	2	26	2	54	5	98	15	6	2	47	23	4	2	55	12
CMKEMPE	6	2	21	0	0	23	25	5	0	0	0	75	27	186	25	189	31	2	0	175	17	0	3	—	1
CMKENTSE	0	0	0	1	1	7	12	0	2	0	0	6	7	40	27	106	—	3	—	57	17	4	10	6	3
CMLAMBET	3	0	18	4	3	21	15	4	0	0	—	46	1	111	22	118	97	3	1	160	10	0	22	25	2
CMLAW	1	14	35	0	—	43	151	8	0	0	3	96	23	247	17	685	5	12	12	120	5	11	4	17	17
CMLUDUS	1	—	1	5	3	14	2	6	0	1	2	8	10	49	3	47	15	4	1	40	14	0	26	79	11
CMMALORY	9	2	13	6	3	40	45	6	4	4	0	36	17	90	17	227	57	18	8	51	1	4	14	26	8
CMMANDEV	9	5	15	6	6	33	26	4	4	4	7	16	22	90	6	248	11	3	2	33	—	6	4	0	0
CMMANKIN	0	—	1	3	—	11	20	2	0	0	6	12	6	43	0	75	12	4	1	26	—	1	42	46	5
CMMARGA	1	0	3	4	1	3	6	0	0	0	3	18	6	43	3	98	37	0	7	47	11	0	2	22	4
CMMETHAM	3	0	1	0	—	9	0	1	0	0	0	18	7	103	4	16	5	5	0	43	1	0	2	15	5
CMMIRK	1	2	7	11	—	14	14	3	0	0	—	18	6	38	0	63	19	0	—	53	—	0	2	1	0
CMMOON	0	0	0	0	0	2	0	0	0	2	2	1	0	5	1	4	1	5	0	3	0	4	0	47	9
CMNORHOM	1	0	3	0	0	10	16	8	0	2	2	24	26	131	5	135	29	9	5	86	16	0	3	47	5
CMNTEST	1	2	17	3	7	12	13	10	0	5	0	37	39	207	53	259	15	5	5	289	0	0	3	28	5

The main prepositions in the HCME

Preposition/Text	aboute	aboue	after	ageins	among	at	bi	bifore	bihinde	biside	bitwine	for	from	in	into	of	on	out of	ouer	to	burgh	under	up-on	wiþ	wiþut
CMOFFIC3	0	0	8	0	4	18	27	2	0	0	3	21	15	97	6	239	5	0	0	51	1	1	8	32	3
CMOFFIC4	2	0	11	11	0	20	44	6	0	0	2	5	6	71	0	162	7	0	1	36	0	0	7	6	0
CMORM	5	2	18	0	9	7	4	20	1	0	14	38	13	80	3	122	63	16	2	57	99	0	15	100	6
CMOTEST	4	3	14	28	3	7	49	22	1	3	9	49	53	185	62	445	46	7	0	120	4	1	0	50	8
CMPERIDI	6	0	16	8	0	2	2	2	0	0	1	2	9	8	1	72	121	5	1	71	24	4	17	13	0
CMPETERB	4	0	7	7	0	7	6	0	0	0	5	10	3	22	4	39	30	3	0	28	5	0	2	3	1
CMPHLEBO	4	1	22	4	5	3	19	2	0	0	0	18	1	82	2	215	5	2	6	26	0	2	0	17	7
CMPOEMH	0	1	5	5	0	10	17	3	0	0	1	8	3	26	3	88	10	4	5	40	2	1	5	13	1
CMPOEMS	0	0	0	1	0	4	5	0	0	0	0	5	3	17	0	31	14	0	1	17	1	0	2	17	3
CMPOLYCH	14	2	24	11	5	41	38	7	0	0	10	21	7	88	10	306	6	6	0	75	0	3	6	53	0
CMPRICK	3	0	14	2	0	9	3	0	0	0	2	17	11	96	0	160	17	3	3	9	15	0	2	29	11
CMPRIV	3	2	23	4	5	175	95	6	0	0	5	82	47	165	6	318	52	1	9	132	1	3	9	84	4
CMPURVEY	2	0	6	5	2	9	26	6	0	2	6	14	4	63	28	104	9	9	0	21	0	6	0	21	0
CMREYNAR	3	6	8	0	0	15	36	0	1	3	4	32	25	111	7	114	31	3	10	81	7	1	15	21	1
CMREYNES	7	2	33	4	0	48	14	1	1	0	15	96	23	143	8	342	28	1	5	134	3	2	15	38	11
CMROBGLO	12	0	11	14	5	55	26	5	1	0	0	0	15	151	8	331	5	15	11	101	29	0	0	31	18
CMROLLBE	0	0	0	2	0	0	0	0	0	2	0	4	7	12	0	23	1	0	2	5	0	0	0	3	0
CMROLLPS	1	11	12	11	2	12	6	6	0	2	0	61	36	460	0	383	6	6	0	9	26	0	2	45	29
CMROLLTR	0	3	7	8	0	6	4	6	0	0	0	21	6	164	5	267	3	2	6	75	6	1	5	23	17
CMROOD	2	0	11	2	0	0	4	3	0	0	6	28	6	13	12	40	168	3	5	121	45	1	0	8	1
CMSAWLES	3	0	12	9	0	2	36	4	0	0	0	34	6	103	1	78	20	0	0	32	3	0	0	22	6
CMSELEG	1	1	8	2	1	29	14	0	0	0	1	22	26	22	2	121	17	6	0	62	9	4	4	22	6
CMSIEGE	3	2	12	3	2	23	11	7	0	0	0	39	14	105	25	207	30	3	2	76	0	0	9	54	6
CMSIRITH	0	0	0	1	0	0	4	0	0	0	0	17	1	6	1	29	18	1	4	23	2	0	3	14	3
CMTHORN	2	0	7	0	2	22	2	6	0	0	0	11	5	114	1	216	19	0	16	47	16	2	2	49	5
CMTHRUSH	0	0	0	0	0	0	6	0	0	0	2	3	2	14	1	29	5	0	0	14	2	2	0	9	0
CMTOWNEL	0	1	1	1	0	6	4	1	0	0	1	20	13	58	7	41	16	3	1	56	1	0	2	24	10
CMTRINIT	2	1	6	6	0	6	11	4	0	0	0	17	7	31	8	70	115	2	2	0	2	1	8	7	0

The main prepositions in the HCME

Preposition/Text	about	aboue	after	ageins	among	at	bi	bifore	bihinde	biside	bitwine	for	from	in	into	of	on	out of	ouer	to	burgh	under	up-on	wiþ	wiþut
CMVESHOM	5	0	11	0	0	0	0	1	0	0	0	21	19	0	1	18	128	0	0	42	12	2	3	8	0
CMVICES1	0	0	23	17	2	12	2	2	0	0	1	54	18	22	19	169	120	13	7	61	51	3	23	4	5
CMVICES4	1	2	0	0	1	10	24	0	0	0	0	32	6	114	0	175	10	9	3	82	3	1	3	23	27
CMWYCSER	2	1	41	0	16	13	71	14	2	3	3	61	31	274	9	418	20	0	5	196	0	0	9	54	20
CMYORK	0	0	3	6	0	18	5	3	0	0	0	32	13	53	1	56	5	0	2	47	5	0	0	27	4
TOTAL	209	122	1001	353	170	1555	2290	305	24	42	218	2397	1154	9437	704	16255	2691	364	371	6305	862	261	656	3563	538

Number of instances   51,822

PRIMARY SOURCES

This list contains the full titles of the texts sampled in the ME section of the HC which correspond to the abbreviated titles used in the body of this study when quoting extracts from the HC.

CMAELR3: *Aelred of Rievaulx's De Institutione Inclusarum.* E.E.T.S., 287. Ed. J. Ayto and A. Barratt. London, 1984.
CMAELR4: *Aelred of Rievaulx's De Institutione Inclusarum.* E.E.T.S., 287. Ed. J. Ayto and A. Barratt. London, 1984.
CMALISAU: *Kyng Alisaunder, Vol. I.* E.E.T.S., 227. Ed. G. V. Smithers. London, 1952. Bodleian Ms Laud Misc. 622(B).
CMANCRE: *Ancrene Wisse.* E.E.T.S., 249. Ed. J. R. R. Tolkien. London, 1962.
CMASTRO: Chaucer, Geoffrey. *A Treatise on the Astrolabe.*
The Riverside Chaucer. Third edition. General editor L. D. Benson. Based on the works of Geoffrey Chaucer, edited by F. N. Robinson. Boston: Houghton Mifflin Company, 1987.
CMAYENBI: Michel, Dan. *Dan Michel's Ayenbite of Inwyt or Remorse of Conscience, Vol. I.* E.E.T.S., O.S. 23. Ed. R. Morris and P. Gradon. London, 1965(1866).
CMBEVIS: *The Romance of Sir Beues of Hamtoun, Vols. I—III.* E.E.T.S., E.S. 46, 48, 65. Ed. E. Koelbing. New York, 1973(1885—1894).
CMBENRUL: *The Benedictine Rule.*
Three Middle—English Versions of the Rule of St. Benet and Two Contemporary Rituals for the Ordination of Nuns. E.E.T.S., O.S. 120. Ed. E. A. Kock. London, 1902.
CMBESTIA: *A Bestiary.*
An Old English Miscellany Containing A Bestiary, Kentish Sermons, Proverbs of Alfred, Religious Poems of the Thirteenth Century. E.E.T.S., O.S. 49. Ed. R. Morris. London, 1872.

CMBODLEY: *Bodley Homilies.*
  Twelfth—Century Homilies in Ms. Bodley 343, Part I. Bod12 E.E.T.S., O.S. 137. Ed. A. O. Belfour. London, 1962(1909).
CMBOETH: Chaucer, Geoffrey. *Boethius.*
  The Riverside Chaucer. Third edition. General editor L. D. Benson. Based on the works of Geoffrey Chaucer, edited by F. N. Robinson. Boston: Houghton Mifflin Company, 1987.
CMBRUT1: *Layamon's Brut, Vols. I, II.* E.E.T.S., 250, 277. Ed. G. L. Brook and R. F. Leslie. London, 1963, 1978. B.L. Ms Cotton Caligula A.Ix.
CMBRUT3: *The Brut or the Chronicles of England Part I.* E.E.T.S., O.S. 131. Ed. F. W. D. Brie. London, 1960(1906).
CMCAPCHR: Capgrave, John. *Capgrave's Chronicle.*
  John Capgrave's Abbreuiacion of Cronicles. E.E.T.S., 285. Ed. P. J. Lucas. Oxford, 1983.
CMCAPSER: Capgrave, John.
  Capgrave's Sermon. John Capgrave's Lives of St. Augustine and St. Gilbert of Sempringham, and a Sermon. E.E.T.S., O.S. 140. Ed. J. J. Munro. New York, 1971(1910).
CMCAXPRO: Caxton, William. *The Prologues and Epilogues of William Caxton.* E.E.T.S., 176. Ed. W. J. B. Crotch. London, 1956(1928).
CMCHAULI: *The Cyrurgie of Guy de Chauliac.* E.E.T.S., 265. Ed. M. S. Ogden. London, 1971.
CMCTPROS: Chaucer, Geoffrey. *The Parson's Tale.*
  The Tale of Melibee.
  The Riverside Chaucer. Third edition. General editor L. D. Benson. Based on the works of Geoffrey Chaucer, edited by F. N. Robinson. Boston: Houghton Mifflin Company, 1987.
CMCTVERS Chaucer, Geoffrey. *The General Prologue to the Canterbury Tales.*
  The Merchant's Tale.
  The Summoner's Tale.
  The Wife Of Bath's Prologue.
  The Riverside Chaucer. Third edition. General editor L. D. Benson. Based on the works of Geoffrey Chaucer, edited by F. N. Robinson. Boston: Houghton Mifflin Company, 1987.
CMCLOUD: *The Cloud of Unknowing.*
  The Cloud of Unknowing and the Book of Privy Counselling. E.E.T.S., 218. Ed. P. Hodgson. London, 1958(1944).
CMCURSOR: *Cursor Mundi.* E.E.T.S., O.S. 57, 59, 62, 66, 68. Ed. R. Morris. London, 1874, 1875, 1876, 1877, 1878. Cotton Ms Vespasian A.III:
CMDIGBY: *Digby Plays.*

The Late Medieval Religious Plays of Bodleian Mss Digby 133 and E Museo 160. E.E.T.S., 283. Ed. D. C. Baker, J. L. Murphy & L. B. Hall, Jr. Oxford, 1982.
CMDOCU2: *The Proclamation of Henry III. Early Middle English Texts.* Ed. B. Dickins and R. M. Wilson. London: Bowes & Bowes, 1956(1951).
CMDOCU3: *Proclamations, London.*
Judgements, London.
Returns, London.
Testaments and Wills, London.
Usk, Thomas. *Appeals.*
Petitions (M3), London.
A Book of London English 1384—1425. Ed. R. W. Chambers and M. Daunt. Oxford: Clarendon Press, 1967(1931).
Petitions (M3), London.
An Anthology of Chancery English. Ed. J. H. Fisher, M. Richardson and J. L. Fisher. Knoxville: The University of Tennessee Press, 1984.
CMDOCU4: *Petitions (M4), London.*
Depositions.
Indenture.
An Anthology of Chancery English. Ed. J. H. Fisher, M. Richardson and J. L. Fisher. Knoxville: The University of Tennessee Press, 1984.

Shillingford, John. *Documents.*
Letters and Papers of John Shillingford, Mayor of Exeter 1447—50. Camden Society, N.S. II. Ed. S. A. Moore. New York, 1965(1871).
CMEARLPS: *The Earliest Complete English Prose Psalter.* E.E.T.S., O.S. 97. Ed. K. D. Buelbring. London, 1891.
CMEDMUND: *The Life of St. Edmund.*
Middle English Religious Prose. York Medieval Texts. Ed. N. F. Blake. London: Edward Arnold, 1972. Pp. 163.1 — 173.313
CMEQUATO: *The Equatorie of the Planetis.* Ed. D. J. Price. Cambridge: Cambridge University Press, 1955.
CMFITZJA: Fitzjames, Richard. *Sermo Die Lune in Ebdomada Pasche. Westminster, Wynkyn De Worde(1495?).* Ed. F. Jenkinson (Facsimile). Cambridge: Cambridge University Press, 1907.
CMFOXWO: *The Fox and Wolf in the Well.*
Middle English Humorous Tales in Verse. Ed. G. H. Mcknight. New York: Gordian Press, 1971(1913).

CMGAYTRY: Gaytryge, Dan Jon. *Dan Jon Gaytryge's Sermon.*
Religious Pieces in Prose and Verse. E.E.T.S., O.S. 26. Ed. G. G. Perry. New York, 1969(1914).
CMGOWER: Gower, John. *Confessio Amantis.*
The English Works of John Gower, Vols. *I, II.* E.E.T.S., E.S. 81, 82. Ed. G. C. Macaulay. London, 1957(1900), 1957(1901).
CMGREGOR: Gregory, William. *Gregory's Chronicle.*
The Historical Collections of A Citizen of London in the Fifteenth Century. Camden Society, N.S. XVII. Ed. J. Gairdner. Westminster, 1876.
CMHALI: *Hali Meidhad.*
*The erine Group. edit*ed From Ms. Bodley 34. Bibliothèque de La Faculté de Philosophie et Lettres de L'université de Liège, CCXV. Ed. S. T. R. O. D'ardenne. Paris: Société D'édition "Les Belles Lettres", 1977.
CMHANSYN: Mannyng, Robert. *Robert of Brunne's «Handlyng Synne», Part I.* E.E.T.S., O.S. 119. Ed. F. J. Furnivall. London, 1901.
CMHAVELO: *Havelok.* Ed. G. V. Smithers. Oxford: Clarendon Press, 1987.
CMHILTON: Hilton, Walter. *Walter Hilton's Eight Chapters on Perfection.* Ed. F. Kuriyagawa. Tokyo: The Keio Institute of Cultural and Linguistic Studies, 1967.
CMHORN: *King Horn.*
King Horn, Floriz and Blauncheflur, the Assumption of Our Lady, Vol I. E.E.T.S., O.S. 14. Ed. J. R. Lumby and G. H. Mcknight. London, 1962(1866).
CMHORSES: *A Late Middle English Treatise on Horses.* Stockholm Studies in English, XLVII. Ed. A. C. Svinhufvud. Stockholm: Almqvist & Wiksell International, 1978.
CMINNOCE: *In Die Innocencium. Two Sermons Preached by the Boy Bishop, At St. Paul's Temp. Henry VII, and At Gloucester, Temp. Mary.* Camden Society Miscellany, VII. Camden Society, N.S. Xiv. Ed. J. G. Nichols. London, 1875.
CMJULIA: *Juliane.*
*The Katherine Group. edit*ed From Ms. Bodley 34. Bibliothèque de La Faculté de Philosophie et Lettres de L'université de Liège, CCXV. Ed. S. T. R. O. D'ardenne. Paris: Société D'édition "Les Belles Lettres", 1977.
CMJULNOR: Julian of Norwich. *Julian of Norwich's Revelations of Divine Love. The Shorter Version Ed. From B.L. Add. Ms 37790.* Middle English Texts. Ed. F. Beer. Heidelberg: Carl Winter Universitaetsverlag, 1978.

CMKATHE: *Katherine.*
    *The Katherine Group. edit*ed From Ms. Bodley 34. Bibliothèque de La Faculté de Philosophie et Lettres de L'université de Liège, CCXV. Ed. S. T. R. O. D'ardenne. Paris: Société D'édition "Les Belles Lettres", 1977.
CMKEMPE: Kempe, Margery. *The Book of Margery Kempe, Vol. I.* E.E.T.S., 212. Ed. S. B. Meech and H. E. Allen. London, 1940.
CMKENTSE: *Kentish Sermons.*
    Selections From Early Middle English 1130—1250, Part I. Ed. J. Hall. Oxford: The Clarendon Press, 1963(1920).
CMLAMBET: *Lambeth Homilies.*
    Old English Homilies and Homiletic Treatises of the Twelfth and Thirteenth Centuries. First Series. E.E.T.S., O.S. 29, 34. Ed. R. Morris. New York, 1969(1868).
CMLAW: *Statutes.*
    The Statutes of the Realm. Printed by Command of His Majesty King George the Third in Pursuance of an Address of the House of Commons of Great Britain, Vol. II. London: Dawsons of Pall Mall, 1963(1816).
CMLUDUS: *Ludus Coventriae or the Plaie Called Corpus Christi.* Cotton Ms. Vespasian D. VIII. E.E.T.S., E.S. 120. Ed. K. S. Block. London, 1960(1922).
CMMALORY: Malory, Thomas. *Morte DArthur.*
    Sir Thomas Malory. Ed. E. Vinaver. London: Oxford University Press, 1954.
CMMOON: *Man in the Moon.*
    Early Middle English Verse and Prose. Ed. J. A. W. Bennett and G. V. Smithers. Oxford: Clarendon Press, 1968(1966).
CMMANDEV: *Mandeville's Travels, Translated From the French of Jean D'outremeuse, Vol. I.* The E.E.T.S., O.S. 153. Ed. P. Hamelius. London, 1919.
CMMANKIN: *Mankind.*
    The Macro Plays. E.E.T.S., 262. Ed. M. Eccles. London, 1969.
CMMARGA: *Margarete.*
    The Katherine Group. Edited From Ms. Bodley 34. Bibliothèque de La Faculté de Philosophie et Lettres de L'université de Liège, CCXV. Ed. S. T. R. O. D'ardenne. Paris: Société D'édition «Les Belles Lettres», 1977.
CMMETHAM: Metham, John.: *Days of the Moon.*
    Physiognomy.
    The Works of John Metham Including the Romance of Amoryus and Cleopes. E.E.T.S., O.S. 132. Ed. H. Craig. London, 1916.

CMMIRK: Mirk, John. *Mirk's Festial: A Collection of Homilies, by Johannes Mirkus (John Mirk), Part I.* E.E.T.S., E.S. 96. Ed. T. Erbe. London, 1905.
CMNTEST: *The New Testament.*
The New Testament in English according to the Version by John Wycliffe About A. D. 1380 and Revised by John Purvey About A. D. 1388. Ed. J. Forshall and F. Madden. Oxford: Clarendon Press, 1879. John I.1 — Xi,56
CMOFFIC3: Henry V. *Letters.*
An Anthology of Chancery English. Ed. J. H. Fisher, M. Richardson and J. L. Fisher. Knoxville: The University of Tennessee Press, 1984.
Henry V. *Letters.*
Letters, London.
A Book of London English 1384—1425. Ed. R. W. Chambers and M. Daunt. Oxford: Clarendon Press, 1967(1931).
CMOFFIC4: Paston, William. *Letter(s).*
Paston Letters and Papers of the Fifteenth Century, Part I. Ed. N. Davis. Oxford: Clarendon Press, 1971.
CMNORHOM: *The Northern Homily Cycle, Parts II, III. The Expanded Version in Mss Harley 4196 and Cotton Tiberius E VII.* Société Néophilologique De Helsinki, 41, 43. Ed. S. Nevanlinna. Helsinki: Société Néophilologique, 1973, 1984.
CMOTEST: *The Old Testament.*
The Holy Bible, Containing the Old and New Testaments, With the Apocryphal Books, in the Earliest English Versions Made From the Latin Vulgate by John Wycliffe and His Followers, Vol. I. Ed. J. Forshall and F. Madden. Oxford: University Press, 1850.
CMORM: Orm. *The Ormulum, Vols. I—II. With the Notes and Glossary of R. M. White.* Ed. R. Holt. Oxford: The Clarendon Press, 1878.
CMPERIDI: *Peri Didaxeon. Leechdoms, Wortcunning, and Starcraft of Early England, Vol. III.* Rolls Series, 35. Ed. O. Cockayne. London, 1866.
CMPETERB: *The Peterborough Chronicle, 1070—1154.* Ed. C. Clark. London: Oxford University Press, 1958.
CMPHLEBO: *A Latin Technical Phlebotomy and its Middle English Translation. Transactions of the American Philosophical Society, 74, Part 2.* Ed. L. E. Voigts and M. R. Mcvaugh. Philadelphia, 1984.
CMPOEMH: *Historical Poems (Harley 2253).*
Historical Poems of the XIVth and XVth Centuries. Ed. R. H. Robbins. New York: Columbia University Press, 1959.

CMPOEMS: *Satire on the Consistory Courts.*
Song of the Husbandman.
Satire on the Retinues of the Great
Historical Poems of the XIVth and XVth Centuries. Ed. R. H. Robbins. New York: Columbia University Press, 1959.
CMPOLYCH: Trevisa, John. *Polychronicon Ranulphi Higden, Monachi Cestrensis, Vols. VI, VIII. English Translations of John Trevisa and of An Unknown Writer of the Fifteenth Century. Rolls Series, 41.* Ed. J. R. Lumby. London, 1876, 1882.
CMPRICK: *The Pricke of Conscience(Stimulus Conscientiae).* Ed. R. Morris. Berlin: A. Asher & Co., 1863.
CMPRIV: Paston, Clement. *Letters.*
Paston, John. *Letters.*
Paston, Margaret. *Letters.*
Paston Letters and Papers of the Fifteenth Century, Part I. Ed. N. Davis. Oxford: Clarendon Press, 1971.
Shillingford, John. *Letters.*
Letters and Papers of John Shillingford, Mayor of Exeter 1447—50. Camden Society, N.S. II. Ed. S. A. Moore. New York, 1965(1871).
Mull, Thomas. *Letters.*
Stonor, Elizabeth. *Letters.*
Betson, Thomas. Letters
The Stonor Letters and Papers, 1290—1483, Vols. I—II. Camden Society, Third Series, XXIX—XXX. Ed. C. L. Kingsford. London, 1919.
Cely, George. *Letters.*
Cely, Richard (The Younger).*Letters.*
The Cely Letters 1472—1488. E.E.T.S., 273. Ed. A. Hanham. London, 1975.
CMPURVEY: Purvey, John. *The Prologue to the Bible. The Holy Bible, Containing the Old and New Testaments, with the Apocryphal Books, in the Earliest English Versions made from the Latin Vulgate by John Wycliffe and his followers, Vol. I.* Ed. J. Forshall and F. Madden. Oxford: University Press, 1850.
CMREYNAR: Caxton, William. *The History of Reynard the Fox. Translated From the Dutch Original by William Caxton. E.E.T.S., 263.* Ed. N. F. Blake. London, 1970.
CMREYNES: Reynes, Robert. *The Commonplace Book of Robert Reynes of Acle. An edition of Tanner Ms 407. Garland Medieval Texts, 1.* Ed. C. Louis. New York and London: Garland Publishing, Inc., 1980.

CMROBGLO: Robert of Gloucester. *The Metrical Chronicle of Robert of Gloucester, Part II.* Rolls Series, 86. Ed. W. A. Wright. London, 1887.
CMROLLBE: Rolle, Richard. *The Bee and the Stork.*
A Handbook of Middle English. Ed. F. Mosse. Translated by J. A. Walker. Baltimore: The Johns Hopkins Press, 1952.
CMROLLTR: Rolle, Richard. *Prose Treatises.*
English Prose Treatises of Richard Rolle De Hampole. E.E.T.S., O.S. 20. Ed. G. G. Perry. London, 1921(1866).
CMROLLPS: Rolle, Richard. *The Psalter or Psalms of David.*
The Psalter or Psalms of David and certain Canticles with a Translation and Exposition in English by Richard Rolle of Hampole. Ed. H. R. Bramley. Oxford: Clarendon Press, 1884.
CMROYAL: *Middle English Sermons, edited From British Museum Ms. Royal 18 B. XXIII.* E.E.T.S., 209. Ed. W. O. Ross. London, 1940.
CMROOD: *History of the Holy Rood—Tree.* E.E.T.S., O.S. 103. Ed. A. S. Napier. London, 1894.
CMSAWLES: *Sawles Warde.*
*The Katherine Group. edit*ed From Ms. Bodley 34. Bibliothèque de La Faculté de Philosophie et Lettres de L'université de Liège, CCXV. Ed. S. T. R. O. D'ardenne. Paris: Société D'édition «Les Belles Lettres», 1977. .
CMSELEG: *The Life of St. Edmund.*
The Early South—English Legendary or Lives of Saints. E.E.T.S., O.S. 87. Ed. C. Horstmann. London, 1887.
CMSIEGE: *The Siege of Jerusalem in Prose.* Memoires de la Société Néophilologique De Helsinki, XXXIV. Ed. A. Kurvinen. Helsinki: Société Néophilologique, 1969.
CMSIRITH: *Dame Sirith. Interlude.(Appendix To Dame Sirith).*
Middle English Humorous Tales in Verse. Ed. G. H. Mcknight. New York: Gordian Press, 1971(1913).
CMTHORN: *The 'Liber De Diversis Medicinis' in the Thornton Manuscript (Ms. Lincoln Cathedral A.5.2.)* E.E.T.S., 207. Ed. M. S. Ogden. London, 1938.
CMTOWNEL: *The Wakefield Pageants in the Towneley Cycle. Old and Middle English Texts.* Ed. A. C. Cawley. Manchester: The Manchester University Press, 1958.
CMTHRUSH: *The Thrush and the Nightingale.*
English Lyrics of the XIIIth Century. Ed. C. Brown. Oxford: Clarendon Press, 1932.
CMTRINIT: *Trinity Homilies.*
Old English Homilies of the Twelfth Century. Second Series. E.E.T.S., O.S. 53. Ed. R. Morris. London, 1873.

CMVESHOM: *Vespasian Homilies.*
        Early English Homilies From the Twelfth Century Ms. Vesp. D. XIV. E.E.T.S., O.S. 152. Ed. R. D—N. Warner. New York, 1971(1917).)
CMVICES1: *Vices and Virtues. Part I.* E.E.T.S., O.S. 89. Ed. F. Holthausen. London, 1888.
CMVICES4: *The Book of Vices and Virtues. A Fourteenth Century English Translation of the Somme Le Roi of Lorens D'orleans.* E.E.T.S., 217. Ed. W. N. Francis. London, 1942.
CMWYCSER: *English Wycliffite Sermons, Vol. I.* Ed. A. Hudson. Oxford: Clarendon Press,
CMYORK: *The York Plays.* Ed. R. Beadle. London: Edward Arnold Ltd, 1982.

BIBLIOGRAPHY

Akimoto, Minoji (1983). *Idiomaticity*. Tokyo: Shinozaki Shorin.
Allerton, David and Paul Skandera (2004). *Phraseological Units: Basic Concepts and their Applications*. Basel: Schwabe.
Altenberg, Bengt (1998). "On the phraseology of spoken English: the evidence of recurrent word-combinations". In: Cowie, Anthony P. (ed.): 101-124.
Anderson, Stephen R. and Paul Kiparsky (1973). *A Festschrift for Morris Halle*. New York: Holt, Rinehart and Wiston.
ATILF: *Analyse et Traitement Informatique de la Langue Française*. Paris: Centre National de la Recherche Scientifique.
Backus, Ad (2003). "Units in code-switching: evidence for multimorphemic elements in the lexicon". *Linguistics* 14(1): 83-132.
Baker, Mona, Francis Gill and Elena Tognini-Bonelli (1993). *Text and Technology*. Amsterdam: John Benjamins.
Bennett, David C. (1975). *Spatial and Temporal Uses of English Prepositions*. London: Longman.
Benson, Morton (1990). "Collocations and general-purpose dictionaries". *International Journal of Lexicography* 3(1): 23-34.
Björkman, Sven (1978). *Le type avoir besoin. Étude sur la coalescence verbo-nominale en français*. Uppsala: Borgstöms Tryceri.
Bosworth, Joseph and T. Northcote Toller (1972) [1898]. *An Anglo-Saxon Dictionary*. London: Oxford Univ. Press.
Botelho da Silva, Teresa and Anne Cutler (1993). "Ill-formedness and transformability in Portuguese idioms". In: Cacciari, Cristina and Patrizia Tabossi (eds.): 129-144.
Bresnan, Joan (1982). *The Mental Representation of Grammatical Relations*. Cambridge, Massachusetts: MIT Press.
Brinton, Laurel J. and Minoji Akimoto (1999). *Collocational and Idiomatic Aspects of Composite Predicates in the History of English*. Amsterdam: John Benjamins.
Brinton, Laurel J. (2004). "Subject clitics in English: A case of degrammaticalization". In: Lindkvist, Hans and Christian Mair (eds.): 227-256.

Brinton, Laurel J. and Elizabeth Closs Traugott. (2005). *Lexicalisation and Language Change*. Cambridge: Cambridge University Press.

Bybee, Joan L. (2003). "Mechanisms of cange in grammaticalization: The role of frequency". In: Joseph, Brian D. and Richard D. Janda (eds.): 602.623.

Bybee, Joan L. and Östen Dahl (1989). "The creation of tense and aspect systems in the languages of the world". *Studies in Language* 13: 51-103.

Bybee, Joan, Revere Perkins and William Pagliuca (1994). *The Evolution of Grammar*. Chicago and London: The University of Chicago Press.

Cacciari, Cristina (1993). "The place of idioms in a literal and metaphorical world". In: Cacciari, Cristina and Patrizia Tabossi (eds.): 27-56.

Cacciari, Cristina and Sam Glucksberg (1990). "Understanding idiomatic expressions: the contribution of word meanings". In: Simpson, Greg B. (ed.): 217-240.

Cacciari, Cristina and Patrizia Tabossi (1988). "The comprehension of idioms". *Journal of Memory and Language* 27: 668-683.

Cacciari, Cristina and Patrizia Tabossi (1993). *Idioms. Processing, Structure and Interpretation*. Hillsdale, New Jersey and Hove: Lawrence Erlbaum Associates.

Cadiot, Pierre (2002). "Schematics and motifs in the semantics of prepositions". In: Feigenbaum, Susanne and Dennis Kurzon (eds.): 41-57.

Carter, Ronald (1987). *Vocabulary: Applied Linguistic Perspectives*. London: Routledge.

Carter, Ronald and Michael McCarthy (1988). *Vocabulary and Language Teaching*. London: Longman.

Cermák, František. (2001). "Substance of idioms: perennial problems, lack of data or theory?". *International Journal of Lexicography* 14(1): 1-20.

Chafe, Wallace (1968). "Idiomaticity as an anomaly in the Chomskyan paradigm". *Foundations of Language* 4: 109-125.

Choueka, Yakov (1988). "Looking for needles in a haystack". In: Fluhr, Christian and Donald E. Walker (eds.): 609-623.

Church, Kenneth and Patrick Hanks (1989). "Word association norms, Mutual Information and Lexicography". *Computational Linguistics* 16(1): 22-29.

Claudi, Ulrike and Bernd Heine (1986). "On the metaphorical base of grammar". *Studies in Language* 10: 297-335.

Clear, Jeremy (1993). "From Firth principles. Collocational tools for the study of collocation". In: Baker, Mona, Francis Gill and Elena Tognini-Bonelli (eds): 271-292.

Colson, Jean-Pierre (2008). "Cross-linguistic phraseological studies: An overview". In: Granger, Sylviane and Fanny Meunier (eds.): 191-206.

Cooper, Gloria S. (1968). *A Semantic Analysis of English Locative Prepositions*. Bolt, Beranek, and Newman, report 1587.

Coriston-Oliver, Monica (2001). "Central meaning of polysemous prepositions: challenging the assumptions". Paper read at International Cognitive Linguistics Conference, Santa Barbara, CA.

Coseriu, Eugenio (1967). "Lexical solidarities". *Poetica* 1: 293-303.

Coseriu, Eugenio (1975). *Esquisses Linguistiques II*. Munich : Fink.

Coulthard, Malcolm (1994). *Advances in Written Text Analysis*. London: Routledge

Cowie, Anthony P. (1998). *Phraseology*. Oxford: Clarendon Press.

Cowie, Anthony P. (1988). "Stable and creative aspects of vocabulary use". In: Carter, Ronald and Michael McCarthy (eds.): 126-137.

Craig, Colette (1991). "Ways to go in Rama: A case study in polygrammaticalization". In: Traugott, Elizabeth Closs and Bernd Heine (eds.): 455-492.

Croft, William (1991). *Syntactic Categories and Grammatical Relations*. Chicago: University of Chicago Press.

Cruz, Juan M. de la (1978). "A late 13th century change in English structure". *Orbis* 22(1): 171-80.

Dirven, René (1993). "Dividing up physical and mental space into conceptual categories by means of English prepositions". In: Zelinsky-Wibbelt, Cornelia (ed): 73-97.

Donner, Morton (1991). "Adverb form in Middle English". *English Studies* 72: 1-11.

Estill, Robert and Susan Kemper (1982. "Interpreting idioms". *Journal of Psycholinguistic Research* 9: 559-568.

Everaert, Martin, Erik-Jan van der Linden, André Schenk, and Rob Schreuder (1995). *Idioms*. Hillsdale, New Jersey and Hove: Lawrence Erlbaum Associates.

Evert, Stefan (2004). *The Statistics of Word Cooccurrences: Word Pairs and Collocations*. PhD dissertation, University of Stuttgart.

Falz, Leonard M. (1985). *Reflexivization: A Study in Universal Syntax*. New York: Garland.

Feigenbaum, Susanne and Dennis Kurzon (2002). *Prepositions in their Syntactic, Semantic and Pragmatic Context*. Amsterdam: John Benjamins.

Feilke, Helmuth (1996). *Sprache als soziale Gestalt*. Frankfurt: Suhrkamp.

Feilke, Helmuth (2003). "Kontext – Zeichen – Kompetenz. Wortverbindungen unter sprachtheoretischem Aspekt". In: Steyer, Kathrin (ed.): 41-64.

Fischer, Olga, Muriel Norde and Harry Perridon (2004). *Up and down the Cline. The Nature of Grammaticalization*. Amsterdam: John Benjamins.

Fisiak, Jacek (1985). *Historical Semantics. Historical Word-Formation*. Berlin: Mouton.

Fisiak, Jacek (1996). *Advances in English Historical Linguistcs*. Berlin: Mouton.

Flores D'Arcais, Giovanni B. (1993). "The comprehension and semantic interpretation of idioms". In: Cacciari, Cristina and Patrizia Tabossi (eds.): 79-98.

Fónagy, Ivan (2000). *Languages within Language. An Evolutive Approach.* Amsterdam: John Benjamins.

Fluhr, Christian and Donald E. Walker (1988). *Computer-Assisted Information Retrieval* (RIAO). Massachusetts, Cambridge: Proceedings. CID.

Fraser, Bruce (1970). "Idioms within a transformational grammar". *Foundations of Language* 6: 22-42.

Fries, Udo, Gunnel Tottie and Peter Schneider (1994). *Creating and Using English Language Corpora.* Amsterdam: Rodopi.

Gazdar, Gerald, Ewan Klein, Geoffrey Pullum and Ivan Sag (1985). *Generalized Phrase Structure Grammar.* London: Basil Blackwell.

Gibbs, Raymond W. Jr. and Nandini P. Nayak (1989). "Psycholinguistic studies on the syntactic behavior of idioms". *Cognitive Psychology* 21: 100-138.

Gibbs, Raymond W. Jr. (1980). "Spilling the beans on understanding and memory for idioms in conversation". *Memory and Cognition* 8: 449-456.

Gibbs, Raymond W. Jr. (1986). "Skating on thin ice: literal meaning and understanding idioms in conversation". *Discourse Processes* 9: 17-30.

Gibbs, Raymond W. Jr. (1995). "Idiomaticity and human cognition". In: Everaert, Martin, Erik-Jan van der Linden, André Schenk, and Rob Schreuder (eds.): 97-116.

Gibbs, Raymond W. Jr., Nandini P. Nayak and Cooper Cutting (1989). "How to kick the bucket and not decompose: Analyzability and idiom processing". *Journal of Memory and Language* 28: 576-593.

Gitsaki, Christina (1996). *The Development of ESL Collocational Knowledge.* Unpublished PhD. Thesis. Brisbane, Australia. The University of Queensland.

Givón, Talmy (1975). "Serial verbs and syntactic change: Niger-Congo". In: Li, Charles N. (ed.): 47-112.

Givón, Talmy (1979). *On Understanding Grammar.* New York: Academic Press.

Gläser, Rosemarie (1988). "The grading of idiomaticity as a presupposition for a taxonomy of idioms". In: Hüllen, Werner and Rainer Schulze (eds.): 264-79.

Gläser, Rosemarie (1998). "The stylistic potential of phraseological units in the light of genre analysis". In: Cowie, Anthony P. (ed.): 125-144.

Gledhill, Chris J. (2000). *Collocation in Science Writing.* Tübingen: Gunter Narr Verlag.

Glucksberg, Sam (1993). "Idiom meanings and allusional content". In: Cacciari, Cristina and Patrizia Tabossi (eds.): 3-26.

Godefroy, Frédéric (1880-1895) [Reprint 1969]. *Dictionnaire de l'ancienne langue française et de tous ses dialectes.* Nendeln/Liechtenstein: Kraus-Thomson.

Granger, Sylviane (1998). "Prefabricated patterns in advanced EFL writing: collocations and formulae". In: Cowie, Anthony P. (ed.): 145-160.

Granger, Sylviane and Fanny Meunier (2008). *Phraseology. An interdisciplinary perspective.* Amsterdam: John Benjamins.

Granger, Sylviane and Magali Paquot (2008). "Disentangling the phraseological web". In: Granger, Sylviane and Fanny Meunier (eds.): 27-50.
Gross, Maurice (1986). "Les nominalizations d'expressions figées". *Langue Française* 69: 64-84.
Grossmann, Francis and Agnès Tutin (2003). *Les collocations: analyse et traitement.* Amsterdam: De Werelt.
Haiman, John (1994). "Ritualization and the development of language". In: Pagliuca, William (ed.): 3-28.
Haiman, John (1985). *Iconicity in Syntax.* Amsterdam: John Benjamins.
Handl, Susanne (2008). "Essential collocations for learners of English: The role of collocational direction and weight". In: Meunier, Fanny and Sylviane Granger (eds.): 43-66.
Haspelmath, Martin (2004). "On directionality in language change with particular reference to grammaticalization". In: Fischer, Olga, Muriel Norde and Harry Perridon (eds.): 17-44.
Hattori, Shiro and Kazuko Inoue (1983). *Proceedings of the XIIIth International Congress of Linguists.* Tokyo: CILP.
Hausmann, Franz Josef (2003). "Was sind eigentlich Kollokationen?". In: Steyer, Kathrin (ed.): 309- 334.
Hawkins, Bruce W. (1984). *The Semantics of English Spatial Prepositions.* Ph. D. dissertation. University of California, San Diego.
Heine, Bernd and Mechtild Reh (1984). *Grammaticalization and Reanalysis in African Languages.* Hamburg: Buske.
Heine, Bernd and Tania Kuteva (2002). *World Lexicon of Grammaticalization.* Cambridge: Cambridge University Press.
Heine, Bernd and Tania Kuteva (2005). *Language Contact and Grammatical Change.* Cambridge: Cambridge University Press.
Heine, Bernd, Ulrike Claudi and Friederike Hünnemeyer (1991). *Grammaticalization: A Conceptual Framework.* Chicago: University of Chicago Press.
Hoffmann, Sebastian (2004). "Are low-frequency complex prepositions grammaticalized? On the limits of corpus data and the importance of intuition". In: Lindkvist, Hans and Christian Mair 2004 (eds.): 171-210.
Hoffmann, Sebastian (2005). *Grammaticalization and English Complex Prepositions. A Corpus-Based Study.* New York: Routledge.
Hopper, Paul J. (1991). "On some principles of grammaticization". In: Traugott, Elizabeth Closs and Bernd Heine (eds.): 17-35.
Hopper, Paul J. and Elizabeth Closs Traugott (1993 [2nd ed. 2003]. *Grammaticalization.* Cambridge: Cambridge University Press.
Hopper, Paul J. and Sandra A. Thompson (1985). "The iconicity of the universal categories "noun" and "verb"". In: Haiman, John (ed.): 151-183.

Horgan, Dorothy M. (1981). "The lexical and syntactic variants shared by two of the later manuscripts of King Alfred's translation of Gregory's *Cura Pastoralis*". *Anglo-Saxon England* 9: 213-21. Cambridge: Cambridge University Press.

Hornero Corisco, Ana Mª (1997). "French influence on English prepositions: A study of *Ancrene Wisse*". *Studia Anglica Posnaniensia* 32: 33-45.

Howarth, Peter A. (1996). *Phraseology in English Academic Writing: Some Implications for Language Learning and Dictionary Making*. Lexicographica, Series maior 75. Tübingen: Max Niemeyer.

Howarth, Peter A. (1998). "The phraseology of learners' academic writing". In: Cowie, Anthony P. (ed.): 161-188.

Hüllen, Werner and Rainer Schulze (1988). *Understanding the Lexicon: Meaning, Sense and World Knowledge in Lexical Semantics*. Tübingen: Max Niemeyer.

Iglesias-Rábade, Luis (2003). "French influence in Middle English phrasing: some evidence from *at*-prepositional phrases". *Neuphilologische Mitteilungen* 104(3): 281-301.

Iglesias-Rábade, Luis (2001). "Composite predicates in Middle English with the verbs *nimen* and *taken*". *Studia Neophilologica* 73: 143-163.

Iglesias-Rábade, Luis (2007). "Twin lexical collocations in legal late Middle English". *Studia Anglica Posnaniensia* 43: 17-41.

Inkpen, Diana Zaiu and Graeme Hirst (2006). "Building and using a lexical knowledge base of near-synonym differences". *Computational Linguistics* 32(2): 223-262.

Jackendoff, Ray (1973) "The base rules of prepositional phrases". In: Anderson, Stephen R. and Paul Kiparsky (eds.): 345-56.

Jespersen, Otto (1942). *A Modern English Grammar on Historical Principles*. Part VI: *Morphology*. London: George Allen and Unwin.

Joseph, Brian D. and Richard D. Janda (2003). *The Handbook of Historical Linguistics*. Oxford: Blackwell Publishing.

Kahr, Joan Casper (1976). "The renewal of case morphology: sources and constraints". *Working Papers on Language Universals* 20: 107-151.

Kastovsky, Dieter (1991). *Historical English Syntax*. Berlin: Mouton de Gruyter.

Kastovsky, Dieter (1994). *Studies in Early Modern English*. Berlin: Mouton de Gruyter.

Katz, Jerrold (1973). "Compositionality, idiomaticity, and lexical substitution". In: Anderson, Stephen R. and Paul Kiparsky (eds.): 357-376.

Keizer, Evelien (2008). "English prepositions in functional discourse grammar". *Functions of Language* 15(2): 216-256.

Killie, Kristin (2007). "On the development and use of appearance/attribute adverbs in English". *Diachronica* 24(2): 327-372.

Kjellmer, Göran (1984). "Why *great: greatly* but not *big: *bigly*? On the formation of English adverbs in *–ly*". *Studia Linguistica* 38(1): 1-19.

Kjellmer, Göran (1987). "Aspects of English collocations". In: Meijs, Willem (ed): 133-140.
Kjellmer, Göran (1994). *A Dictionary of English Collocations*. Oxford: Clarendon Press.
Klausenburger, Jurgen (2000). *Grammaticalization. Studies in Latin and Romance Morphosyntax*. Amsterdam/Philadelphia: John Benjamins.
Kniezsa, Veronika (1991). "Prepositional phrases expressing adverbs of time from late Old English to early Middle English". In: Kastovsky, Dieter (ed.): 221-231.
Kreitzer, Anatol (1997). "Multiple levels of schematization: A study in the conceptualization of space". *Cognitive Linguistics* 8(4): 291-325.
Kurylowicz, Jerzy (1965). "The evolution of grammatical categories". In: Coseriu, Eugenio (ed.): 38-54.
Lakoff, George and Mark Johnson (1980). *Metaphors we Live by*. Chicago: University of Chicago Press.
Langacker, Ronald (1987). *Foundations of Cognitive Grammar. Vol. I: Theoretical Prerequisites*. Stanford: Stanford University Press.
Leech, Geoffrey Neil (1969). *Towards a semantic description of English*. London : Longman.
Lehmann, Christian (1985). "Grammaticalization: Synchronic variation and diachronic change". *Lingua e Stile* 20(3): 303-318.
Lehmann, Christian (1995). *Thoughts on Grammaticalization*. Munich-Newcastle: Lincom Europa.
Lehmann, Winfred Philipp and Yakov Malkiel (1982). *Perspectives on Historical Linguistics*. Amsterdam: John Benjamins.
Levorato, M. Chiara (1993). "The acquisition of idioms and the development of figurative competence". In: Cacciari, Cristina and Patrizia Tabossi (eds.): 101-128.
Li, Charles N. (1975). *Word Order and Word Order Change*. Austin: University of Texas Press.
Lichtenberk, Frantisek (1991). "Semantic change and heterosemy in grammaticalization". *Language* 67: 475-509.
Lindkvist, Karl-Gunnar 1978). "AT versus ON, IN, BY: on the early history of spatial AT and certain primary ideas distinguishing AT from ON, IN, BY". *Acta Universitatis Stockholmiensis, Stockholm Studies in English* XLVIII. Stockholm: Almquist and Wiksell International.
Lindkvist, Hans and Christian Mair (2004). *Corpus Approaches to Grammaticalization in English*. Amsterdam: John Benjamins.
Live, Anna H. (1973). "The *take-have* phrasal in English". *Linguistics* 9: 31-50.
Lundskær-Nielsen, Tom (1993). *Prepositions in Old and Middle English*. Odense: Odense University Press.

Malmkjær, Kirsten (1991). *The Linguistics Encyclopedia*. London: Routledge.
Marchello-Nizia, Christiane (2006). *Grammaticalisation et changement linguistique*. Bruxelles: de Boeck.
Matsumoto, Meiko (1999). "Composite predicates in Middle English". In: Brinton, Laurel J. and Minoji Akimoto (eds.): 59-96.
McInnes, Bridget T. (2004). *Extending the Log Likelihood Measure to Improve Collocation Identification*. M.S. Thesis, Department of Computer Science, University of Minnesota, Duluth.
McIntosh, Angus (1991). "Old English adjectives with derivative *-lic* partners: Some semantic problems". *Neuphilologische Mitteilungen* 92: 297-310.
MED (1959-) (*Middle English Dictionary*). Eds. Kurath, Hans and Sherman M. Kuhn. Ann Arbor: The University of Michigan Press.
Meijs, Willem (1987). *Corpus Linguistics and Beyond*. Amsterdam: Rodopi.
Mel'čuk Igor (1988). "Semantic description of lexical units in an explanatory combinatorial dictionary: Basic principles and heuristic criteria". *International Journal of Lexicography* 1(3): 165-188.
Mel'čuk, Igor (1995). "Phrasemes in language and phraseology in linguistics". In: Everaert, Martin, Erik-Jan van der Linden, André Schenk, and Rob Schreuder (eds.): 167-232.
Mel'čuk, Igor (1998). "Collocations and lexical functions". In: Cowie, Anthony P. (ed.): 23-54.
Mitchell, Bruce (1978). "Prepositions, adverbs, prepositional adverbs, post-positions, separable prefixes, or inseparable prefixes in Old English?". *Neuphilologische Mitteilungen* 79: 240-57.
Meunier, Fanny and Sylviane Granger (2008). *Phraseology in Foreign Language Learning and Teaching*. Amsterdam: John Benjamins.
Moon, Rosamund (1994). "The analysis of fixed expressions in text". In: Coulthard, Malcolm (ed): 117-135.
Moon, Rosamund (1998). "Frequencies and forms of phrasal lexemes in English". In: Cowie, Anthony P. (ed.): 79-100.
Moskowich-Spiegel Fandiño, Isabel (2002). "The adjective in English. The French type and its place in the history of the language". *Folia Linguistica Historica* 23(1-2): 59-71.
Moskowich-Spiegel Fandiño, Isabel and Begoña Crespo García (2002). "Adjectival forms in late Middle English. Syntactic and semantic implications". *Studia Neophilologica* 74: 161-170.
Mourón Figueroa, Cristina (2008). "A semantic analysis of by-phrases in the York Cycle". *Studia Neophilologica* 80: 1-14.
Mourón Figueroa, Cristina (2008). "At-phrases in the York Cycle: A semantic analysis". *Neuphilologische Mitteilungen* CVII(4): 471-486.
Nattinger James R. and Jeanette S. DeCarrico (1992). *Lexical Phrases and Language Teaching*. Oxford: Oxford University Press.

Nesselhauf, Nadja (2004). "What are collocations"?. In: Allerton, David and Paul Skandera (eds.): 1-21.
Nevalainen, Terttu (1991). *BUT, ONLY, JUST. Focusing Adverbial Change in Modern English 1500-1900* (Mémoires de la Societé Néophilologique 51). Helsinki: Societé Néophilologique.
Nevalainen, Terttu (1994a). "Aspects of adverbial change in early Modern English". In: Kastovsky, Dieter. (ed.): 243-259.
Nevalainen, Terttu (1994b). "Diachronic issues in English adverb derivation". In: Fries, Udo, Gunnel Tottie, and Peter Schneider (eds.): 139-147.
Nevalainen, Terttu (1997). "The processes of adverb derivation in late Middle and early Modern English". In: Rissanen, Matti, Merja Kytö and Kirsi Heikkonen (eds.): 145-189.
Nevalainen, Terttu (2004). "Three perspectives on grammaticalization: lexico-grammar, corpora and historical sociolinguistics". In: Lindkvist, Hans and Christian Mair (eds.): 1-32.
Nevalainen, Terttu (2008). "Social variation in intensifier use: Constraint on -ly adverbialization?". *English Language and Linguistics* 12(2): 289–315.
Nichols, Johanna and Alan Timberlake. (1991). "Grammaticalization as retextualization". In: Traugott, Elizabeth. Closs and Bernd Heine (eds.): 129-146.
Nicolas, Tim (1995). "Semantics of idiom modification". In: Everaert, Martin, Erik-Jan van der Linden, André Schenk, and Rob Schreuder (eds.): 233-252.
Nunberg, Geoffrey (1978). *The Pragmatics of Reference*. Bloomington: Indiana University Linguistics Club.
O'Dowd, Elizabeth M. (1998). *Prepositions and Particles in English. A Discourse-Functional Account*. New York and Oxford: Oxford University Press.
OED (*The Oxford English Dictionary*). (1989). Eds. Simpson, John A. and Edmund S. C. Weiner. 2nd edition. Oxford: The Clarendon Press.
Omazič, Marija (2008). "Processsing of idioms and idiom modification: A view from cognitive linguistics". In: Granger, Sylviane and Fanny Meunier (eds.): 67-80.
Ortony, Andrew, Diane L. Schallert, Ralph E. Reynolds, Stephen J. Antos (1978). "Interpreting metaphors and idioms: Some effects of context on comprehension". *Journal of Verbal Learning and Verbal Behavior* 17: 465-477.
Pagliuca, William (1994). *Perspectives on Grammaticalization*. [Current Issues in Linguistic Theory 109] Amsterdam/Philadelphia: John Benjamins.
Palander-Collin, Minna (1999).*Grammaticalization and Social Embedding*. Helsinki: Société Néophilologique.
Piirainen, Elisabeth. (2008). "Figurative phraseology and culture". In: Granger, Sylviane and Fanny Meunier (eds.): 207-228.

Pivaut, Laurent (1994). "Quelques aspects sémantiques d'une construction à verbe support *faire*". *Lingvisticae Investigationes* 18(1): 49-88.
Pounder, Amanda (2001). "Adverb-marking in German and English: system and standardization". *Diachronica* 18(2): 301-358.
Prins, Anton A. (1952). *French Influence in English Phrasing*. Leiden: University Press.
Puhvel, Jann (1969). *Substance and Structure of Language*. Berkeley: University of California Press.
Ramat, Paolo (1980). *Linguistic Reconstruction in Indo-European Syntax*. Amsterdam: Current Issues in Linguistic Theory 19.
Rauh, Gisa (1991). *Approaches to Prepositions*. Tübingen: Gunter Narr Verlag.
Rissanen, Matti (2004). "Grammaticalization from side to side: On the development of *beside(s)*". In: Lindkvist, Hans and Christian Mair (eds.): 151-170.
Rissanen, Matti, Merja Kytö and Kirsi Heikkonen (1997). *Grammaticalization at Work*. Berlin-New York: Mouton de Gruyter.
Rosenbach, Anette (2004). "The English *s*-genitive: A case of degrammaticalization"?. In: Fischer, Olga, Muriel Norde and Harry Perridon (eds.): 73-96.
Rothkegel, Annely (1973). *Feste Syntagmen, Grundlagen, Strukturbeschreibung und automatische Analyse*. Tübingen: Niemeyer.
Samuels, Michael L. (1972). *Linguistic Evolution with Special Reference to English*. Cambridge: Cambridge University Press.
Schenk, André (1995). "The syntactic behavior of idioms". In: Everaert, Martin, Erik-Jan van der Linden, André Schenk, and Rob Schreuder (eds.): 253-272.
Siepmann, Dirk (2005a). "Collocation, colligation and encoding dictionaries. Part I: Lexicological aspects". *International Journal of Lexicography* 18(4): 409-444.
Siepmann, Dirk (2005b). "Collocation, colligation and encoding dictionaries. Part II: Lexicographical aspects". *International Journal of Lexicography* 19(1): 1-40.
Simpson, Greg B. (1990). *Understanding Word and Sentence*. Amsterdam: Elsevier.
Sinclair John McH. (1991). *Corpus Concordance Collocation*. Oxford: Oxford University Press.
Sinclair John McH. (2004). *Trust the Text. Language, Corpus and Discourse*. New York/London: Routledge.
Smadja, Frank (1993). "Retrieving Collocations from Text: Xtract". *Computational Linguistics* 19(1): 143-177.
Steyer, Kathrin (2003). *Wortverbindungen - mehr oder weniger fest. Jahrbuch des Instituts für Deutsche Sprache*. Berlin: Mouton de Gruyter.
Svensson, Maria Helena (2008). "A very complex criterion of fixedness: Non-compositionality". In: Granger, Sylviane and Fanny Meunier (eds.): 81-94.
Swan, Toril (1984). *Sentence Adverbials en English*. Oslo: Novus.

Swan, Toril (1988). "The development of sentence adverbs in English". *Studia Linguistica* 42(1): 1-17.
Sweetser, Eve E. (1990). *From Etymology to Pragmatics*. [Cambridge Studies in Linguistics 54]. Cambridge: Cambridge University Press.
Swinney, David A. and Anne Cutler (1979). "The access and processing of idiomatic expressions". *Journal of Verbal Learning and Verbal Behavior* 18: 523-534.
Tabossi, Patrizia and Francesco Zardon (1993). "The activation of idiomatic meaning in spoken language comprehension". In: Cacciari, Cristina and Patrizia Tabossi (eds.): 145-162.
Talmy, Leonard (2000). *Towards a Cognitive Semantics* (2 vols). Boston: MIT Press.
Teliya, Veronika, Natalya Bragina, Elena Oparina and Irina Sandomirskaya (1998). "Phraseology as a language culture: its role in the representation of a cultural mentality". In: Cowie, Anthony P. (ed.): 55-78.
Tobler-Lommatzsch (1954-). *Altfranzösisches Wörterbuch*. Wiesbaden: Franz Steiner Verlag GMBH.
Traugott, Elizabeth Closs (1982). "From prepositional to textual and expressive meanings: some semantic-pragmatic aspects of grammaticalization". In: Lehmann, Winfred Philipp and Yakov Malkiel (eds.): 245-71.
Traugott, Elizabeth Closs (1989). "On the rise of epistemic meaning: An example of subjectification in semantic change". *Language* 65: 31-55.
Traugott, Elizabeth Closs and Bernd Heine (1991). *Approaches to Grammaticalization*. 2 vols. Amsterdam/Philadelphia: John Benjamins.
Traugott, Elizabeth Closs and Ekkehard König (1991). "The semantics-pragmatics of grammaticalization revisited". In: Traugott, Elizabeth Closs and Bernd Heine (eds.): 189-218.
Tyler, Andrea and Vyvyan Evans (2003). *The Semantics of English Prepositions. Spatial Scenes, Embodied Meaning and Cognition*. Cambridge: Cambridge University Press.
Vandeloise, Claude (1986). *L'Espace en français*. Paris: Le Seuil.
Van Gelderen, Elly (2004). *Grammaticalization as Economy*. Amsterdam: John Benjamins.
Van Kemenade, Ans (1987). *Syntactic Case and Morphological Case in the History of English*. Dordrecht: Foris Publications.
Van Lancker, Diana and Gerald J. Canter (1981). "Idiomatic versus literal interpretations of ditropically ambiguous sentences". *Journal of Speech and Hearing Research* 24: 64-69.
Vincent, Nigel 1980. "Iconic and symbolic aspects of syntax: Prospects for reconstruction". In: Ramat, Paolo (ed.): 47-68.
Visser, Fredericus T. (1963). *An Historical Syntax of the English Language*. Leiden. University Press.

Wasaw, Thomas, Ivan Sag and Geoffrey Nunberg (1983). "Idioms. An interim report". In: Hattori, Shiro and Kazuko Inoue (eds.).
Weinreich, Uriel (1969). "Problems in the analysis of idioms". In: Puhvel, Jann (ed.): 23-81.
Wood, Frederick T. (1967). *English Prepositional Idioms*. London: Macmillan.
Wright, Laura (2004). "Life after degrammaticalisation: Plural *be*". In: Lindkvist, Hans and Christian Mair (2004) (eds.): 211-226.
Zelinsky-Wibbelt, Cornelia (1993). *The Semantics of Prepositions*. Berlin, New York: Mouton de Gruyter.
Zelinsky-Wibbelt, Cornelia (1993). "Interpreting and translating prepositions: A cognitive based formalization". In: Zelinsky-Wibbelt, Cornelia (ed.): 351-390.

Studies in English Medieval Language and Literature

Edited by Jacek Fisiak

Vol. 1 Dieter Kastovsky / Arthur Mettinger (eds.): Language Contact in the History of English. 2nd, revised edition. 2003.

Vol. 2 Studies in English Historical Linguistics and Philology. A Festschrift for Akio Oizumi. Edited by Jacek Fisiak. 2002.

Vol. 3 Liliana Sikorska: *In a Manner of Morall Playe*: Social Ideologies in English Moralities and Interludes (1350–1517). 2002.

Vol. 4 Peter J. Lucas / Angela M. Lucas (eds.): Middle English from Tongue to Text. Selected Papers from the Third International Conference on Middle English: Language and Text, held at Dublin, Ireland, 1–4 July 1999. 2002.

Vol. 5 Chaucer and the Challenges of Medievalism. Studies in Honor of H. A. Kelly. Edited by Donka Minkova and Theresa Tinkle. 2003.

Vol. 6 Hanna Rutkowska: Graphemics and Morphosyntax in the *Cely Letters* (1472–88). 2003.

Vol. 7 The *Ancrene Wisse*. A Four-Manuscript Parallel Text. Preface and Parts 1–4. Edited by Tadao Kubouchi and Keiko Ikegami with John Scahill, Shoko Ono, Harumi Tanabe, Yoshi-ko Ota, Ayako Kobayashi and Koichi Nakamura. 2003.

Vol. 8 Joanna Bugaj: Middle Scots Inflectional System in the South-west of Scotland. 2004.

Vol. 9 Rafal Boryslawski: The Old English Riddles and the Riddlic Elements of Old English Poetry. 2004.

Vol. 10 Nikolaus Ritt / Herbert Schendl (eds.): Rethinking Middle English. Linguistic and Literary Approaches. 2005.

Vol. 11 The *Ancrene Wisse*. A Four-Manuscript Parallel Text. Parts 5–8 with Wordlists. Edited by Tadao Kubouchi and Keiko Ikegami with John Scahill, Shoko Ono, Harumi Tanabe, Yoshi-ko Ota, Ayako Kobayashi, Koichi Nakamura. 2005.

Vol. 12 Text and Language in Medieval English Prose. A Festschrift for Tadao Kubouchi. Edited by Akio Oizumi, Jacek Fisiak and John Scahill. 2005.

Vol. 13 Michiko Ogura (ed.): Textual and Contextual Studies in Medieval English. Towards the Reunion of Linguistics and Philology. 2006.

Vol. 14 Keiko Hamaguchi: Non-European Women in Chaucer. A Postcolonial Study. 2006.

Vol. 15 Ursula Schaefer (ed.): The Beginnings of Standardization. Language and Culture in Fourteenth-Century England. 2006.

Vol. 16 Nikolaus Ritt / Herbert Schendl / Christiane Dalton-Puffer / Dieter Kastovsky (eds): Medieval English and its Heritage. Structure, Meaning and Mechanisms of Change. 2006.

Vol. 17 Matylda Włodarczyk: Pragmatic Aspects of Reported Speech. The Case of Early Modern English Courtroom Discourse. 2007.

Vol. 18 Hans Sauer / Renate Bauer (eds.): *Beowulf* and Beyond. 2007.

Vol. 19 Gabriella Mazzon (ed.): Studies in Middle English Forms and Meanings. 2007.

Vol. 20 Alexander Bergs / Janne Skaffari (eds.): The Language of the Peterborough Chronicle. 2007.

Vol. 21 Liliana Sikorska (ed.). With the assistance of Joanna Maciulewicz: Medievalisms. The Poetics of Literary Re-Reading. 2008.

Vol. 22 Masachiyo Amano / Michiko Ogura / Masayuki Ohkado (eds.): Historical Englishes in Varieties of Texts and Contexts. The Global COE Program, International Conference 2007. 2008.

Vol. 23 Ewa Ciszek: Word Derivation in Early Middle English. 2008.

Vol. 24 Andrzej M. Łęcki: Grammaticalisation Paths of *Have* in English. 2010.

Vol. 25 Osamu Imahayashi / Yoshiyuki Nakao / Michiko Ogura (eds.): Aspects of the History of English Language and Literature. Selected Papers Read at SHELL 2009, Hiroshima. 2010.

Vol. 26 Magdalena Bator: Obsolete Scandinavian Loanwords in English. 2010.

Vol. 27 Anna Cichosz: The Influence of Text Type on Word Order of Old Germanic Languages. A Corpus-Based Contrastive Study of Old English and Old High German. 2010.

Vol. 28 Jacek Fisiak / Magdalena Bator (eds.): Foreign Influences on Medieval English. 2011.

Vol. 29 Władysław Witalisz: The Trojan Mirror. Middle English Narratives of Troy as Books of Princely Advice. 2011.

Vol. 30 Luis Iglesias-Rábade: Semantic Erosion of Middle English Prepositions. 2011.

www.peterlang.de